TAYLOR
THE WHOLE STORY
SWIFT

TAYLOR
THE WHOLE STORY
SWIFT

THE FULLY UPDATED
UNAUTHORIZED BIOGRAPHY

by Chas Newkey-Burden

HarperCollins*Publishers*

HarperCollins*Publishers*
1 London Bridge Street,
London SE1 9GF

www.harpercollins.co.uk

HarperCollins*Publishers*
Macken House, 39/40 Mayor Street Upper
Dublin 1, D01 C9W8, Ireland

First published by HarperCollins*Publishers* 2014
This updated edition published in 2024

24 25 26 27 28 LBC 7 6 5 4 3

A catalogue record of this book is
available from the British Library

ISBN: 978-0-00-868071-8

Printed and bound at Lakeside

Introduction

As Taylor Swift looked back over the year 2013, she could hardly believe what a momentous twelve months it had been for her. Sales of her fourth album, *Red*, had taken her total record sales beyond 26 million. Meanwhile, her songs had now been downloaded 75 million times, making her the number-one digital singles artist of all time.

Taylor's achievements become ever more impressive when you measure them against those of other artists. For instance, at the start of the year she became the first artist since The Beatles to spend six or more weeks at number one with three consecutive albums.

She notched up all these remarkable accomplishments before she turned 24. Yet young Taylor was treated like an industry veteran when, in November 2013, the Country Music Association Awards handed her its Pinnacle Award, which is its equivalent of the lifetime achievement gong. Most awards hand such honours to artists in their fifties or beyond. At the ceremony, a video tribute was aired, in which Julia Roberts, Justin Timberlake and Mick Jagger gushed over the youngster's talent and influence.

While the middle-aged country music industry treats Taylor like an elder stateswoman, the teenage-driven pop market screams its appreciation for her as one of its own. Serious music magazines treat her with reverence, while celebrity gossip rags obsess over her love life. And who else but Taylor could carry the banjo into the pop world with such effortless grace and hipness?

She is the princess of paradox. While some artists feel constrained by the boundaries of music and image, she flutters lightly over them. As well as dipping her feet in the waters of pop, she has written bold arena rock tunes and even experimented with dubstep.

This bewitching young lady of contrasts can, within one album, softly whisper lyrics which offer sweet, touching perspectives on love and romance, then spit out furious choruses of vengeance, defiance and denunciation. She is a conventionally attractive blonde who nonetheless plays the part of the perennial gawky outsider.

In an era of X-rated stage productions from the likes of Rihanna and Lady Gaga, Taylor stands tall as a clean-cut wholesome American – a demure diva of apple-pie sweetness. Just weeks after her friend Miley Cyrus created a global storm by 'twerking' at an awards ceremony, the elegantly turned-out Taylor was grabbing the headlines her own way by sharing a microphone with Prince William and Jon Bon Jovi at a posh charity event in Kensington Gardens.

And so a year that began with her kissing One Direction heart-throb Harry Styles in Manhattan ended with her high-fiving the man in line to be the future King of England. Meanwhile, the front cover of the influential *New Yorker* magazine named her 'The biggest pop star in the world'. The respected – and rather serious – music monthly *Rolling Stone* was also joining in the cacophony of praise for Taylor. Focusing on her performances during the *Red* tour, it gushed: 'Seeing Taylor Swift live in 2013 is seeing a maestro at the top of her or anyone's game.'

On the surface, Taylor played it cool and acted as if all these experiences were just a normal part of life. Inside, though, she could scarcely believe how thrilling her existence had become. It is all so far from the world in which she grew up.

Chapter One

How different it could all have been ... Taylor Swift was never meant to be a singer-songwriter; she was supposed to become a stockbroker. Her parents even chose her Christian name with a business path in mind. Her mother, Andrea, selected a gender-neutral name for her baby girl so that when she grew up and applied for jobs in the male-dominated finance industry no one would know if she were male or female. It was a plan that came from a loving place, but it was not one that would ever be realised. Instead, millions and millions of fans across the world would know exactly which gender Andrea's first-born was, without ever meeting her.

In Taylor's track 'The Best Day', which touchingly evokes a childhood full of wonder, she sings of her 'excellent' father whose 'strength is making me stronger'. That excellent father is Scott Kingsley Swift, who studied business at the University of Delaware. He lived in the Brown residence hall. There, he made lots of friends, one of whom, Michael DiMuzio, would later cross paths with Taylor professionally. Scott graduated with a first-class degree and set about building his career in similarly impressive style. Perhaps a knack for business is in the blood: his father and grandfather also worked in finance.

Scott set up his own investment-banking firm called the Swift Group, which offered clear, well-informed financial advice under the Merrill Lynch umbrella. He had joined the world-renowned firm in the 1980s and rose quickly, eventually becoming the first vice president. He often travelled with his work and it was on one such trip, to Harris, in Texas, that he met a young lady, six years his junior, called Andrea Gardner Finlay. Like him, she worked in finance, as a marketing manager in an advertising agency, and was a determined and highly driven soul.

Although the two found that they had a great deal in common, Andrea was focused more on her career than thoughts of marriage when Scott first crossed her path. She had needed to work hard to break into the finance industry, which in the late 1970s was an almost entirely male sector. Yet break in she did, and she could afford to feel immense satisfaction at having done so. As Taylor later told a television interviewer, her mother had, prior to meeting Scott, 'a career on her own and lived alone' and was financially independent. Taylor's knowledge of this dimension of her mother's past has filled her with respect for Andrea and shaped her own approach to work and life.

Having worked so hard and been so strong, Andrea was not in the mood to take her eye off the ball. Yet when she met Scott he melted her heart and they quickly fell in love. They married in Texas on 20 February 1988 but moved to Pennsylvania, settling in West Reading in Berks County. Then, at the age of 30, Andrea found out she was pregnant with her first child. The girl was born on 13 December 1989 in Wyomissing. They named her Taylor Alison, and she showed very early signs of the star quality that would propel her to fame later in life. Within hours of her birth, the baby girl had already made quite an impression on a member of staff at the hospital. A paediatrician told Andrea: 'She's a really good-natured baby, but she knows exactly what she wants and how to get it!' At the time, Andrea wondered what on earth the man was talking about. How could he possibly read the personality of a baby just a few hours old? In time, Andrea would have to agree that his description had been right on the money.

For those who believe in 'birth order' – the theory that a significant amount of your character and life experience is determined by the order in which you are born into your family: as first, middle, last or only child – Taylor's firstborn status is pertinent. Firstborns enjoy uninterrupted attention from their parents until a sibling arrives. Typical characteristics of firstborns are a pronounced eagerness to please, and an increased tendency to conform to rules. However, firstborns are likely to show responsibility or leadership in crisis situations.

They can also be nurturing and caring, but are vulnerable to episodes of self-criticism and jealousy – emotions that were first sparked the day they realised they were no longer the only child of the household, and saw their parents' attention and affections move in part towards someone else. As for astrologers, they ascribe mixed traits to Taylor's star sign of Sagittarius. Those born under this sign are said to be, on the positive side, honest, generous and oozing with charisma. Less positively, they can also be reckless, superficial and lacking in tact. Other famous Sagittarians include Nicki Minaj, Jimi Hendrix, Frank Sinatra and Brad Pitt.

Taylor first lived on the 11-acre Christmas-tree farm that had been the property of Scott's father in the past. Based in the town of Cumru, it provided a useful additional income for the family and allowed them to live in increasing splendour as Taylor grew up. To her, the place seemed enormous. 'And it was the most magical, wonderful place in the world,' she has said. She could run free and let her imagination run riot, which would prove key to her emotional and creative development. While some childhoods squeeze all artistic aspirations out of a youngster, Taylor's childhood nurtured and encouraged her dreams. In her inspirational book *The Artist's Way*, Julia Cameron outlines compellingly how important this is to any young creative. Had Taylor's dreams been squashed as a child, she might well have ended up working in finance as her parents had originally envisaged; another would-be artist who slipped through the net.

At three years of age, Taylor got a younger sibling in the form of brother Austin, who was born on 11 March 1992. Within two years of his arrival, Andrea decided to set her career to one side and become a full-time mother. Andrea's influence on Taylor remained profound. 'She totally raised me to be logical and practical,' said Taylor. 'I was brought up with such a strong woman in my life and I think that had a lot to do with me not wanting to do anything halfway.' Taylor speaks about her parents in contrasting yet balancing tones. Andrea's rational and down-to-earth nature is balanced by Scott, who, says Taylor, is 'just a big teddy bear who tells me that everything I do is perfect'. Where Andrea is described as 'realistic', Scott is described as 'head-in-the-clouds' and optimistic.

Yet he is not all dreamy glass-half-full chirpiness: his sound financial know-how has been of great help to Taylor, particularly since she became famous. 'Business-wise, he's brilliant,' she said. Although her parents had a financial route already mapped out for Taylor in their minds, she had other ideas. At the age of three she began singing, even delivering an impressive rendition of the vocally tricky Righteous Brothers' classic 'Unchained Melody'. She enjoyed the feeling of sweetly singing the lyrics of songs, and she found she had a strong memory for words and melodies. When Scott and Andrea took her to see films at the cinema, she would sing songs from the soundtrack on the way home, having somehow been able to commit the lyrics and tune to memory during one listen. Taylor told the *Daily Mail* that her parents would be 'freaked out' by this feat of musical memory. 'I retained music more than anything else,' she added.

Where had this magic come from? To find musical deftness in the family tree, we need to hop back a generation to Taylor's maternal grandmother, Marjorie Finlay. A charismatic and lively lady, Finlay became a successful opera singer, admired in many countries across the world. She had married a man whose work in the oil industry took him around the world. This meant she performed in countries as far apart as America, Singapore and Puerto Rico.

Ten years after giving birth to Andrea, Finlay and her family settled in America. Here, she was handed a host of new opportunities, including membership of the Houston Grand Opera. She appeared in musicals of an operatic bent – such as Rossini's *The Barber of Seville* and Smetana's *The Bartered Bride* – and in other, more mainstream productions, including Bernstein's *West Side Story*. She also became a television presenter, working in Latin America as the hostess of a leading television variety show called *The Pan American Show*. She was a vivacious and occasionally comical figure. Taylor told *Wood & Steel* magazine that her grandmother's Spanish was so bad that she became a joke among some viewers, who found her 'hysterically funny'.

Yet her charisma passed down the family tree to her granddaughter. Scott has noted several similarities between his mother-in-law and Taylor. 'The two of them had some sort of magic where they could walk into a room and remember everyone's name,' he said. 'Taylor has the grace and the same physique of Andrea's mother. Andrea's mother had this unique quality: if she was going into a room, literally everybody loved Marjorie.' Taylor, who remembers the 'thrill' of hearing her grandmother sing, also noted Marjorie's charisma – and she liked what she saw. 'When she would walk into a room, everyone would look at her, no matter what,' Taylor told the *Sunday Times*. For young Taylor, the 'it factor' she identified in Marjorie gave her something that many children are scanning people for. It made her grandmother, said Taylor, 'different from everyone else'. The youngster keenly wanted to be the same.

Yet despite this entertainment-industry heritage further up the family tree, Taylor grew up among a wholesome clan. The Swifts are a Catholic family. Taylor attended pre-school at Alvernia Montessori School, which is run by nuns. 'She always liked to sing,' the school's head, Sister Anne Marie Coll, told the *Reading Eagle*. The family were regulars in church, and these services gave Taylor yet more experience of singing, as she joined in the hymns. When she was six years of age, Taylor began to listen to music seriously. An early artist to grab her attention was LeAnn Rimes, the country/pop singer who became famous at the age of 14.

Swift had to go her own way to discover the charms of Rimes, as that sort of music was not commonplace in the family home. Andrea, for instance, was a fan of rockier sounds, such as Def Leppard. Taylor says that her mother listened to a lot of their music when she was pregnant with her. However, the Swifts were a 'random family when it comes to musical tastes', which meant Taylor could find her own place within it all. 'LeAnn Rimes was my first impression of country music,' she told the *Guardian*. 'I got her first album when I was six. I just really loved how she could be making music and having a career at such a young age.'

She also fell in love with other artists including Shania Twain and Dixie Chicks. Then she explored the history of country music, digging deep enough to discover, to her joy, older acts such as Patsy Cline and Dolly Parton. She became, she said, 'infatuated' with the sound and the 'storytelling' of the genre. 'I could relate to it. I can't really tell you why. With me, it's instinctual.' At the age of 10 she was bowled over with admiration for Shania Twain. Taylor was impressed by Twain's independent nature, and the fact that she 'wrote all her own songs'. She told *Time* magazine: 'That meant so much to me, even as a 10-year-old. Just knowing that the stories she was telling on those songs – those were her stories.'

Meanwhile, Taylor was continuing to show flashes of the same star quality that her famous ancestor possessed. Perhaps it was her grandmother who directly bequeathed Taylor her charisma. Andrea still remembers how, when Taylor was five years of age, she arranged for family photographs to be taken for Christmas cards. Her daughter was, recalled Andrea in an interview with *Sugar* magazine, 'really posing' in the snaps. So much so, in fact, that the photographer suggested that Taylor could have a career as a child model in Los Angeles. Mindful of the potentially seedy elements of that industry, Andrea decided that this was not the path she wanted her girl to follow.

Instead, Taylor continued to tread a more artistic path – but not one that was solely musical. She told the *Washington Post* that writing became an obsession for her from an early age. 'Writing is pretty involuntary to me,' she said. 'I'm always writing.' That obsession began with a fascination for poetry, and 'trying to figure out the perfect combination of words, with the perfect amount of syllables and the perfect rhyme to make it completely pop off the page'. As with music, she found that poems she read would stay with her; she would replay the catchy rhymes she had read and then try and conjure up some of her own. In English classes at school, many of Taylor's classmates would groan when the teacher asked them to write poems of their own. Not Taylor. Before she knew it, she had written three pages of rhymes. Many of these were strong efforts.

In fourth grade, she entered a national poetry contest with a piece of work she had written entitled *Monster In My Closet*. She was so excited to compete. It included the lines: 'There's a monster in my closet and I don't know what to do / Have you ever seen him? / Has he ever pounced on you?' It turned into a long poem and one that Taylor selected carefully from her collection. 'I picked the most gimmicky one I had; I didn't want to get too dark on them,' she said. She was delighted to win and became 'consumed' with building on the success to write ever more impressive couplets.

She also loved stories: reading them, including *The Giving Tree*, a children's picture book written and illustrated by Shel Silverstein. First published during the 1960s, it is a story about a female tree and a male human who become friends. Taylor also enjoyed the *Amelia Bedelia* series, which was written by Peggy Parish and, more recently, by her nephew Herman Parish. Stories became a passion for the young Swift; she loved hearing them and telling them. 'All I wanted to do was talk and all I wanted to do was hear stories,' she told journalist and talk-show host Katie Couric. 'I would drive my mom insane,' she added. She usually refused to go to bed unless a story was read to her. 'And I always wanted to hear a new one,' she said. These readings lit a creative spark in the girl. Andrea remembered that Taylor 'wrote all the time' as a child. She believes that if her daughter had not made it as a musician she would have tried to become an author or journalist. It is conceivable that she may still take the former path. One summer, during the long holidays from school, Taylor even wrote a novel. It was a 350-page effort that she has scarcely elaborated on. But neither has she ruled out publishing it one day, so Swifties may yet get to read her story. It would be guaranteed plenty of attention and sales.

Readers should not be surprised if her novel turns out to have a dark side to it. As a kid she often dreamt up imaginary conversations and storylines involving the dead squirrels and birds that had been killed near the house by barn cats. These morbid moments suggest a darker side to her character, beneath the blonde-haired wholesome American girl. She also wrote short stories, which impressed her tutors, who felt she had a strong grasp of English far beyond her years. She credits her surroundings at the Christmas-tree farm for her creative imagination. There, as she ran free, she could 'create stories and fairy tales out of everyday life', she remembered.

The farm also provided some gainful employment for Taylor during her childhood. She was given a peculiar odd job – picking the eggs of praying mantises off trees. This task was important to avoid local homes becoming infested with the creatures. So she would move between the many Christmas trees and remove as many of the eggs as she could. The importance of this job was highlighted when she forgot to check the trees on one occasion and praying mantises hatched in homes around the neighbourhood. 'There were hundreds of thousands of them,' she recalled during an interview with Jay Leno on *The Tonight Show*. 'And they had little kids and they couldn't kill them because that'd be a bad Christmas.'

However, despite mishaps such as this, she was rarely disciplined harshly as a child – mostly because she proved to be her own toughest critic, a self-disciplinarian of sorts. 'When I was naughty as a kid, I used to send myself to my own room,' she told the *Daily Mail*. Andrea was no pushover – far from it, in fact – but she hesitated to discipline Taylor because her daughter was 'so hard on herself'. Taylor did not know at this stage what she wanted to do for a living when she grew up. She would often tell people she was going to become a stockbroker, but, despite her family heritage in that sphere, she admits that she did not even know what this meant. Friends of hers would say they wanted to become a ballerina or an astronaut. 'And I'm, like, "I'm gonna be a financial adviser,"' she said.

Adjusting to the realities of country life had been something of a strain for Scott and Andrea – particularly Scott, whose existence was one of stark contrasts: high-powered financial work in the city by day, and bumpkin duties in the countryside in the evening. As for Taylor, she thrived on rural life. She would ride ponies across trails, take rides on tractors, build forts in the hayloft, roam around the fruit orchards and adopt pets from the plentiful woodland creatures. This earthy existence and love of nature would influence her music in the years ahead. More immediately, though, it had the effect of influencing her appearance: her hair became tangled and messy. Taylor has since said that she is delighted she lived in a 'space' where she was free to be 'a crazy kid with tangled hair'.

As she approached the childhood milestone age of 10, the country-keen Taylor was adding pop to her musical tastes – or trying to, at least. Among the acts she listened to were Natasha Bedingfield, the Spice Girls and Hanson. Hints of these three acts can be heard on her fourth studio album, *Red*. She also listened to Backstreet Boys and Britney Spears, choreographing dance moves to their biggest hits alongside a friend of hers. Pop was not a lasting flirtation for Taylor, but it was fun while it lasted.

At the age of 10, she decided she wanted to perform. She had already taken parts in small local productions, including a male character called Freddy Fast Talk in one such play. To Taylor, the fact that the character was a guy, and a *bad* guy at that, made no difference. 'I was like, "I will dress up like a guy; I want to sing that song,"' she said. The next push in that direction came when she saw a local children's theatre, called the Berks County Youth Theater Academy, put on a production of *Charlie and the Chocolate Factory*, the Roald Dahl classic. She loved it when she went to watch, and felt drawn to being on the stage herself. Within days she was back at the theatre to audition for a part in a forthcoming production of *Annie*. She impressed enough to be welcomed into the group. There, she met other youngsters who were, in an important way, like her: they had a hunger to perform and to succeed. There was plenty of competitiveness and sometimes jealousy, too, yet at least the drive of these children would give Taylor a lift, ensuring that she upped her game and remained focused. It was within these walls that Taylor's ambitions were nurtured.

In time, she would find she had several things going for her at the BYTA: she was tall, for one thing, so she could command the stage as required for lead roles. When she first arrived there, however, she found her height to be a disadvantage – it made her stand out awkwardly among her peers. This only added to the pangs of anxiety she felt in those early days. Fortunately, she still managed to get a part in *Annie*, albeit a very small one in the ensemble. According to one source, practically everyone who auditioned managed to get a part in the production.

Yet the confidence she drew from her experience in *Annie* helped her to land her first lead role – in the well-known musical *The Sound of Music*. She took to the part with aplomb – so much so that, contrary to usual BYTA procedures, she was not rested for half the weekend shows. Instead, she appeared in all of them. She then landed another starring role, as Sandy in the theatre's production of *Grease*.

As she performed Sandy's songs, Taylor found that her vocals were sounding distinctly country in flavour. 'It was all I had listened to, so I guess it was just kind of natural,' she told the Great American Country channel. It is from this moment that the rest of her story flows: she said she decided right there that 'country music was what I needed to be doing'.

All the while, she was serious about making a go of it in musicals. She travelled to New York to audition for roles in Broadway and off-Broadway productions. Her voice teacher, Kirk Cremer, became her unofficial manager for such ventures. He had professional-looking headshots taken of Taylor and he would be at her side as she travelled to the Manhattan auditions. She would, she recalled during a chat with *Inquirer Entertainment*, 'stand in line in a long hallway with a lot of people'. Later, back in her home town, she took another lead part, in a production of *Bye Bye Birdie*. In this play she took the role of Kim MacAfee, who has a secret crush on a rock star. This play was less successful than her previous outings and the production was struck with a number of problems. But by now she had decided that country music was her future, so she was able to cope with the disappointment.

From this realisation, she began a process that, in increasingly voluminous form, continues to this day: she sought out opportunities to sing her favourite songs in front of a live audience. This began with karaoke, initially using the theatre's own karaoke unit. She chose songs she liked and sang them to her fellow cast members at parties, loving the experience so much that it felt like 'my favourite thing in the world'. She received plentiful praise for her karaoke performances. One evening, as Taylor stood there belting out another country classic, someone approached her mother and said that this was what Taylor should be doing for a living. It was a sentiment that Taylor and her family increasingly felt themselves.

She just needed to get out there and sing to new audiences. One venue she turned up at was the Pat Garrett Roadhouse, where she took part in karaoke competitions. This smoky bar was an incongruous place for a pre-teen girl to be, but her parents understood what it meant to her and allowed her to go and compete, provided they were physically accompanying her every inch of the way. Although one parent at the BYTA reportedly accused

Taylor's mother and father of being that dreaded species, the 'pushy parents', Taylor prefers to view their encouragement as 'empowerment' rather than pressure.

Speaking to Country Music Television, she expanded on her view of parenting and pressure. She felt that simply telling a child that they can be whatever they want to be and that they should chase their dreams was only half of the process. The other half was for the parents to genuinely believe those sentiments – 'My parents actually believed it,' she said. She is clear, however, that her mother and father 'never pushed' her. Indeed, she added, had they done so, she would probably have been a lot less, rather than more, successful.

So she continued to turn up at Pat Garrett's venue every week. Her parents might not have been pushy, but Taylor was – proudly so. 'I was kind of like an annoying flag around the place,' she told *CMT News*. 'I would not leave them alone. What they would do is have these karaoke contests … I would go until I won.' She also played her guitar at a wide range of other venues, including coffee shops, and even at Boy Scout meetings.

Her persistence paid off and further success was quickly coming her way. On one significant occasion, she won a karaoke contest singing the LeAnn Rimes song 'Big Deal'. As part of her victory, she was given a slot opening for the country music legend Charlie Daniels. Having wowed the often-sparse audiences at her karaoke performances, Taylor then began to target larger crowds. High on her target list were sports teams who needed someone to sing the national anthem at their matches. The Reading Phillies, the local baseball outfit, were one of the first teams to invite her to sing. With a handful of performances for them under her belt, she aimed even higher. For her, this was a simple equation. 'I figured out that if you could sing that one song, you could get in front of 20,000 people without even having a record deal,' she would tell *Rolling Stone* later.

She sang at the US Open tennis tournament and then at a Philadelphia 76ers match. It was April 2002. Taylor looked marvellously patriotic as she took to the stage with a top covered in small American flags. When she looked back on the night later, she laughed at how nervous she had seemed. She was indeed 'nervous', she said, but she still found it to be an 'awesome' experience.

As she left the court after this latter performance, she saw the famous rapper Jay-Z sitting in the audience. As she walked past, he leaned in and gave the youngster a congratulatory high-five. She was so thrilled: she has said that she boasted about that encounter 'for, like, a year straight'. What a badge of honour for a budding singer to have! Singing the national anthem became easier for her the more she did it, but she admitted that she did feel nerves when she sang at a World Series tie between the Philadelphia Phillies and the Tampa Bay Rays. She said the 'challenge' came due to the 'utter silence that comes over 40,000 people in a baseball stadium and you're the only one singing it'. Taylor recalled how that first moment of silence would be 'surreal'. Then she would do what all artists yearn to do, however terrifying it can feel: she would fill the silence with her own sweet voice.

'It was a little scary at first,' she told *Elle Girl* magazine. What she would learn in time was that the best answer for nerves was simply to keep performing. 'Every time you play another show it gets better and better,' she added. This worked better for her than other coping strategies. When she tried the technique of imagining each member of the audience wearing just underpants, she found it did not work for her – 'at all'. News of her nerves will be a surprise for some who knew her back then, as she portrayed an air of utter confidence on the surface.

Her *de facto* manager Kirk was so impressed with her continued progress that he arranged for her to record some tracks at the studio owned by his older brother Ronnie. Among the songs she recorded were cover versions of those by some of her favourite artists, including: 'Here You Come Again' (Dolly Parton); 'One Way Ticket' (LeAnn Rimes); 'There's Your Trouble' (Dixie Chicks) and more. She loved being in a recording studio, standing at the microphone with her headphones on, and when she saw the banks of controls at the mixing desk she wondered what they all did; but, most of all, she felt as if she was becoming a professional artist, much like her heroes.

Those heroes influenced her in different ways. She had taken inspiration and guidance from three different stars, as she would later explain during an interview with *Rolling Stone* magazine. 'I saw that Shania Twain brought this independence, this crossover appeal; I saw that Faith Hill brought this classic old-school glamour and beauty and grace; and I saw that the Dixie Chicks brought this complete "We don't care what you think" quirkiness. I loved what all of those women were able to do and what they were able to bring to country music.' She was being inspired as a musician and a female; this was girl power, but with a country drawl.

Her existence was proving exciting on the road, and her family life was pleasant and comfortable, too. Her parents' hard work in business had paid off and delivered a wonderful life for the Swifts. The family's new six-bedroom home was a comfortable and enviable building in a grand location, at 78 Grandview Boulevard, Reading, Pennsylvania, 19609. It had, according to reports, an elevator and an inside pool, complete with hot tub. The classical-revival building was large and spacious, measuring 5,050 square feet. A later listing of the property described a 'bright study', where Taylor would play guitar. When it hit the market in the summer of 2013, it was listed at $799,500. Back then, she was given the attic. Given the stature of the house, this effectively meant she had an entire floor to herself, comprising three rooms, including one bedroom. It was almost as if she had her own apartment at the age of 11. Indeed, when her friends and colleagues from the theatre group visited the house there was a lot of shock and a fair amount of envy among them as they saw the splendour she lived in. The theatre group included kids from a broad range of social backgrounds – some of them barely knew that people could live in such luxury.

Taylor had it good, and did her best to shrug off the envious glances. In the summer, the family would move to their gorgeous holiday home in Stone Harbor, New Jersey. Americans flock there on vacation from several east-coast regions and beyond. The *New York Times* describes the area as featuring 'block after block of gleaming McMansions and elegant shops', and it is among the richest towns in the United States. It has now gained wider recognition thanks to its place on the trashy and fun reality television show *Jersey Shore*. For Taylor, it proved to be a pivotal part of her upbringing: 'That's where most of my childhood memories were formed,' she has said.

Taylor – who once told *Sea Ray* magazine that she had 'lived in a life jacket' since the age of four – loved this seaside resort, where the family first bought property the year she turned two. She found Stone Harbor 'magical' and loved to swim in the sea as well as take part in watersports, including jet-skiing and sailing, even though, in general, she was not a natural at sport. Sometimes they would see a dolphin and it felt so wonderfully life-affirming to be near such natural beauty. 'There were so many places to explore, whether it was finding a new island in the inlet or walking to 96th Street for ice cream,' she said. As she entered Springer's, the ice-cream place she so loved, she would be struck by indecision. As she gazed upwards at the long list of flavours, it was so hard to choose just one. However, cookies 'n' cream became a flavour she would regularly settle upon. The outlet, run proudly by the Humphreys family, was a firm favourite for Taylor. She also enjoyed visiting an Italian restaurant on the same street, where she would devour Caesar salad and pizza. She says that, thanks to the Swifts' long summers in Stone Harbor, 'I could not have had a cooler childhood.'

The family's home was opposite a bird sanctuary, meaning that Taylor could enjoy the sights of our feathered friends without even leaving the house. She would just open her window, put her binoculars to her eyes and delight in the birds. Some days she did little else but this, so entranced was she by them. On other days she got up to mischief, chiefly at the annual boat parade that she watched on Independence Day. 'We used to all gather together on the dock when the boat parades would go by on 4 July and we'd shoot water balloons at them,' she told Philly.com. She also found renewed creative inspiration during these summers, though. Many artists feel that being near water is a magical, creative experience, and it certainly seemed to work for Taylor. 'I was allowed to be kind of weird and quirky and imaginative as a kid, and that was my favourite part of living at the Shore,' she said.

Some of this creative energy showed itself in the form of musical experiments and literary endeavours, including the aforementioned novel. She was moved to write it because she was missing her friends. Putting them on the page made her feel closer to them. 'I would send them back chapters of it,' she said. However, some of it was more domestically orientated. Taylor showed early signs of being a homemaker. She took over the room above the garage and turned it into her own private den, a sanctuary in which she could reign. 'I painted the whole room different colours and used to spend all day in there, just doing nothing but sitting in my little club,' she said, 'because it was mine.'

There was one thing – or, to be precise, one person – that she could not consider hers, however badly she wanted to. A boy who lived next door to the Swifts' holiday home had captured her imagination. He would spend a lot of time in the Swift household, as his parents were friends with Taylor's parents. Soon, she felt strong yearnings for them to become an item. In fact, she decided she wanted to marry him. While Taylor wished that he would ask her out, he instead would tell her at agonising length about other girls he had his sights set on. The rejection she felt over this unrequited crush was the creative spark that led to one of her first songs. 'I felt, well, invisible,' she said. 'Obviously. So I wrote that song about it.' As we shall see, this made it onto her first album, albeit as a bonus track. She also wrote a second track, called 'Smokey Black Nights'. She describes that song, about life at the Shore, as 'a little demo I made when I was 11'.

Despite this heartbreak and the sad song that it spawned, she was relaxing and having lots of fun, but her hunger for new opportunities to perform in front of an audience did not dissipate during the summer breaks. She found fine venues on Third Avenue and 98th Street. 'I used to sing karaoke at Henny's and play acoustic shows for hours on end at Coffee Talk, a little café on 98th Street,' she said. 'I used to drag my parents into those places all the time, and all of their friends would show up and put dollars in my tip jar.' She played really long sets on occasion, and would run out of songs after a while. Not wanting to leave the spotlight, she would make up new songs on the spot. Live performances, dolphins, pranks and an unrequited crush: these were idyllic summers for the Swifts, and Taylor truly basked in the fun and drama of it all.

By now, she had also improved at guitar playing. She had been given her first guitar, an electric, when she was eight years of age. However, she had initially abandoned her attempts to learn the instrument, as she felt baffled and discouraged by it. Much later, a man came to fix the family's computer one day. Seeing the guitar, he offered to show Taylor a few chords. She quickly grew in confidence with the instrument, and the man returned to teach her some more chords. Soon, Andrea noted, Taylor was practising so much that the strings would crack her fingers. 'She was driven beyond anything I had ever witnessed,' her mother observed. The determination of her ancestors, particularly on her mother's side, was really burning brightly in Taylor.

She began to like the idea of playing on a different type of guitar: an acoustic 12-string. When a teacher told her that she would never be able to master such an instrument, there was only one thing Taylor wanted to do – prove him wrong. 'I actually learned on a 12-string, purely because some guy told me that I'd never be able to play it, that my fingers were too small. Anytime someone tells me that I can't do something, I want to do it more.' This stubborn 'I'll-show-them' determination has served Taylor well ever since.

When she returned home to Pennsylvania, she would feel so refreshed and inspired that she became even more determined to make her dream come true. She wanted to become a country music singer. But for that to happen, she realised she would need to convince her family to move hundreds of miles away from home. Easier said than done for a child of 11, but Taylor can be a pushy customer.

Chapter Two

It was actually a singer, not a signpost, who pointed Taylor in the direction of Nashville, Tennessee. As we have seen, one of her earliest country music heroes was the singer Faith Hill. It was only when Hill, who was born in Mississippi in 1967, moved to Nashville that her musical career took off. The heart of country music, Nashville has almost become a byword for that genre.

Known as 'Music City, USA', Nashville's proud musical heritage has been strong since the first half of the nineteenth century. Yet it was during the following century that things really took off in the city. A weekly country music concert, the Grand Ole Opry, was launched in 1925. Over the following decades, so many music labels opened offices in the city that a particular area, just southwest of Downtown Nashville, became known as 'Music Row'. You could scarcely walk a few yards in the area without bumping into an important figure from the music industry, energetically going about their endeavour.

By the middle of the twentieth century, the city had spawned its own musical genre. Known as 'the Nashville sound', this was a combination of country and folk with a hint of pop fun, and it produced some memorably catchy tunes. Decca Records, RCA Records and Columbia Records were the key promoters of this style, which would go on to influence so many, including Taylor. Brenda Lee, Jim Reeves and Dottie West were among the trailblazers. Elvis Presley was also a key figure. Although launched from Nashville and influenced by country, Presley made rock 'n' roll the flavour of the times.

More recently, the likes of Dolly Parton and Garth Brooks have put country, and Nashville, back on the musical map. By the time Taylor, at 11, was falling ever deeper in love with country music, the city was once more the thriving heart of the movement. Taylor decided that if Faith Hill's career had taken off when she moved to Nashville, then that was where she needed to go, too. She recalled later how 'a little bell' went off in her head, making her decide that she simply had to move there herself. She had felt for a while that Wyomissing was 'about the most random place in the world for a country singer to come from'. Something had to change.

So she embarked on a relentless, pushy campaign, regularly asking her parents: 'Hey, Mom and Dad, can we move to Nashville?' Naturally, Andrea and Scott were surprised and nonplussed at first. They had built such a strong and comfortable family home in Pennsylvania, together with their gorgeous holiday home on the coast, that they were understandably a little shaken at the thought of upping sticks to the heart of Tennessee.

Taylor, though, was fierce and focused. Indeed, if there are two themes that run throughout her life, it is determination and a willingness to be persistent and take risks. Those qualities are particularly pronounced in this chapter. In the face of initial opposition to her Nashville plan, Taylor was determined. She continued to plead with them to make the move that she believed would make her dream come true. She particularly put pressure on Andrea, perhaps hoping that her mother – a determined woman herself – would at least relate to her drive. Andrea eventually gave in – partially. She would sanction a one-off trip as an initial step. Taylor's mother said that she was particularly impressed by the fact that her daughter never mentioned fame as the thing she hoped to find in Nashville. Unlike the hopefuls who pop up on our screens during reality television contests to state pleadingly that being famous is all they have ever wanted, Taylor took a different angle. Instead, she only said that she wanted to be there to work alongside the artists whom she loved and respected, and that one day, hopefully, she would be able to move people herself in the way they had moved her. As Andrea explained: 'It was about moving to a place where she could write with people she could learn from.'

Taylor had a double reason to be delighted with Andrea's movement on the Nashville question. She had been experiencing unpleasant bullying from classmates at school. Unfortunately for her, a number of factors in her life were enough to make classmates jealous of her –

her comfortable home life and wealthy parents, to name two. To add to their thinly veiled envy, she was beginning to be written about in the media. This press attention was a mixed blessing for Taylor. While it was flattering and helpful for her career, it tended to prompt spikes in the teasing and shunning she was suffering. When one of her national-anthem renditions was reported in a local newspaper, she knew that the following day would be 'a bad day at school for me'.

In addition, her love of country music was also causing her to be picked on. Like many children who take an interest in music beyond the most mainstream of genres, she found that she would be teased for daring to be different. Her classmates were, said Taylor, 'going to sleepovers and breaking into their parents' liquor cabinets on the weekend', whereas she was focusing solely on music. It made her stand out. They even teased her over her sore fingers, which had been worn down by hours of guitar practice. Andrea had taped Taylor's fingers up for her. To the bullies, this was another reason to mark Taylor down as a 'weirdo'. One day, a group of girls whom she had been friendly with for some time decided to shun her. As she sat down to join their table at lunch, they suddenly all got up and moved to a different table. On other occasions, schoolmates would shout unpleasant remarks at her. Andrea became accustomed to helping Taylor get over these 'awful' incidents. 'I'd have to pick her up off the floor,' she said. For her mother, the knowledge that her daughter was in such pain was torturous.

Taylor was, she realised, 'uncool' thanks to her individuality. Under the pressure of the teasing and ostracism, Taylor went against her individualist nature and took steps to try to blend in with her classmates. Here, though, she learned a valuable lesson. She discovered that the harder she tried to fit in with the in-crowd at school, the more their respect for her declined. 'So I found that trying to be like everyone else doesn't work,' she said.

On one especially hurtful day, she suggested to some girls she knew that they all meet up together for a visit to the local shopping mall. To Taylor, this seemed like a fun thing to do, so she was disappointed when they all said they had other plans. She chose to go with Andrea instead. When she and her mother walked into the mall, she saw that the group of friends was indeed there. 'I remember what happened … like it was yesterday,' Andrea told *Elle Girl*. 'Taylor and I walked into a store and these six little girls who had all claimed to be "really busy" were there together.'

Taylor felt enormously shocked and hurt. Andrea gathered her up and they drove to a different mall far away and did their shopping there. Remembering that horrible day, Taylor said the memory of it is 'one of those painful ones you'll never fully get over'. She was grateful for Andrea's lead that day. By travelling to a different shopping mall and having a fun time there, they had given as good a response as they could to those who had spurned her. The King of Prussia mall was a 90-minute drive away, but the trip felt well worth it.

Taylor was not entirely socially isolated, though. She had made friends with a girl called Britany Maack when they were both mere toddlers, and that friendship continued to blossom during and beyond her childhood. 'We were more sisters than friends,' Maack told the *Reading Eagle*. 'Taylor's family was my family.' Yet this bond was not enough to paper over the cracks of hurt that Taylor felt when kids bullied her. Lots of kids found her 'annoying' and 'uncool'. Among her offences to coolness was the fact that she was not interested in getting drunk. She knew they thought her weird, but she in turn found 12-year-olds getting drunk at parties weird. Once, during a mass sleepover at a friend's house, it was suggested they decamp to the house of a guy they knew who had access to some beer. Where her friends were excited, Taylor was appalled. She felt like phoning Andrea and asking her to take her home.

With the benefit of hindsight, she can see how all the kids at middle school, popular or not, bullies and bullied, were battling with their own personal insecurities. But back then it hurt. She would arrive at school and not know whom, if anyone, she would hang out with and chat to that day. 'And that's a really terrifying thing for somebody who's 12,' she said. She described her existence in those difficult times as that of an outsider who was forever 'looking in', but hindsight again delivers a healthy perspective on the matter. These painful moments provided vivid creative sparks for her music. The theme of the outsider, which has featured in so many songs across so many genres, was to be rich and fertile ground for her. It was first touched upon in a song she wrote when she was 12 and has, as we shall see, surfaced in several songs since.

Her isolation during her middle-school years also gave her plenty of time to focus on music. Had she still been running with the in-crowd she would have spent more time on normal schoolgirl pursuits, rather than solitary sessions with her guitar and imagination – those two dear friends who have served her so loyally ever since. The fact that she had her guitar to turn to when she was feeling low also prevented her from needing to use alcohol or drugs as a form of escape. 'Music has always been that escape for me,' she said.

So now Taylor looks back with gratitude at those who rejected her, recognising the gift their bullying gave her. Sadness has proved to be the most fertile creative ground for so many artists, but that inspiration comes, by definition, at a price, and being tormented and excluded was the price Taylor paid.

So imagine her huge relief when she learned that Andrea had begun to buckle in the face of her determination to move to the city of her dreams. As we have seen, however, Andrea only agreed to take Taylor to Nashville for a temporary visit to begin with. During a school holiday, Andrea took Taylor and her brother on the 650-mile trip to Nashville. Taylor would distribute her demo tape to the record labels and hope that one of them would snap her up once they heard her music.

Although Andrea sanctioned and organised the trip, she also drew a clear line in the sand over her own role within it. It was one that was supportive but strictly defined. 'I made it really clear,' she told TV show *Teen Superstar*. 'Okay, if this is something you want, you've got to do it,' she told Taylor. She added that she had never signed up to be Taylor's manager and she certainly did not see herself as a 'stage mom'. So she would walk only as far as the front door of the label companies with Taylor. From then on, the youngster would have to walk on alone. Remembering her pride over her own career achievements, Andrea was keen for her daughter to feel the same.

Taylor had given the demo CD a simple design. The front cover had a photograph of her face on it and the words 'Call me'. On the back cover were her telephone number and her email address. As they drove down the road, Taylor would suddenly shriek as she saw a label. 'That's Mercury Records!' she would cry. 'Pull over! I need to give them my demo tape!' When she arrived at the reception desk she would hand over her homemade CD and tell them, 'Hey, I'm 11, and I want a record deal.' Then, echoing the slogan printed on the front cover, she would add with a smile: 'Call me!' It was a sweet pitch, but not a finely honed one. Later, looking back at this with the advantage of time and experience, she was able to smile. She would say: 'How did that work out for me? It didn't!'

In the immediate wake of her trip, she was enormously disappointed when all but one of the labels she had visited failed to contact her. She waited for the phone to ring or the email to ping, but nothing happened. These were crushing days – they felt more like weeks, so slowly and emptily did they drag along. Until, one day, a man from one of the record companies rang her back to tell her that the way she was going about her pitch was unlikely to work. 'He was so sweet,' she recalled later.

She had thought she was special, but in time she realised that there were 'hundreds of people' also trying to make it in Nashville and that they all had 'the same dream'. She realised that she was not inherently as special as she had hoped, and that she would have to make a real effort to show how much she could stand out. While this was news to her, she did not take it as bad news. Instead, she stepped up again. Taylor is usually good when there is a challenge on. 'I thought,' she told *Teen Superstar*, 'you don't just make it in Nashville. I've got to really work on something that would make me different.'

The short trip to Nashville had not reaped the immediate results that Taylor had hoped for. In fact, she would get her first attention from a major label as a result of her being spotted at one of her sporting performances by a man called Dan Dymtrow. He was then managing the career of the pop princess Britney Spears. He approached Taylor and asked if she could provide some more evidence of her talent and personality. Scott decided that the best way to do this would be for them to film a quirky home video, showing Taylor in an interesting light. 'My dad put together this typical "dad video" type of thing, with the cat chewing the [guitar] neck and stuff like that,' Taylor told *Wood & Steel*. This was enough for Dymtrow to invite her to his office, so she showed up with her trusty 12-string guitar and played some music for him.

He was impressed. But the first project he got her involved in was closer to modelling than music. She posed in Abercrombie & Fitch clothes in a shoot for *Vanity Fair* magazine called 'Rising Stars'. This promotional gimmick saw the retailer link up with potential stars of the future and drape them in its autumnal range. After Dymtrow had sent them a press kit about Taylor, they invited her to take part in the shoot. In Taylor's photos, she wore a white top with denim jeans. She portrayed a heartbroken girl, even wiping away a tear from her eye with a handkerchief. She was holding a guitar in the photos, but this was still far away from what she really wanted to do. She also worried that she was not 'cool' enough to be in such a position – a legacy of her school experiences, perhaps.

The irony was that she certainly *was* cool enough to take part, and by doing so she was showing her bullies that she could be very much the insider after all. To be part of the well-known label's 'Rising Stars' campaign was a significant honour. Among those selected by Abercrombie & Fitch before they became household names were Channing Tatum, Jennifer Lawrence, Ashton Kutcher and Penn Badgley. More recently, the label has chosen *Glee* star Jacob Artist, *American Horror Story*'s Lily Rabe, *Texas Chainsaw 3D*'s Scott Eastwood and a slew of other young talent. Now, Taylor stands tall among this list, but at the time she felt out of her depth.

She worried about all sorts of scenarios, including her photograph being dropped from the publication. So imagine her excitement when, in July 2004, her photo appeared on the news stands in *Vanity Fair* magazine. There she was, featured in a full-page photograph, alongside a passage of text in which she explained to readers who she was. 'After I sang the national anthem at the US Open last year,' she began, 'a top music manager signed me as his client.' She went on to describe her love of country music: 'I love the sound of fiddles and mandolins ringing in my ears and I love the stories that you hear in country ballads. I sometimes write about teenage love, but I am presently a 14-year-old girl without a boyfriend. Sometimes I worry that I must be wearing some kind of guy repellent, but then I realise that I'm just discovering who I am as a person.' She concluded: 'Right now, music is the most important thing in my life, and I want to touch people with my songs.'

She was aiming for the top but was not shy of taking on more apprentice-style roles within the country music scene. For instance, she grabbed an intern slot at the four-day CMA Music Festival, held each year by the Country Music Association in Nashville. She was handed a clipboard and set to work in an administrative role. She was entranced as she watched autograph hunters approach the stars she was serving. 'I remember just feeling like, if there was ever a chance that one day people would line up to have me sign something of theirs, then that would be a really, really good day for me,' she said.

Another promotional activity at this stage saw her signed-up to a compilation album assembled by the cosmetics firm Maybelline. One of her songs appeared on the album *Chicks With Attitude*. Her manager then took her on a breathless tour of meetings with record labels. The tour would pay off – in a way. Meetings such as these come with a wide scale of outcomes. Sometimes, executives cannot contain their excitement for the young act in front of them. Other times, they are summarily dismissive of them. It is also far from unheard of for an act to be turned away before they even get past the receptionist.

Taylor was keen for more musical projects to get involved in and she was, initially, delighted when Dymtrow got her a deal with RCA Records. It seemed to be just what she wanted – recognition from a major label in Nashville. For a while, she felt that she had finally made the big step she had dreamed of. It felt so exciting. 'I was elated,' she told *CMT Insider* later. 'I was just, "Oh my gosh! This huge record label wants to sign me to a development deal. I'm so excited!"' There seemed to be, on the face of it, so much to be optimistic about. RCA gave her sponsorship money and recording time.

However, the agreement turned out to be not quite as exciting as she hoped. 'A development deal is an in-between record deal,' she told NBC. 'It's like a guy saying that he wants to date you but not be your boyfriend. You know, they don't want to sign you to an actual record deal or put an album out on you. They want to watch your progress for a year.' At 14 years of age she was being told by the label that they wanted to keep her on ice until she was 18. For a girl in her mid-teens this was unbearable – four years seemed so far away. She felt she was running out of time. For Taylor, her teenage years were not an inconvenience to get beyond before she could become a singer-songwriter. She wanted to be that creature there and then. 'I wanted to capture these years of my life on an album while they still represented what I was going through,' she recalled.

Her self-belief would soon be rewarded when her parents agreed to a more fixed move to Nashville in the wake of the RCA development. 'My father had a job he could do from anywhere,' she told *Blender* magazine. 'My parents moved across the country so I could pursue a dream.' Put like that, it slightly downplayed the sacrifice Scott and Andrea had made. Taylor was aware of the extent of that sacrifice, despite the fact that her parents went to some effort to minimise it. There was no pressure heaped on her, no guilt trips laid at her feet. Instead, they acted as if this was a choice they had made themselves, on their own terms.

It did not fool Taylor for a moment. She told *Self* magazine: 'I knew I was the reason they were moving. But they tried to put no pressure on me. They were like, "Well, we need a change of scenery anyway," and, "I love how friendly people in Tennessee are."' Crucially, they took steps to ensure that as little expectation was placed on Taylor's shoulders as possible. With the entire family moving hundreds of miles for her, it would be easy for Taylor to feel that she had let everyone down if she were not to hit the big time. But as Andrea told *Entertainment Weekly*, 'I never wanted to make that move about her "making it".' She feared it would be too 'horrible' if Taylor had not succeeded.

As she house-hunted in Nashville, Andrea found a place on Old Hickory Lane that she liked the look of. She arranged for the rest of the family to go and look at it. Scott told the Sea Ray website how quickly he was sold on it. 'We stopped at the dock on the way to check up on the house,' he recalled. 'I looked down the cove toward the lake, imagined my Sea Ray tied up there and said, "I'll take it."' Even the estate agent was shocked: 'Don't you want to see the house first?' she asked.

He felt at home and so did his children. Taylor and Austin joined a local high school called Hendersonville. Here, to Taylor's relief, her fellow pupils were not suspicious or envious of her musical endeavours. Quite to the contrary – they were impressed by her efforts and delighted to help her make her dreams come true. 'Everybody was so nice to me,' she told the *New Yorker* later. 'They're all, like, "We heard you're a singer. We have a talent show next week – do you want to enter?"' What a breath of fresh air for her; she could hardly believe how well the move to Nashville was turning out. It felt a world apart from the troubled existence she'd had in Pennsylvania. 'They were so supportive,' she recalled of her new neighbours.

She had her first ever kiss at the age of 15. However, it was a subsequent boyfriend, called Brandon Borello, who inspired her to write a song. She was in the freshman year of high school when she was asked to write a song for a ninth-grade talent-show project. 'I was sitting there thinking, I've got to write an upbeat song that's going to relate to everyone,' she told AOL. 'And at the time I was dating a guy and we didn't have a song. So I wrote us one, and I played it at the show. Months later, people would come up to me and say, "I loved the song you played." They'd only heard it once, so I thought, there must be something here.'

On her first day at school she sat down next to a girl in English class. They began to chat and quickly became close friends. The girl's name was Abigail Anderson. They felt an instinctive bond, grounded in the fact that they both felt like outsiders but both had defined ambitions: Anderson's was to become a professional swimmer. Finally, Taylor had a friend she could relate to on several levels. They were the outsiders who wanted to become, in the widest sense, champions. They also shared an impish sense of humour.

Anderson was not the only good thing about English classes for Taylor. A lover of words and writing, she often enjoyed these lessons enormously. Among the books that they studied in these classes was that staple feature of so many youngsters' education: Harper Lee's novel *To Kill a*

Mockingbird. This classic American novel inspired her greatly. 'You know, you hear storytelling like in Harper Lee's *To Kill a Mockingbird* and it just … it makes your mind wander,' she has said. 'It makes you feel like it makes your world more vast. And you think about more things and greater concepts after you read something like that.'

After studying like any other schoolgirl during the day, in the evening she would enter a much more adult world, as she teamed up with established songwriters for creative sessions. She later described the curious duality of these days as 'a really weird existence – I was a teenager during the day when I was at school, and then at night it was like I was 45. My mom would pick me up from school and I'd go downtown and sit and write songs with these hit songwriters.'

She told *American Songwriter* magazine that she realised what an opportunity these sessions were for her. Yet she was also aware that it was important for her to appear as confident as possible. 'I knew that, being a 14-year-old girl, anybody would – understandably – think, I'm going to have to write a song for a kid today.' She was determined that this would not happen. 'So I would walk in with 10 or 15 almost-finished melodies or choruses. I just wanted to make sure that everybody knew I was serious about it.'

Throughout her waking hours she was on the hunt for new inspiration and for the opportunity to record it. When moments of lyrical inspiration struck she would scribble down the words on whatever came to hand: her school exercise books, a tissue. This sometimes caused awkward moments. Teachers would sometimes call in a random notebook check and they would be surprised to find Taylor's scribbled lyrics of anguish alongside her schoolwork. 'But they learned to deal with me,' she said. Other times a melody would come into her head. She would record it by humming it into her mobile phone. It was not unheard of for her classmates to spot – and hear – her in the toilets, humming a rough tune into her phone.

Here, we turn to a crucial difference between her new school and her old one. Previously, her fellow pupils gave her inspiration only via the cruellest and most unintentional of routes. By excluding her and bullying her, they sent Taylor into such pits of unhappiness that she would compose her way out of them. Now, however, her schoolmates offered deliberate and positive inspiration. Groups of them would join Taylor around a campfire at night and listen to her singing her songs as she strummed her guitar. These youngsters were of the age that Taylor wanted to appeal to, so they were the perfect test audience for her songs and ideas.

This obsessive documentation and regular road testing meant that Taylor turned up to her writing sessions with plenty to put on the table. There would be no question of her being a young passenger, incomplete without the patronage of those older and wiser. For instance, she wrote with a fellow composer called Liz Rose. 'I think she ended up just writing with me because I didn't change what she was doing,' Rose told *American Songwriter*. 'I tried to make it better and mould it and hone it, and [said] "hang on there" and "write it down"; that's why it worked with us. I really respected her and got what she was trying to do, and I didn't want to make her write in the Nashville cookie-cutter songwriting mould.'

Rose was impressed with her young collaborator. In time, she felt that she was little more than Taylor's editor. 'She'd write about what happened in school that day,' Rose told *Blender*. 'She had such a clear vision of what she was trying to say. And she'd come in with the most incredible hooks.' The two found they complemented one another well in these sessions. Out of them came the song that would launch Taylor's career properly – 'Tim McGraw'. The earliest origins of the song came during a maths class. She began to hum a new melody in the lesson and then, Taylor said, it took her just a quarter of an hour to write the basic structure of the song. When she got home she smoothed it out and improved it a bit, adding some piano melody. Then she was ready to take it to a session with Rose.

The song, which was originally going to be entitled 'When You Think Tim McGraw', is a bittersweet affair in which Taylor looks back on a real-life relationship she had with a boy, who is widely believed to be her ex-boyfriend Brandon Borello. The lyrics take the form of a letter written to her former partner. Borello was a senior when he dated Taylor, who was then still a freshman. This leads to the month of tears in September in the song when they were parted.

Explaining what she felt was the power of the song, Taylor said: 'It was reminiscent, and it was thinking about a relationship you had and then lost.' She added: 'I think one of the most powerful human emotions is what should have been and wasn't. That was a really good song to start out on, just because a lot of people can relate to wanting what you can't have.' She knew what made a good song, intellectually as well as instinctively. 'Tim McGraw' would be track one on her debut album – and it had all started in a maths class.

Taylor soon felt that she was on a roll. She told the *Washington Post* that she could 'draw inspiration from anything'. She expanded on what this meant for her. 'If you're a good storyteller, you can take a dirty look some-body gives you, or if a guy you used to have flirtations with starts dating a new girl or somebody you're casually talking to says something that makes you sooooo mad – you can create an entire scenario around that.'

Another early track she wrote was called 'Lucky You'. 'It was about this girl who dares to be different,' she said. The autobiographical parallels are clear. 'At that time I was describing myself,' she added. Following that and 'Tim McGraw', she then wrote a song about a guy called Drew Hardwick, on whom she had a 'huge crush', but an unrequited one. Speaking to *Country Standard Time*, she added: '[He] would sit there every day talking to me about another girl: how beautiful she was, how nice and how smart and perfect she was.' It was as if she was back in her younger years, with her unrequited crush of her summer holiday. Again, she would do her best to fake smiles for him as he told her all about other girls, and wonder if he knew that she would think about him all night.

The song, which would namecheck Drew directly, would be called 'Teardrops on My Guitar'. She began composing this track on her way home from school one day. Given its power, maturity and poise, it's remarkable that the song was conjured out of this circumstance. In the song, she yearns for Drew's flawless looks, which take her breath away. Taylor can only hope, with a slice of bitterness, that Drew's perfect girl will look after him properly. The imagery of a guy being the song she sings in her car gives this track a universal appeal of the sort that drive-time radio shows adore. When the listener truly connects with Taylor's lyrics and the emotions they describe, they will find themselves shedding a few teardrops, too.

Her songs were proving to be rich little numbers. Word soon spread around town about this incredible kid who was writing with such aplomb and deftness. Soon, she would be contacted by the mighty Sony. They snapped her up as a songwriter to compose potential tracks for their existing artists. She agreed and duly became the youngest staff songwriter ever hired by the esteemed Sony/Tree publishing house. The significance and symbolism of this is stark: a girl in her mid-teens was signed by one of the world's biggest record labels to compose songs for artists many years older than her.

So came the bold move: Taylor decided to leave RCA and go in search of a label that would truly believe in her. This was a difficult decision and one she only reached after much soul-searching. What courage and self-belief it showed to reject a major label's interest in her. However, the fault line between artist and label was significant: she felt she was 'good to go' right then. The label felt she needed time and development, not least because it was the country music market she wanted to move into – complete with its world-weary lyrics and ageing fanbase – rather than pop, which is far more geared for teenage stars.

But Taylor was quite sure. 'I figured, if they didn't believe in me then, they weren't ever going to believe in me,' she said. She took a deep breath, walked away and continued to prepare for the day when she would make it big. She even spent ages practising her autograph, filling a notebook with her scrawl in preparation for the day when she would be famous enough to sign her name for fans. Even though the humble autograph would have been surpassed by the smartphone photograph as the favoured proof of a celebrity encounter by the time she made it big – particularly for Taylor's generation – these signature rehearsals showed that she was determined to be an authentic star.

Again, her courage was rewarded. The moment soon came that changed everything: enter Scott Borchetta, the man who would make her a queen. For him, the decision to sign her would be a no-brainer. 'I fell in love with her,' he said. 'It's really that simple.' Born in the 1960s, Borchetta was always a competitive and driven soul. In middle school he competed in car races with friends. He found, he told *Forbes* later, that he had a 'race devil' inside him. After school he decided to try to make it in the music industry. He took a job in the mail room of his dad's independent promotion company. He was not the first record company executive to have joined the industry via the mail room – the famed Simon Cowell took a similar route. Borchetta moved from California to Nashville and took a job working for the promotional department of Mary Tyler Moore's MTM record label. He then ran his own independent promotions firm for a while before joining MCA Records.

Then he joined Universal Music Group, under whose umbrella he launched DreamWorks Nashville. Here, he was part of one of the planet's biggest record labels. However, in 2005, his division was closed down. He was looking for a new star to really launch his next label. Taylor, who would be the perfect person, crossed his path at the famous Nashville showcase, the Bluebird Café. This regular event was an exciting prospect for Taylor, who would get to play in front of an audience of local record industry talent hunters. The institution had its success stories, and none – prior to Taylor's arrival – came bigger than Garth Brooks. He was spotted there in 1987 and signed up to Capitol Records. The rest is history.

History would be made the night that Taylor showed up for her own slot. She carried her guitar onto the stage and performed an acoustic set. By now she was comfortable with live performance, but she was also aware that this was no usual audience. Somewhere out there, she hoped, would be a record label figure able to make her dreams come true. Borchetta, meanwhile, had turned up with a corresponding dream. He wanted to find a talent he could turn into an international star.

When Taylor first sat down onstage, both she and Borchetta – who were at this point more or less strangers to one another, despite a brief encounter during his days at DreamWorks Nashville – took a deep breath and hoped for the best. Borchetta remembers sitting with his eyes closed and wondering: 'Is this going to hit me? And it absolutely did.' He told Great American Country: 'I was just smitten on the spot. It was like a lightning bolt.' Straight afterwards he arranged to meet Taylor and the Swifts to pitch what he could do for them.

He told Taylor: 'I have good news and I have bad news: the good news is that I want to sign you to a record deal; the bad news is that I'm no longer with Universal Records.' He explained that he wanted her to wait for him, as he was about to launch a new record label of his own. 'I'm working on something,' he said. Taylor found him convincing; he made her feel that he had something up his sleeve that she would want to take part in.

Looking back on how she won him over, Borchetta told NBC: 'I think it was in August of 2005. Taylor played me a song called "When You Think Tim McGraw". She finished the song and I said, "Do you realise what you

51

have just written? Do you have any idea?" That was that moment of, "Oh my God." And the grenade dropped in the still pond.' Inspired, he went away and told friends that he had found a future country music sensation. When he went on to tell them that she was a teenage schoolgirl, he could see the scepticism draw across their faces. 'People would look at me cross-eyed,' he said. 'I would feel like they were deleting me from their BlackBerrys as I was telling them.' To him, though, Taylor seemed as great a prospect as his previous big catches, Sugarland and Trisha Yearwood.

So what was this project Borchetta had up his sleeve for Taylor? The new label he was working on would be called Big Machine Records. ('The name Big Machine is kind of a joke,' he said during an interview with Fast Company, 'because, really, we're anything but.') He started it within months of his DreamWorks Nashville label coming to an end. His criteria for whether to sign an artist for Big Machine has always been the same: 'I either fall in love with an artist's music or I don't,' he said. He also set out a bold mission statement for his new label, which would, he hoped, put 'the music first and the artist first'. He added: 'It's the *music* business. It's not the *business* of music.' Borchetta has also happily defined himself and his team as dedicated workaholics. 'There are no shortcuts,' he told an industry gathering. 'We work 24/7, and we love it.'

He had truly fallen in love with Taylor's material, so Taylor finally had someone on her side who, she felt convinced, could take her where she wanted to go. She had needed to hold her nerve several times, but she was at last on her way to something big. She had shrugged off school bullies, moved hundreds of miles away from home, weathered several rejections, walked away from an unsatisfactory arrangement with a big label and maintained her self-belief as best she could throughout. With such optimism in the air following her first meetings with Borchetta, she could afford to feel truly proud of herself.

Yet she was always in touch, and still is, with her greatest source of support – her parents. To be reminded of their role in her success, she only has to look to a friend of hers. 'I'm really good friends with Kellie [Pickler], whose Mom abandoned her,' Taylor told the *Washington Post*. 'I look at my mom, who's been there for everything, and I think, like, if I'd been in Kellie's situation, I probably wouldn't have made it. I look at other people who have absentee fathers or self-consumed mothers, and I'm so lucky.' The Swifts were proving to be a mighty fine team.

Chapter Three

As an artist, Taylor sees herself as one who avoids the temptation to succumb to cheap gimmicks, however superficially enticing they may seem in the short term. With her record deal signed and her parents on board with the whole project, it was time for Taylor to take the music she had been working on for some years and channel it into a package that would become her first album. Her inner artist wanted to produce a record she would be proud of. Her business-savvy side was keen for the album to succeed commercially.

The latter emotion was the one that invited temptation – and the more she worked on the songs, the more aware she became of how her youthful conceits would stand out in the adult-centred, middle-age-dominated country world. 'All the songs I heard on the radio were about marriage and kids and settling down,' she said. She found these themes hard to relate to. Rather than become a gimmicky act, singing songs on topics clearly beyond her years, she resolved to stick to what she knew. She had no wish to become one of those child performers who sing incongruously mature ballads as some sort of ghastly cabaret act.

As far as Taylor was concerned, there was no rule that stated country music songs should not tell the stories of young people. If she had to overcome the doubting tones of many industry authorities on this point, that was fine by her – she has always been comfortable sticking to her guns. Indeed, some of those close to her swear she is at her best when there is some sense of fight in the air. 'I kept writing songs about the guy I dated for a couple of weeks and who cheated on me, about things I was going through,' she told *Entertainment Weekly*. 'There was no reason why country music shouldn't relate to someone my age if someone my age was writing it.' She returned to the theme during an interview with *Billboard*: 'I was writing about the same things that I'm writing about now, of course – boys. And I've always been fascinated by the way that people treat each other and the way that they interact. Stuff like that just really, really fascinates me and always has.'

These themes would form the backdrop of her debut album. A team of producers were involved in putting it together, but the first and main talent called in was Nathan Chapman. He came to the project after he met Liz Rose. Though he had produced music before, he had never produced an album in full. Ever since he graduated from Lee University in 2001 with a degree in English, he had been looking for his big break. He would certainly get that by working with Taylor. As for the lady herself, she was quickly impressed by his way with the studio controls. She had begun to work with him on her demos. When he stayed on for the album proper, he did not disappoint. As she told Country Music Television (CMT) in 2006: 'I got to record with a bunch of really awesome producers in Nashville, but none of [it] sounded the way it did with Nathan ... the right chemistry hit.'

She had the right man for the job – and she was ready to give him the space to shine. Unlike some divas, Taylor acknowledges the importance of producers to the creative process, but she takes a hands-on approach in the studio. For she is an artist who feels she can bring a lot to the production table herself. 'When I write a song, I hear how it is supposed to sound in my head,' she said. 'I can hear the production. I can hear what the drums are doing, what the mandolin is doing, what the bass is doing, when I'm writing that song. So usually, when we go to the studio, all I have to do is sit down with Nathan for 10 minutes and say, "This is how I want this to sound," and he [brings] it all to life.'

How the drums, mandolin, bass and other instruments would sound on her debut would be a pleasing mix. It took her four months to complete the album – and she was delighted with the final product. Little wonder, then, that her eponymous debut album would prove a fascinating collection of music. Here was the first substantial glimpse she gave to the world of her vision. We have already looked at the genesis of the album's opener, 'Tim McGraw'. The final production was a rich tune, complete with slide guitars – all the better for setting the tone from the start. During the song, Taylor reflects on the relationship it concerns as 'bittersweet'. The song itself is also a mixed bag emotionally – it is at once romantic and uplifting, as well as sad and heart-breaking. It includes moments of humour – like the tendency of the guy's truck to become 'stuck' in secluded side roads at night – and vivid imagery, such as the moon acting like a spotlight on a lake. It is a fine and fitting opener to her debut.

Some songs by Taylor are growers, which creep up on the listener only after several plays. Others grab the listener immediately. A song in the latter category is 'Picture to Burn', in which we first come across Taylor's tendency to vent immense anger through her material. Indeed, it is the song's very fury that makes it a true throat-grabber. She has spoken about the story behind the song. 'It's about a guy I liked who didn't like me back, and I got really mad, you know?' she said. They never actually dated, because Taylor was deeply troubled by how 'cocky' and narcissistic the guy was – 'and that's where that song came from'.

Discussing the track with *CMT Insider*, Taylor admitted: 'This song is my angry song on my album.' It is not just about ire, though. She showcases her knack for sassy vocal delivery in the song's second line – in which she sings knowingly that the narcissist will always love himself more than he could love her. She also replaced a subsequent line, which joked about her telling her friends that the guy was 'gay', for the radio release, as she was keen not to offend any listeners unintentionally.

The chorus is chanted, heaping some good, fun, hands-in-the-air infectiousness into proceedings. With its rich banjo and instantly catchy guitar line, 'Picture to Burn' seems to be influenced musically in part by Amy Dalley and Ashlee Simpson – and is all the better for it. Yet the anger continues to be striking. As Taylor repeatedly chants the word 'burn' at the end of the song, it turns into something quite aggressive for such a sweet young girl. The overall theme of the song ties into the 'defiant lady' motif employed by many of country music's female singers. For instance, 'Goodbye Earl' by the Dixie Chicks – one of Taylor's favourite songs during her karaoke era – is of this genre, though it does not burn as angrily as Taylor's track.

Yet, as she told *CMT Insider*, there is also some wit and fun in the song. 'I think girls can relate to the song, because basically it's about just being mad,' she said. 'And it's okay to be mad after a break-up or after something goes wrong with a relationship. It's just, like, completely, brutally honest. It's also kind of funny. It's got a comedic edge to it.' The critics loved it: among the tributes paid to it by reviewers were that it was 'bluntly relatable', and a 'clever, sassy, upbeat' song.

Moving to the real-life experiences behind the track, the song itself paints an unflattering picture of the guy she is raging against. He comes across as angry and lacking in self-awareness. Perhaps the strongest hint of his narcissism is that he is, as far as Taylor is concerned, oblivious to the fact that the song is about him. That he did not connect any of the dots and point the finger at himself suggests considerable delusion on his part. In the years since the album's release, as Taylor has matured and evolved as both a songwriter and a person, she had changed from the angry teen who wrote this song. 'I had this song called "Picture to Burn" that's talking about how "I hate your truck" and "I hate that you ignored me", "I hate you",' she told MTV. 'Now, the way that I would say that and the way that I would feel that kind of pain is a lot different.' Yet, as we shall see, she has stood by the overall album in the main.

Track three is the now-iconic 'Teardrops On My Guitar'. This song is cooler and calmer than its predecessor, but no less arresting or inspiring for that. As we know, Taylor wrote this song about her friend Drew Chadwick. She had a crippling crush on him, which was unrequited. 'I had it bad for him, and I just kept thinking, why am I so invisible to him? Why does he have to have a girlfriend?' I never told him that I liked him, but I did write a song with his name on it.'

The final version, which appeared on the album, is a sweetly produced mid-tempo number. It begins gently, with Taylor singing the opening to the verse in a semi-detached, almost Bieberesque style. Yet as the verse builds into the bridge, the pace and intensity both pick up. The chorus arrives in a rush of energy. The overall effect is one of Taylor at her best and most earnest. This is the track that grabbed the attention of the media and, indeed, the world. It took Taylor out of the country and teen markets and spread her appeal to all. As *Billboard* magazine put it, the song is 'ultimately relatable' and Taylor 'makes the heartbreak palpable'. It is a tender song.

Where the opening tracks dealt with experiences that are universal, track four tells a story that is very particular to Taylor. And while 'A Place in this World' is a song that many listeners will be able to relate to, the lyrics are explicitly autobiographical to Taylor, concerning her own efforts to make it in the music industry and the world itself. She was inspired to write this song during her earliest days in Nashville. Her initial dream had come true – she had moved to the heart of the industry she wanted to conquer. However, having got there, she felt overwhelmed by the scale of the challenge ahead. As she explained to TV network Great American Country (GAC), she was 'just sort of looking around at all these big buildings and these important people, wondering how I was going to fit in'.

Every listener could understand that emotion and pinpoint an example of it in their own life: perhaps their first day at university or in a new job. Moving to a new district, even. Arguably, human existence is driven by a desire to find a place in this world. And that desire is never truly satisfied, however old one gets. Not for the first – or last – time, Taylor had struck lyrical gold: a theme that all ages, genders and backgrounds could empathise with. Commercially speaking, this is songwriting of the smartest kind. Musically, it has a stadium feel, which makes it seem as much like a song from the *Red* era as it does from her debut album.

'Cold As You' includes 'some of the best lyrics I've ever written in my life', according to Taylor. The lyrics are certainly astonishingly adult and dark for those penned by a girl in her mid teens. She has never specified which real-life person, if any, this song is about. Perhaps that is just as well; whoever he is, he comes across appallingly. Some of the subjects of her break-up songs emerge as men who were just not right for Taylor, rather than just not right. The protagonist of this song – real or otherwise – seems a troubled figure.

The song will send shivers down the spines of many listeners. This is not the wistful, unrequited love found in previous efforts, but one of dark and chilling imbalance. While musically it is by no means a highlight on the album, the words – with their condescending smiles, rainy days and emotional walls painted a shade of grey – transport it into a career highlight in the opinion of many Swifties (as her fans are known). Taylor gets excited about the musical structure of songs, but what seems to animate her most is a powerful, punchy lyric. 'I love a line on a song where afterward you're just, like, burn,' she told *Rolling Stone*. There are, ironically, several burning moments in 'Cold As You'. It is another song that has considerable poise and is steeped in maturity.

In the aforementioned track 'The Outside', Taylor lays some demons of her younger years to rest. As we have seen, she wrote this song when she was just 12 years old. Finding it hard to fit in with the 'in' crowd at school, she penned these lyrics to try to make sense of what she was going through. 'I wrote that about the scariest feeling I've ever felt: going to school, walking down the hall, looking at those faces and not knowing who you're gonna talk to that day,' she told *Entertainment Weekly*.

Ironically, she went on to explain, the rejection she felt at school thickened her skin and toughened her will, to the extent that it made her unafraid of rejection from record labels when she presented herself to them. She knew that anything the labels said to her could never sting as much as her schooldays had. It is fascinating to reflect on what an inadvertent gift her school tormentors were. There is always a positive to be found in any bitter challenge life throws at us.

Musically speaking, this is essentially an upbeat tune that sets up a fiery juxtaposition: sad lyrics about loneliness set against the feel-good melody and production. Artists throughout pop history have found that, when done correctly, this is an effective trick. In its very essence, though, 'The Outside' emits the message that there is an upside to life's trials. Its position in the track sequencing is inspired: it lifts the pace of the album precisely when that surge is needed.

Not only does 'The Outside' partially conceal its sad theme under a happy track, it also to an extent reflects the essence of track seven. In 'Tied Together with a Smile', Taylor sings about how people put a brave public face on their problems. They tie themselves together with a smile, she sings, even as their lives come apart. The inspiration for the song came when she discovered that a friend – widely considered by their contemporaries to be 'the golden one' – was bulimic. When Taylor was told about her friend's problem, she said it was 'one of those moments when your heart kind of stops'. Therefore, she added, it was a 'tough' song to write, because it was about something so painful and 'real'.

However, she aimed to flavour the song with an element of redemption and hope. The song is, she hopes, ultimately about 'how, no matter what my friends go through, I'm always going to love them'. In a sense, this song is a sibling to 'The Outside'. There, she indirectly channelled the advantages of being an outsider; here, she shows that being very much on the inside can come at a bitter price. She loves to turn assumptions on their head, give them a good shake and see what falls out. Said Taylor: 'It's about that moment [when] you realise someone isn't all you thought they were and you've been trying to make excuses for someone who doesn't deserve them. And that some people are just never going to love you,' she said. Musically the song is no great shakes compared to some of the bigger tracks on the album, yet its theme has struck many listeners deeply.

Heartache, unrequited love, bullying and bulimia – the album has been a tough journey so far. In 'Stay Beautiful' she lightens the load as she celebrates the beauty of a boy who seems unaware of his stunning looks. Seeing him merely walk past her on the street is a highlight of her day – and as she sings, she is far from alone in her admiration of him. She hopes one day that he will choose her door to knock on, but even if he does not, she hopes he will stay beautiful. The feelings behind the song are reminiscent of 'You're Beautiful' by James Blunt. With its slide guitar and sway-in-your-seat tempo, this is a happy tune. It's a welcome one, too: it sets aside the growing sense of gloom its predecessors had set.

However, it's straight back to darker shades in 'Should've Said No', an anthem that has become one of her signature tunes. Here it is glowering anger that rules. She steps outside the country sphere and enters the terrain of the classic teenage anthem. This was the final song to be written for the album and she says it took just minutes to put the basics of it together. She says she wrote it 20 minutes before she recorded it. 'It just kind of fell out of my mouth and now it is in my CD player,' she explained. In it, she addresses a boy called Sam who cheated on her. The pop-rock format lends itself perfectly to her indignant yet defiant anger. Some critics, particularly a handful in the country music community, felt it was too angry. But this vengeful song was absolutely lapped up by mainstream audiences. It is also perfect for the live arena and has been covered by television talent-show hopefuls to great effect.

Taylor says that she has learned a lesson from the incident behind the song and others like it. She has concluded that a crucial decision or temptation comes before any

problem in life. If one would only say no to that temptation, she believes, life could be so much simpler. She uses
the ever-influential Andrea to strengthen this argument.
'Before I can make decisions, I always think: what is my
mom going to think if I tell her this? Is my mom going to
be really upset if she finds out about this?' This thought
experiment is often enough to convince her to say no at
the right times.

Therefore, a wider concern can perhaps be identified
here. Does Taylor, who has long aimed to position herself
as the wholesome daughter of the sometimes-debauched
pop world, mean that we should all say no to temptation?
Is this, in part, a Christian-influenced message of restraint
and abstinence in a world of snakes? One thing is for
sure: the protagonist of the song felt uncomfortable about
the track. By capitalising certain words in the lyrics sheet
of the CD, she spelt out the word 'Sam' repeatedly, offering a partial identification of her villain. He began to send
Taylor nervous texts. He was worried that she would turn
even more attention onto him during interviews, and that
she would 'crucify' him on television. 'All I could think
was, well, you should've said no,' she told *Women's
Health*. 'That's what the song is about.'

Finally, after all the anger, heartbreak and accusation,
in 'Mary's Song (Oh My My My)' Taylor offers some
hope. In this redemptive song she tracks the life of a
loving, happy couple. Inspiration for it struck after a
real-life couple who lived next door came for dinner with
the Swifts. As Taylor listened to their tales of how they

met and stayed together, she wanted to set their story to song. The tales of the Swifts' neighbours were a great boost to Taylor. They formed a warming contrast to what she saw elsewhere in the world. 'I thought it was so sweet, because you can go to the grocery store and read the tabloids, and see who's breaking up and cheating on each other – or just listen to some of my songs, ha-ha. But it was really comforting to know that all I had to do was go home and look next door to see a perfect example of forever.'

If 'Mary's Song (Oh My My My)' lifted the mood of the album, then 'Our Song' lifts it even higher. It came about when she was at Henderson High and realised that she and her boyfriend did not have a song to define their relationship. So she put this right in the best possible style. Rather than choosing one for them, she 'sat down one day with my guitar and got in the groove'. From this session came 'Our Song'. The production is impish and fun, and the banjos and fiddles give the song a festive feel.

Most people, were they to look back at their teenage diaries later in life, would feel a little embarrassed by their adolescent feelings and ramblings. Luckily, they can keep what they created back then to themselves. For Taylor, her innermost thoughts, as recorded on this album, are forever public and known to millions of listeners. These songs reflect her feelings during her pre- and mid-teenage years.

It is nice for Taylor, then, that she regards this early part of her work with such pride. 'I look back on the record I made when I was 16, and I'm so happy I made it,' she told MTV in 2011. 'I got to immortalise those emotions that when you're so angry you hate everything. It's like recording your diary over the years, and that's a gift.' The album has stood the test of time for Taylor, who is, as we have seen, the harshest of self-critics.

The press critics were impressed when the album was revealed to them. The *New York Times* admired how she wrote her debut 'in diaristic fashion, with incriminating names and details left intact'. The authenticity of Taylor's approach was being admired not only by listeners, but also by journalists. Jon Caramanica added: 'The result was a small masterpiece of pop-minded country, both wide-eyed and cynical, held together by Ms Swift's firm, pleading voice. Her best songs – "Picture to Burn", "Should've Said No" – were a little vicious, too, animated by something sharper than traditional teenage angst.'

Chris Neal of *Country Weekly* magazine said that on her debut Taylor showed 'an honesty, intelligence and ideal-ism with which listeners of any age will be able to connect'. He also ventured that 'the more thoughtful material suggests a talent poised to last well past high school'. The website AllMusic criticised elements of the album's production, which it felt was a little too polished in parts. However, the reviewer separated this misgiving from the artist herself. 'Swift has no trouble overcoming any blandness taking place around her,' said the review.

'She's come up with a commendable starter album that's as accomplished as any by a 10-year veteran who's seen a lot more road and felt a lot more emotion.'

Country Standard Time magazine said that the album was a commendable balance between two genres, lending it 'an iPod feel, with as much pop as country among the 11 cuts'. Rick Bell, the reviewer, continued: 'Swift's best efforts come on her deeply personal, self-penned songs, particularly "The Outside" and "Our Song", which she sings with stirring conviction.' He added: 'It's an impressive debut.'

The album was finally released on 24 October 2006 – a proud day for Taylor. An anxious one, too: she was so nervous that she woke up at 5 a.m. She was staying in a hotel in Manhattan, as she was booked to appear on the TV show *Good Morning America*. Such a high-profile promotional slot was a coup for her – many established artists try unsuccessfully to get such a spot themselves. Amid the promotional activity, Taylor wanted to do one other thing now her album was on sale – buy a copy of it. 'I just want to do that and put it on the register face down,' she said. 'I can't even express how excited/ nervous I am. It's such a cool day, because I am in New York City and it feels like that's the place where your album should be released.' Her own purchase would ultimately be lost in a sea of sales that would take the album to number 19 in the *Billboard* 200 chart.

So what can we learn from Taylor's debut album about the lady herself? We can see how uncompromising she is:

her songs are often sad or dark; there is a generous slice of anger in the album, too. As the *New York Times* reflected, her ire seems to reach beyond the angst that is so 'traditional' among adolescents. Despite her country/ pop blend, there is an almost grunge or punk-rock dimension to her fury. In 'Picture to Burn' and 'Should've Said No' in particular, so much rage flies forth that the listener can't help feeling it is a good thing Taylor has her musical outlet. Bottling up such anger would not have been healthy.

As we have seen, the people around Taylor began to feel nervous or excited at the thought that she might be writing about them in her songs. 'I think it's one of every-body's favourite things to talk about – who my songs are written about,' she told *Entertainment Weekly*. 'There are definitely a few more people who think that I've written a song about them than there actually are,' she added. However, she did not deny that her material was grounded in her own experiences – 'It's very autobiographical,' she said. Therefore, her life and mind are laid bare in many of the song's lyrics.

The songs are largely about real-life experiences, in keeping with Taylor's insistence that her music is as authentic as possible. This approach is a growing trend among twenty-first-century female artists. Amy Winehouse famously – or infamously, perhaps – wrote her two albums about specific lovers. *Back to Black* – the track and the album of the same name – chronicled her tumultuous relationship with Blake Fielder-Civil. Pain and heartache pour out of the tracks, which are all the more heart-rending to listen to in the wake of Winehouse's untimely death. It is tempting to speculate that there was a degree of self-sabotage in Amy's life, so as to inspire her all the more to write breathtaking tracks of heartbreak and despair. What an ugly price such musical beauty came with for her. (This is not quite so outlandish a proposition as it might seem: singer Lily Allen admitted in an interview with the *Radio Times* that she had broken up with boyfriends purely for musical inspiration. 'When I hit a period of not being able to write music, I get up and walk away,' she said. 'It's pretty mean, but it's true.')

Adele – in some musical senses a successor to Winehouse – also believes that music should always reflect real-life experiences. Since recording her memories of heartache in her albums *19* and *21*, Adele has found considerable personal stability and happiness. She is in a settled relationship and has a young son to complete the bliss. While this is great news for Adele personally, it remains to be seen what it means for Adele the artist. Songs such as 'Rolling in the Deep' and 'Someone Like You' came out of sorrow and loneliness. What sort of music – if any – will spring forth from happier times for the much-adored London singer?

This is a longstanding issue for musicians. Eminent British songwriter Noel Gallagher – formerly of Mancunian rock band Oasis and now a successful solo artist and elder statesman of British rock – has reflected on how much easier it was to write relatable songs when he was a hungry youngster, on the dole and dreaming of oblivion at the weekend. When he became a famous multi-millionaire, living in glamour and comfort while basking in the adoration of millions, he suddenly found his life experiences were not so much ones that his everyday fanbase could relate to. And while the decline in his band's critical success was for a number of reasons, this songwriting dilemma was certainly one of them.

Taylor was aware of the concern. She was asked whether this might cause a problem for her in the future, but she nonchalantly shrugged off the matter. 'You know, songwriting is all about being able to paint a story and tell a story, and sometimes that's telling a story to yourself,' she said. 'Sometimes that's using your imagination to transplant yourself back to when you got lied to. I write when I'm happy, too. The number-one song that I had, I wrote when I was in a relationship.' Now we know that her confidence was well placed. Famously, Taylor continues to have an eventful and turbulent personal life deep into her years of fame and fortune. This means her songs have continued to pack a hefty emotional punch, even as her career has seen her life become much more comfortable in material terms. It was by putting her foot down early in her career, insisting that she would aim to write as authentically as possible, that her knockout delivery was set up.

She has outlined the extent of her own autonomy in her career. 'When I'm in management meetings, when we're deciding my future, those decisions are left up to me,' she said in an interview with *Harper's Bazaar*. 'I'm the one who has to go out and fulfil all these obligations, so I should be able to choose which ones I do or not. That's part of my life where I feel most in control.' She also took, she said, a hands-on role in the promotion of her album. She had been very mindful of the power of the internet and social networking for several years, as she later explained during a Q&A interview with *Billboard*. 'I was, like, 12 when we secured taylorswift.com and started putting up different versions of a website,' she said. 'And when we moved to Nashville, my mom and I got really proactive with trying to make it really, really cool. We went to Mad Dancer Media, and we told them we wanted it to look like a scrapbook. And there are all these buttons on it and it opens the book and there are all these tabs and pages and we wanted it to be really interactive and really appropriate for where I was in my life at that point. I didn't want a sleek, too-cool site. I wanted it to be reflective of who I was as a person and who I am as a person. And that's kind of casual.'

Another aspect of her online presence was her account on the then-hip social-networking website MySpace. The website had been used to great effect to launch two of the biggest UK artists, in the shape of Lily Allen and Arctic Monkeys. Both acts had used it to create and maintain a following, thus bypassing to a great extent the main-stream media. By the time Taylor became a recognised young artist, MySpace had passed its peak. Too many would-be stars had flooded the network, hoping some magic dust would come their way. Also, Facebook had made its first steps onto the internet, gradually putting a dent into MySpace's popularity.

Therefore, for any user to make their name via the site – famous, non-famous or somewhere in between – they would need to use it cleverly. Taylor stepped up to the challenge. She's admitted that she spent 'so much time on MySpace', and went on to explain that, here, she was personally responsible for her image. 'My MySpace is something that I made,' she said. 'The background that you see on there, I went to a website and copied the code and copy-and-pasted my "About me" section. I upload all the pictures, I check the comments, I am in charge of everything on that page. It really is important to me and really special to me when someone comes up to me and says, "I'm your friend on MySpace." I've always taken so much pride in it, just because it's really personal to me.' She also used the social network as a fan. She loved discovering new artists on it. Many of those she went on to love she had first seen recommended on the MySpace page of her friend Abigail. 'Whatever [she] has playing on her MySpace is usually something new and cool that I'll most likely end up downloading,' said Taylor.

However, the most important dimension of her MySpace activity was how it completed the promotion of her debut single and album. The way that Scott Borchetta got her single added to the playlists of country music radio stations shows how wise this tactic was. He made sure that her online presence was strong. He also released the video for 'Tim McGraw' before the single. As a result, by the time he visited the all-important country music stations to ask them to add the single to their playlists, he could do so from a position of strength. 'We said: "We have you surrounded and you don't even know it,"' he said. Most artists, particularly those at the beginning of their career, arrive to meet radio stations in a far less confident and more servile frame of mind.

In fact, he presents a somewhat more brutal and aggressive approach than the reality. Taylor added some sweet charm to the mix. For instance, she wrote personal, hand-written notes to any station that played her song. These charming teenage notes melted the hearts of many a cold scheduler and disc jockey. It had a spiritual authenticity to it, too. Taylor and Andrea had personally hand-packed many of the demo CDs of the single that had been sent out. As she packed each one, Taylor had personally whispered a good-luck message to it. With radio stations on-song, the single sold well. It made number six on the *Billboard* Hot Country Songs chart and stayed in the top 10 for 35 weeks. In the main *Billboard* chart it went to number 40.

Her life had changed as a result of her newfound fame and fortune, but Taylor tried to eschew the temptation to complain about it. Many modern celebrities have become infamous for moaning about their life in the spotlight. Robbie Williams, for instance, veered between chirpy, can't-believe-my-luck delight in his fame and life-is-terrible-when-you-are-famous self-pity. Taylor trod a more measured path, even though she had to combine school-work into the mix. 'Balancing all this is not hard,' she said. 'I mean, what do I have to complain about? I have the best time in the world. I'm so lucky. When I go out in public and I go to a mall, yeah, it's a lot different than it was two years ago, but it's a beautiful kind of different. It's the kind of different that I've wanted my entire life. I'm a strong believer that if you work your entire life for something, and you work so hard and you want this one thing so much, you should never complain once you get it.'

However, there were changes all the time. One of them was that she would have to leave school and take the home-schooling option. It became unfeasible for her to promote her music properly and conform to traditional school hours and demands. There was also a concern that her fame and increasingly exciting lifestyle might spark envy among classmates. Nobody in the family wanted to risk Taylor returning to the dark days when she was cruelly targeted by her fellow pupils. However, this was perhaps an overly cautious move, as she was leaving a school where she had many friends and much fun. Taylor was sad to be leaving and her best friend Abigail Anderson had to adjust to life at school without her dear Tay. Anderson admits that it took a lot of adjustment: 'I mean, any girl knows that if your best friend leaves you in tenth grade, it's just like, "Okay, what do I do now?" So, it was hard for both of us,' she told the newspaper *Lawrence Journal-World*. 'I had to kind of make a new name for myself around school, and she had to do her own thing out there and miss everything that had been her life for the previous few years. But she just immediately started doing so well … you just couldn't really think about anything else.'

During her summer holidays, she set off on a radio tour to promote her music. With 2,500 stations to target, it would require a breathless effort on her part. She was following a simple equation she had been offered by an adviser: if you want to sell 500,000 records, then you should aim to meet 500,000 people. She slept in the back of the car as Andrea drove them from station to station. Andrea said it was 'a lot of work' to help promote her daughter – 'but a lot of fun, too'. To add another personal touch, Taylor baked cookies to hand to the radio teams.

She will always remember where she was when she first heard one of her songs on the radio. 'I was driving down the road and somebody called in and requested it, and I almost drove off the road – literally,' she told *Seventeen* magazine. 'My record label president still has the message of me screaming at the top of my lungs, screeching; you can barely hear what I'm saying because I was crying – it was amazing.' This was such a milestone for Taylor – suddenly the bullying and isolation she had endured just a few years before at school seemed a long way away. It felt like everybody was taking notice of her now.

During her radio tour she had been delighted with the impression she had made on the programmers. She also received a separate boost when she took a call from the country band Rascal Flatts. The popular three-piece, known for hits including 'Bless the Broken Road' and 'What Hurts the Most', were in a pickle after their support act for their tour had parted company with them. They asked Taylor if she would replace him. The good news was that this gave her the chance to play in front of large live audiences. The bad news was that she would have just 48 hours to prepare. Taylor stepped up to the plate, however, and took on the challenge. 'I'm so excited and I can't even express to you how loud I screamed when I found out,' she wrote on MySpace. She played a six-song mini-set in front of the fans, warming them up for the main act. Critics noted that she built the sort of connection with the audience that only a much older and more experienced artist would usually be able to manage. A typical set list for Taylor around this time would begin with 'I'm Only Me When I'm With You' and end with 'Picture to Burn'. Between these two, she would sing 'Our Song', 'Teardrops On My Guitar', 'Should've Said No' and – of course – her signature hit, 'Tim McGraw'.

Her rapport on the Rascal Flatts tour helped her live appeal to snowball – before long she was receiving invitations from other acts asking her to join them on the road. The veteran country artist George Strait asked her to join the bill for a 20-date tour he had lined up. Known as 'the King of Country', Strait is an industry legend. A nod of approval from him meant a great deal to Taylor. She believes in aiming for authenticity when she performs live, however large the audience or vast the venue. She vowed there and then never to 'go through the motions' on stage, but instead always to perform from a place of passion. She feels there is no hiding place when performing live: 'People can see it on your face and they can see what the song means to you,' she said. She swore never to perform dispassionately. 'I wrote these songs and they all mean something to me,' she went on. 'When you can look at two people in the front row who are singing the words to your songs, I love that. I love to be able to look at someone and make that contact and nod your head and say thanks for being here.'

The Rascal Flatts tour had been a 'perfect match' for her, said Taylor. However, with Strait there was the massive bonus of being able to perform 'in front of a more "traditional country audience".' She wrote on her blog: 'I'm pretty much a George Strait superfan, so this is going to be SO much fun.' After each slot she would watch Strait's performance from the wings. She was fascinated by the intensity of the audience's respect for Strait, which was, she felt, 'like religion'. She felt a moment almost akin to Holy Communion herself when, on the first night of the tour, at the Lafayette in Los Angeles, Strait name-checked her during his own set. 'George Strait SAID MY NAME,' she wrote on her blog later. 'We were watching George's show … and all of a sudden he said, "I'm very happy to have the talented Miss Taylor Swift out here with us." YESSSS. It was pretty awesome, sort of a life-changing moment,' she wrote.

The snowball continued to roll. Next to help it on its way was the country rocker Brad Paisley. 'I was looking at a lot of artists to come out on tour with us,' he told *Blender* magazine, 'but as soon as I downloaded her album, I knew we had to have her. I was floored by the songwriting. I love the fact that she doesn't pretend to be 30 years old in her songs. She has a very genuine voice.' For Taylor, it was thrilling to get another chance to hit the road. Just as satisfying, though, was the fact that Paisley 'got' her approach. Several industry figures had suggested she drop the adolescent nature of her material and write songs in the voice of someone much older. Taylor was pleased that Paisley saw the benefits of her alternative approach. She saw the time on the road with him as a chance to 'pick his brain and learn as much as I can from him'.

Also present on Paisley's *Bonfires & Amplifiers* tour was Kellie Pickler. She and Taylor would become good friends on the road. Born in 1986, Pickler first came to fame as a contestant on the fifth series of the TV music talent contest *American Idol*. Although she finished in sixth place, she had caught the attention of viewers and industry giants alike. She released an album, called *Small Town Girl*, within months of the series ending. Taylor got on well with her from the first time they met. They felt like more than mere buddies – their relationship took on an almost familial stature. 'She's like a sister,' Taylor has said of her friend. 'People say we're such opposites, but that's what makes us such good friends. She's incredibly blunt. I love that about her. If some guy has said or done something to me she doesn't like, she'll grab my cell phone and say, "I'm deleting his number."'

They both enjoy practical jokes, too. They played one on Paisley during the tour. Along with fellow artist Jack Ingram, they donned costumes and joined Paisley on stage one evening, much to his surprise. As he sang his song 'Ticks', he suddenly saw Taylor and Pickler dressed as ticks, dancing around him on the stage. Then Ingram appeared dressed as an exterminator. He performed a pretend spraying motion, at which point the two 'ticks' acted a dramatic death. It was a silly, but fun, exercise. 'I was laughing so hard I could barely breathe,' wrote Taylor on her blog later. 'Then I was lying there on the stage playing dead and I looked up at Brad, and he looked down at me and said, "Nice work." Guess he was a little bit "bugged",' she punned.

Having hit the road with Paisley, she then opened the show for another industry great, the singer Kenny Chesney. As before, she was gushing with praise and excitement over the affair. 'Opening up for Kenny Chesney is one of the coolest things I've ever done,' she said, ever happy to play up her experience. However, this one had a different feel to it when compared to Paisley's. 'His tour has this laid-back vibe to it, and everyone's so cool to work with. And Kenny Chesney is so completely nice. Genuinely nice.' She also noted, with admiration, his work ethic. 'Kenny is up at the crack of dawn, walking around the venue, getting to know everyone, from the sound-check guys to the fans,' she told the newspaper *USA Today*. He lived life in a way that rang true with Taylor's principles, as well as those of her earnest parents.

It was at the end of each tour, as she stepped out of the bubble of being on the road and back into her usual life, that her tender years became plain. Indeed, her online writings give a pleasant insight into the contrast between her life on tour and her day-to-day existence at home. 'I just got back from a five-show run on the road,' she wrote. 'Now I'm sitting in my kitchen … on the counter. Eating Cool Whip. And trying to think of things to do with my cat and making a playlist of sad songs.' Like many a good country girl, Taylor was fine and comfortable at home, even though her time on the road had thrilled her. She was basking in her popularity and the ease with which things were working out for her. Her everyday fans delighted her and so did the many famous, respected industry figures who were backing her. With all that combined, she felt she had respect as well as fame. All true artists yearn for the former at least as much as they hope for the latter.

Her career and life in general were going well. Taylor felt on a roll, and 2007 just kept delivering gold for her – quite literally, on occasion. He debut album earned gold certification, marking the first 500,000 copies sold. This was a symbolic yardstick for another reason: it was the round figure that she had set out to sell. In April she won her first serious music award. The CMT Music Awards handed her one of their 'Buckle' awards (so-called because they are shaped like a buckle) for Breakthrough Video of the Year for the promotional film for 'Tim McGraw'. However, it was in the following month, at the Academy of Country Music Awards, that she truly felt she had arrived. Even though she did not win an award on the night, she felt as if she had hit the jackpot. She sang 'Tim McGraw' to the audience, which contained none other than McGraw himself. Each big step upwards suddenly seemed to lead to another. When she played at the Gold Country Casino & Hotel in the same month, one reviewer wrote: 'I just went to a show by a future superstar.' These were just the sorts of words she longed to hear. Everywhere she looked, Taylor was seeing predictions of future glory. Yet even her present was more glorious than she had expected at this stage.

In June, she played at the Country Music Festival. It was a richly symbolic occasion for her on several levels. While she was there, she learned that her album had gone platinum. It had passed this milestone just eight months after its release – a phenomenal achievement. She measured her success against two former visits to the festival. 'I went the first year as a volunteer (when I was 14) and helped out with getting artists to their radio interviews,' she wrote on her blog. 'The last year, I was there signing autographs (nobody knew who I was, it was funny) and telling anyone who would listen that I had a single coming out called 'Tim McGraw' and would they please request it [on the] radio … ha-ha. Then, one year later, there I was, receiving a platinum plaque for a million copies of my album sold. It's been a good year.' The following month the album reached number one on the *Billboard* Country Albums chart.

She found herself taking on the role of elder sibling to her younger fans. They felt they could listen to her songs and her public statements and learn from them. This put significant pressure on her young shoulders: one wrong move from her could, potentially, have ramifications for many of her fans. Yet she wore that responsibility well. In the autumn she signed up for a public education initiative to raise awareness about online predators and the whole gamut of internet crimes against children. Joining up with the Governor of Tennessee and a police association, she spoke directly to schoolchildren to take care when getting to know people online, 'because when you meet somebody online, you can never really know them'. Speaking with vivid frankness, she added: 'If there are two or three of you here that maybe would get lonely after school, and somebody random [instant messages] you and says that they're a 19-year-old college student at Yale and [do] modelling work on the side, they're probably 45 years old and live in the basement of their parents' house,' Swift said. 'And they're probably an online predator. It's a reality.'

As well as lending her time to good causes, she also handed over money. When Cedar Rapids in Iowa was hit by severe flooding, she promised to donate $100,000 to the Red Cross charity's efforts to clear up and assist the community. 'They've stood by me; they gave me a sold-out show,' she explained to *People* magazine. 'You've got to pay it forward in life – that's all I did in Cedar Rapids.'

Meanwhile, in October 2007 she released a festive album for the forthcoming holiday season. It was a limited-edition album, featuring some original compositions and four cover versions of Christmas classics: 'Santa Baby', 'Silent Night', 'Last Christmas' and 'White Christmas'. Although the cover versions lent a festive familiarity to the collection, Taylor insisted that it include original tracks, too. 'There's got to be something really original and different about it,' she said, avoiding the temptation to lazily toss out a collection of cheesy songs. Taylor is a fan of Christmas, in both religious and traditional terms. 'I love everything about this time of year, but mostly the way that people find ways to be with the ones they love,' she wrote on her blog. One of her original songs on the album, 'Christmases When You Were Mine', is among the most powerful and heartbreaking tracks she has ever composed. It is a shame it is tucked away on an obscure release.

The same can be said of some of the tracks that only appeared on the bonus edition of *Taylor Swift*. For instance, 'I'm Only Me When I'm With You' is a festive romp of a barn dance. The verses are pregnant with the sense that something immensely beautiful is on its way, and the chorus partially satisfies that yearning. Still, there is a feeling that more is to come. That more does indeed come after the chorus; as the violins and drums come to the foreground, it is as if the song has taken the listener up to heaven, where their arrival is greeted with party-poppers, champagne corks and fireworks. Somewhere amid the chorus and its immediate aftermath, it is as if the listener has been injected with a feeling of invincibility.

At the 2007 Country Music Awards (CMAs) ceremony, Taylor won the much-coveted Horizon Award, which celebrates the best new artist. In landing the trophy, she joined a prestigious roll of honour. Past winners include Garth Brooks, Dixie Chicks and Carrie Underwood. Indeed, the 2007 ceremony, which was held at the Sommet Center (now the Bridgestone Arena), turned into a big night for Underwood. For the second year in a row, she won two significant honours – for the best single and best female vocalist. At 24 years of age, the fair-haired country artist – who thanked 'God' during her speech – stood as a fascinating role model for Taylor.

Taylor sang her latest hit, 'Our Song', at the ceremony. She might have reflected on the symbolism of her centre-stage position at this huge event in the Nashville calendar. She was the first of the five Horizon Award nominees to sing on the night. She was wearing a short black dress with long gloves. If she showed a few nerves during the performance, they truly came to the surface when she returned to the stage to accept her Horizon Award. It was presented to her by the ubiquitous Underwood.

Taylor – who, following a costume change, certainly looked a winner in her golden dress – threw her hands to her face in shock when her name was announced. She turned to Andrea, who was sitting next to her, and mother and daughter embraced in celebration. She had to lift up her long dress as she ascended the stairs to the stage. She was breathless and trembling as she started her acceptance speech. 'I can't even believe that this is real,' she said. She then took a religious turn before finishing on a schooldays note. 'I want to thank God, and my family for moving to Nashville so I could do this. I want to thank Country Radio; I will never forget the chance you took on me. Brad Paisley, thank you for letting me tour with you.' She also thanked Scott Borchetta and 'everyone at Big Machine Records'. As the tears rose, she concluded with a thanks to 'the fans – you have changed my life. This is definitely the highlight of my senior year!'

The 'senior year' line provoked much mirth in the audience. It had been a charming speech from Taylor. The following month she was charm personified again as she joined in with the announcing of the Grammy Award nominees. As she stood on the stage, revealing some of the names up for gongs at the fiftieth annual ceremony, she seemed surprised when she heard the Foo Fighters announce her name as a nominee in the category of Best New Artist.

She ran over to Foo Fighters members Dave Grohl and Taylor Hawkins and enfolded them in an enthusiastic hug. 'Don't worry, Taylor,' said an amused Grohl, 'you got it in the bag.' She said later: 'It's been a really amazing year, and we had a lot of success at the CMAs this year, and I won the Horizon Award – and that was amazing.' She was asked if she would be losing sleep in the weeks leading up to the Grammys ceremony, now she knew she was a nominee. She replied: 'You know, as far as trouble sleeping – you can't control award shows. I've come to terms with the fact that I can control what I say, I can control how I act, I can control what I do on a stage, but I can't control awards shows, so I try not to get nervous about it.'

It had indeed been an amazing year. It ended with Taylor reaching a personal milestone. On 13 December she turned 18 years of age. Scott and Andrea threw a pink-themed party for their daughter. They felt so proud in so many ways as their firstborn turned 18. 'This party is our birthday gift to her,' her mother told *People* magazine. 'She knows the real gifts in life are relationships.' However, when asked what the best part of turning 18 was, Taylor replied: 'I wanted a number-one record, and I got that. And I got something I didn't even ask for: a Grammy nomination.'

On her Foo-Fighter folding hug, she was straightforward. 'I'm starstruck,' she told *People*. Commenting on her touchy-feely response, she added: 'I've always been a hugger. I honestly did not think I was going to get nominated, so when they said my name I just felt like hugging somebody. I'm glad that everyone started hugging. If we all hugged more, the world would be a better place.'

After what felt like long periods of waiting for something to happen, she was now gliding along at a good pace. 'Sometimes you feel like you have to pinch yourself. It's like, "Am I really here?"' she said. Everything felt great in the land of Taylor. However, Borchetta was concerned. Neither he nor Taylor had expected her career to take off to quite the extent it had with her debut album. He worried that she would peak too soon and then lose some of her motivation.

He particularly wondered how Taylor – so enlivened when she is set a challenge or has a perception to over-turn – might energise herself when she turned from underdog to champion. 'My fear is that she'll conquer the world by the time she's 19,' he confided to the *Washington Post*. 'She'll get to the mountaintop and say: "This is it?" Because she's just knocking down all these goals that we didn't even have for the first album.' He added: 'My job at this point is really to protect her and not burn her out.'

Too many child stars had burned out early and disap-peared from the public eye as fast as they had appeared. The priority for everyone in Taylor's corner was to prevent that from happening to her. As for Taylor, she admitted that she was anxious. 'I can't believe I get to have the life I have, so I've got a complete fear of messing up, of making a misstep where it all comes crumbling down. It's a high-wire act in my brain all the time.' She was, she added to the *Daily Mail*, 'a really big worrier'.

The attention she was focusing on her own feelings was matched by that paid to her by Borchetta and her parents. She had plenty of good people around her, watching over her wellbeing. They were all only too aware of the contradictions in her life: on the one hand, she was a celebrated music starlet, with a critically acclaimed and commercially viable album on the shelves. But she was also still a schoolgirl.

Taylor wore the paradox well, as she had an old head on her young shoulders. That maturity would serve her well in the next chapter of her career. She was about to discover just what an adult world she had entered.

Chapter Four

Like many young celebrities, Taylor attracted much speculation on her personal life as her fame soared. Before she became publicly linked with high-profile men, there was curiosity over why she did not have a partner. In April 2008, she was featured as the cover star of *Blender* magazine. The cover line introduced her as the 'boyfriend trashing, radio ruling, girl next door'. In the accompanying video, she was probed over why she did not have a partner. She claimed that she had not kissed a guy in nearly two years. 'I just don't have the time,' she said. She was asked who her dream prom date would be, and replied that it would be an infamous, and openly gay, celebrity blogger. 'Perez Hilton! Your prom date is supposed to be fun and hilarious, and I think I'd have more fun with Perez than with anyone else.' It was a shrewd deflection of the question.

In keeping with the squeaky-clean, wholesome image that was being sculpted for her, she added that as well as being man free, she also eschewed the party circuit. 'There could be drinking there or whatever,' she said, as if the very prospect was enough to make any *Blender* reader shudder along with her. 'Your career could go up in smoke just like that. It's not worth the risk.' Instead, she said, she preferred simple dining at the family-friendly US restaurant chain Applebee's. This was the ultimate imagery of clean-cut America. While she would retain her good-girl image when it came to partying, she would in time be associated with an eventful, rather than non-existent, love life.

As her *Blender* cover was slotted into newsstands across America, it was time for her to attend another awards ceremony where she would, once more, clean up. The Country Music Television Awards, held in the middle of the month, provided a night of glory for her. She was the belle of the ball at the ceremony, winning two honours, including Video of the Year. The evening was hosted by Miley and Billy Ray Cyrus. 'Are you sure? Are you serious?' Swift said in disbelief as she accepted her first award for Female Video of the Year. Taylor later wrote that she would never forget the expression on Andrea's face when she was announced as the winner. As the newly crowned Taylor looked out into the audience, she wrote later, she was thinking: how am I this lucky ...? How did I get to live this life?

She was barefoot for much of the evening, helping her to stand out even more on the night. This barefooted teenager cut through the corporate sterility that hung over the evening. Of her lack of footwear, she later told *People*, 'I walked by Faith Hill and I was like, "This hurts so bad." And she was like, "Take them off." Faith Hill told me to. So I did it.' Having accepted her award wearing a claret dress, she also performed that evening. Taylor changed into a black dress, fedora and cowboy boots to sing 'Picture to Burn'. For the evening's performance she added a vast, iconic bluesy introduction. She was delivering a statement: I am not merely a teenage gimmick; I am a serious artist. When the song properly kicked in she threw away the hat and flicked her hair. In the second verse she took her microphone on a walkabout and seemed out of breath. It was, though, a masterful and grand performance. With background pyrotechnics emphasising the fiery nature of the song, it made for a visually arresting experience.

Where that performance was about fire, her next rendition at an industry bash was dominated by the opposite element: water. Taylor won the top new female vocalist award at the 43rd Annual Academy of Country Music Awards in Las Vegas in May. She dedicated the award to Andrea, saying: 'Mom, thank you so much. I love you. This is for you!' When she sang 'Should've Said No', it began as a tame performance. She sat in dark clothes, including a hooded black jumper, strumming her acoustic guitar and singing a gentle and slow version of the song. When it was time for the first chorus, she threw her guitar into the wings and stood at the microphone stand. For the second verse, her casual clothing was magically whipped from her by two dancers, leaving her in a black dress far more in keeping with the occasion. Gimmicks galore already, then. For the final chorus she stood under pouring water. Despite the drenching, she continued to strut defiantly, her body language echoing the song's lyrics. As she took her bow at the end of the song, she giggled at the cheek of the production. The media were quick to play, with predictable headlines about what a 'splash' she had made.

Then came the Grammys. In the end, it was British singer Amy Winehouse who won the trophy she and Taylor were both vying for. Indeed, the 24-year-old London songstress landed five awards on the night. She was not present at the ceremony, as her application for a visa to enter the United States had been delayed – ever the wild card. But Taylor quickly found consolation of sorts: she appeared in *People* magazine's '100 Most Beautiful' list. Not quite a Grammy, but better than a slap in the face.

Her increasingly adult existence in public belied the fact that she was a girl who was still finishing her schooling. In the summer of 2008 she finally graduated and was bursting with excitement and pride. The latter feeling was heightened, because she had been tempted to ditch her education altogether as the lure of fame had grown. 'Graduating high school is really, really cool,' she said. 'I'm so proud of it, because I stopped going to high school in tenth grade, but I started home schooling.' For her, it had not ultimately been an either/or choice. With the encouragement of her parents, she had found a way to combine her musical ambitions and a traditional education. 'It's really good to know you don't have to give up on your dreams to graduate high school, and you don't have to quit your education to live your dreams,' she said. 'It's really cool that you can do both.'

What was cooler still was the day that she was told she was occupying both the first and second position on the *Billboard* Country Album Chart. Her CD and DVD pairing *Beautiful Eyes* and her eponymous debut album, which had since gone triple platinum, proudly stood in the number-one and number-two slots respectively. Taylor found it all very amusing. 'It was really, really funny to read the headlines the next day that said, "Taylor Swift gets bumped out of number one – by herself,"' she said. She quipped: 'We're gonna have problems, me and that girl, whoever that is!' *Beautiful Eyes* was an EP released by Taylor in July 2008. It was released exclusively to Walmart stores and online sales. It included an accompanying DVD, which featured promotional videos, an interview with Taylor and footage of a live performance.

In promoting the release, Taylor was at pains to emphasise that this was *not* her second album. She was also aware that she was releasing material at quite a prolific rate. 'This is not my new album that I've been working on all year,' she wrote on her MySpace blog. 'I'm only letting my record company make a small amount of these,' she continued. 'The last thing I want any of you to think is that we are putting out too many releases.' The EP's cover was rich with red and yellow colouring. It featured Taylor in a yellow dress holding a red flower, her own eyes doing justice to the collection's title. *Beautiful Eyes* peaked at number nine on the US *Billboard* 200 and, as we have seen, topped *Billboard*'s Top Country Albums chart, knocking her debut off its perch.

As well as success in the charts, she found herself enjoying increasing recognition from the teenage market. For instance, in the summer she was named Choice Breakout Artist by the Teen Choice Awards. This was a doubly satisfying moment for Taylor. Although she was collecting awards at a rapid rate, such honours still had enough of a novelty factor for her to enjoy them – particularly so with this gong, as it vindicated her insistence that, as a country music artist, she could pitch to and appeal to a teenage market. Kids were lapping up the distinctly Nashville flavour of her music and enjoying how she blended it with very adolescent lyrical themes.

She was handed the chance to return to her roots, in a sense, when she was booked to sing the national anthem at a World Series tie between the Tampa Bay Rays and the Philadelphia Phillies. It was a milestone moment for both Taylor and some of the players. Some in the line-ups had previously played for the minor-league Reading Phillies and recalled Taylor singing ahead of their ties. It was a delicious symmetry: both they and Taylor had now made it to the big time. As she sang, Taylor was preparing to reach for a new championship moment of her own, in the form of the release of her second album, *Fearless*.

Eventually, it was time for her *actual* second album to hit the stores – or to 'drop', as the US market puts it. It would make quite a noise. In working on the album, she had been able to collaborate with some fantasy figures. She wanted something new and felt that to get it she would need new faces around her. As she later recalled: 'My absolute dream collaborators were Shellback and Max Martin on the last project. I've never been so challenged as a songwriter. I've never learned so much.' The first single to be released from the collection was 'Love Story', which hit the stores on 12 September 2008. 'This isn't a fairytale, it's Shakespeare, but Romeo and Juliet were always my favourite couple, because they didn't care, and they loved each other no matter what. And it was always my favourite – except for the ending. So with "Love Story", I just took my favourite characters and gave them the ending that they deserve.'

More significantly, it addressed the question the media had been increasingly asking her. For the song also represented the romantic experience Taylor had been having since she had become famous – or rather the lack of it. 'I used to be in high school where you see [a boyfriend] every day,' she explained to the *Los Angeles Times*. 'Then I was in a situation where it wasn't so easy for me and I wrote this song because I can relate to the whole Romeo and Juliet thing.' Musically, the song has a poise that is emblematic of the journey Taylor had made between albums one and two. This is the sound of an artist quite in control of her craft, who is harnessing it with confidence. The concept had been inspired by the central lyric 'This love is difficult but it's real'. This has become her favourite line to sing live. She smiles with pride as the words roll off her tongue. Yet behind the song is a story of unfulfilled desire: she wrote it about a guy she liked, but who she never got together with properly because she feared that her friends and family would disapprove of him.

The song takes the sad literary and real-life inspirations as springboards and leaps from them into happier terrain. That late key change makes everything warm and glowing with optimism. Yet even within that upbeat tone, Taylor was keen not to enter happy-clappy territory, or to come across as naive. 'I have to believe in fairytales, and I have to believe in love – but not blindly,' she told *Seventeen*. 'If you do meet your Prince Charming, know he is going to have his good days and his bad days. He is going to have days when his hair looks horrible, and days when he's moody and says something that hurts your feelings. You have to base your fairytale not upon happily ever after, but on happy right now.'

The single's most significant legacy was that it took her outside the US and Canada: it reached number three in New Zealand, number one in Australia and number two in Britain. This was a big moment for Taylor, akin to her leaving the country music ghetto. The richness and maturity of the single whetted the fans' appetites for the album itself. When they heard it, they were confronted with a deft, beautiful yet strangely dark body of songs. 'Fearless', the title track, is a strong album opener. The drums and guitars are robust, the production lush and the overall feel is, well, fearless. She says she was inspired to write the title track while she was on tour, in common with several tracks on the album. The lyrical concerns were reflecting, in this sense, the changing life of their composer. Single, due in large part to her focusing on her career, Taylor began to imagine what an ideal first date would be like for 'Fearless'. It led to a song about the courage of returning to the romantic fray. It is what happens after a heart-broken soul has picked themselves up and dusted themselves down. 'This is a song about the fearlessness of falling in love,' she said. 'No matter how many break-up songs you write, no matter how many times you get hurt, you will always fall in love again … I think sometimes, when you're writing love songs, you don't write them about what you're going through at that moment, you write them about what you wish you had.'

Track two is one of the most discussed songs of her career. 'Fifteen' is, said Taylor at the time, 'the best song I have ever written'. It has provoked a great deal of admiration for its composer. Country singer Vince Gill said that 'Fifteen' was a 'great example' of how Taylor writes songs that are 'pointed right at' her young fans. Here again, Taylor was like an elder sibling for many of her listeners, taking on the music mantle of 'spokeswoman for a generation' that she had been handed. Again, she carried it off with commendable grace. 'It says, "I should have known this, I didn't know that, here's what I learned, here's what I still don't know."' She added that it was advice 'to my former self', but also 'advice to any girl going into ninth grade and feeling like you're the smallest person on the planet'.

It is an emotional track. The challenges and heartaches that Taylor describes had happened to her and await many of her fans: the listener is weighed down by the pain of it all. So is the singer: Taylor admits that she cried while recording the song. Listeners of all ages are vulnerable to tears themselves as they mull over the message of the music. The younger ones can relate to what Taylor is telling them, the elders can remember the pain and then feel it afresh as they imagine their own daughters, nieces or other relatives facing it. Ultimately, there is little anyone can do to guard their younger relatives from these sorts of heartaches. This song goes some way towards addressing that; Taylor shows girls that at least they are not alone in feeling these things.

The song has a real-life inspiration. Taylor's friend Abigail went through a painful break-up when she and Taylor were in ninth grade. It was that experience that led Taylor to write the song. As she told CMT, she had never gone through heartbreak as painful as Abigail's. 'Maybe I haven't had that break-up yet,' she said. 'Maybe there will be a break-up where I'll just cry every time I think of it – but the things that make me cry are when the people I love have gone through pain and I've seen it. "Fifteen" talks about how my best friend Abigail got her heart broken … and singing about that absolutely gets me every time.' It was Abigail who was left feeling like she was the smallest person on the planet.

After the aforementioned 'Love Story', the album's tracklist turns to 'Hey Stephen'. This is an entertaining song about a crush she developed while on the road with Love and Theft, who opened for her at some shows during 2008. She went weak at the knees over their singer and guitarist Stephen Barker Liles and penned this song. When the album was released she texted him to let him know. He was flattered and emailed her back to say thanks. He later spoke to *People* magazine about their friendship. 'We've become great friends since Love and Theft started opening shows for her,' he said. 'I think everyone would agree she's a total sweetheart and anyone would be lucky to go out with her.'

However, he has since come out with mixed noises about Taylor and the song. He told Yahoo! Music the inspiration for the song was 'probably just a crush, or lack of people to write about'. Yet later he would write a song about Taylor in return. Not only that, he would state that 'Taylor genuinely loves people in a way only the Lord would,' while speaking to internet TV channel Planet Verge. A bizarre turn of events.

But the song is great fun, lending some light relief to the album. It kicks off with some playful rhyming, while the 'Mmmm' at the end of the chorus is raunchy and was the most adult moment of Taylor's music up to that point. It seems that singing about someone who was just a passing fancy, rather than anything more serious than that, brings out her playful side. Several commentators pointed out that the song is rich in already-familiar Taylor motifs:

kissing a partner in the rain and turning up at their bedroom window.

The festive feel does not last long. Where 'Hey Stephen' is all fun and in-jokes, 'White Horse' is Taylor at her sombre best. It concerns, as Taylor put it, the 'earth-shattering moment' when you realise that the fairytales you had dreamed of enjoying with someone are not going to come true. She sings that this is not 'Hollywood', but a 'small town'. She sings painfully about the number of dreams and happy endings she had in mind with her guy. All she ever wanted, she complains, was the truth.

Interestingly, Taylor has described the studio version as being musically 'sparse'; in reality it is by no means a soft-production track. The guitar, piano and cello combine densely. Taylor's voice – here at its saddest, disappointed best – blends beautifully. On an album not short of sad songs, this is a really gloomy track. The man is no prince, and it is too late, she concedes, for his white horse to come into her life. Few artists do broodingly disappointed as well as Taylor – here, she does it brilliantly.

Although 'White Horse' was originally earmarked for her third album, it was brought onto *Fearless* after the producers of the smash-hit television show *Grey's Anatomy* phoned Taylor's management to ask if they could feature it on the opening episode of Season Five. It was an 'easy yes' for Taylor to sign off the song to them – *Grey's Anatomy* is her favourite television show. An easy 'yes', and an emotional one, as she explained later.

'You should've seen the tears streaming down my face when I got the phone call that they were going to use that song,' she said. 'I have never been that excited. This is my life's goal, to have a song on *Grey's Anatomy*. My love of *Grey's Anatomy* has never wavered. It's my longest relationship to date.' She could hardly believe her fortune.

'You Belong With Me' is another playful track, both musically and thematically. The inspiration for the song came when she was travelling on a tour bus. She heard a male musician placating a girlfriend over the telephone. 'The guy was going, "Baby, of course I love you more than music, I'm sorry. I had to go to sound check. I'm so sorry I didn't stay on the phone."' In the song, Taylor wonders why the guy cannot realise that he has more in common with her than with this distant girl. Lyrically, the song is clever, including a couplet about how the other woman wears 'short skirts', while Taylor wears 'T-shirts'. Musically, it is a decent, functional effort.

A central motif in Taylor's work is the concept of invisibility. We have seen it, of course, in the song 'Invisible', but it also appears in other songs of hers, including 'Teardrops On My Guitar'. It features, too, in 'You Belong With Me'. She sings about how hard it is to see something brilliant right in front of you. While this idea of a great girl being essentially invisible to a man is clearly a driving force for Taylor romantically and musically, it can also be seen as fuelling her overall energy and determination. Her lyrical obsession with the concept suggests that she is inherently haunted by the idea of being invisible to the world, and therefore puts much time and effort into getting as many people as possible to notice her, to see the great thing standing right in front of them. We will see this theme again in subsequent tracks released by Taylor.

After 'You Belong With Me' the album takes a step down in tempo, with 'Breathe'. She wrote it with the Californian singer-songwriter Colbie Caillat and invited the artist to duet with her on the recording. Taylor was a fan, declaring Caillat 'the coolest thing out there right now', adding, 'So for her to be on my next album makes me feel cooler.' Caillat returned the gushing praise, saying of Taylor: 'She is so sweet, so beautiful, so talented, and honestly just a really intelligent young woman. She knows what she is doing and she knows how to handle her career and take charge.' She added: 'I love her.'

The song's title is matched by its mood: here, the album seems to pause and take a breath. More broadly, the track also steps aside from the fury and recrimination that underpins so much of Taylor's music. There is a sense of fate in the lyrics: Taylor notes that there is nothing she can do to save the relationship. 'It's a song about having to say goodbye to somebody, but it never blames anybody. Sometimes that's the most difficult part. When it's nobody's fault.' The lack of blame and bitterness in this track gives the album itself a freshness and poise. It shows that Taylor is not always a fuming finger pointer.

That Taylor, however, reappears in 'Tell Me Why'. Liz Rose, who wrote the song with Taylor, knows how to open up the feelings inside an artist's head. The tin opener she uses is a simple one: perceptive questions. So when Taylor arrived for a songwriting session in a pent-up and fuming mood over a guy in her life, Liz knew just what to do. She turned to Taylor and asked her, if she were given the chance to say everything on her mind to the guy, what she would say first. 'I would say to him, "I'm sick and tired of your attitude, I feel like I don't even know you."' From there, Taylor says, she 'just started rambling'. Yet as she did so, Liz was busily noting down the essence of that rambling. 'We turned it into a song,' said Taylor.

And a lively song at that. We are back to the 'sick and tired' Taylor we are more familiar with. We also see her expressing themes that crop up a lot in her music: the sense that a man dismisses her life and dreams in order to make his own seem more important. She mourns being 'fooled' by the man's smile – an error that many will no doubt be able to relate to. One wonders whether, if the man did attempt to tell her why, she would be a receptive listener or too overcome with anger to deal with the situation. In any case, she ends the song letting him go, with a final declaration that she will not fall for his games any longer.

Arguably the album's most mournful song is 'You're Not Sorry'. While in 'Breathe' Taylor had herself been in openly apologetic mode, in 'You're Not Sorry' she curses the fact that a man in her life has not afforded her the same honour. As in 'Tell Me Why', she feels she has been fooled. 'He came across as Prince Charming,' she said. 'Well, it turned out Prince Charming had a lot of secrets he didn't tell me about. And one by one, I would figure them out. I would find out who he really is.' As she stumbled upon his secrets, he would apologise and vow not to repeat his mistakes. Yet then he would do them 'again and again'. Eventually, she felt she had to 'stand up' to him and point out that he was not, in fact, sorry in any real sense. When she tells him that 'she can have you', the listener discovers that among the secrets was an affair. The production gives this a ballad feel – one could easily imagine a boy band attempting it, perhaps rising from their stools in the final third of the song. However, few male vocalists could deliver the song's message of hurt and defiance with the same gusto as Taylor.

Some journalists, particularly the male of the species, have painted Taylor as a girl who will never be happy. So quick is she to complain about men, they argue, that there will never be a man who lives up to her exacting standards. Instead, they speculate, she is destined to a life of only transient relationships, each of which will be over too soon and then turned into a song. It is a harsh verdict, but not one she would entirely disagree with, as we see in 'The Way I Loved You'. In this song she complains about how, as she dates a nice guy, she secretly wishes she was back with a bad boy. Her current beau is 'sensible', prompting envy from her friends. But she ends up yearning for the drama and volatility of a relationship with a less perfect man.

She explained: 'It's about being in a relationship with a nice, punctual, practical, logical guy and missing the crazy, complicated, frustrating guy.' Taylor co-wrote it with John Rich, a former member of the popular band Lonestar who then went solo. He is also a widely respected songwriter who has penned tunes for the likes of Bon Jovi and Faith Hill. For him, the experience of writing with someone so much younger than him was not a problem. He said: 'Sure, there's an age difference, but she knows herself and her audience very well, and she's so connected to who that audience is. She knows she's still a kid and embraces it. She writes things that are important to her. If she breaks up with a boyfriend, that's traumatic to her, and she'll write about it.'

As for Taylor, she noted that, in Rich, she was to a certain extent writing with the sort of character she was yearning for in the song. 'He was able to relate to it because he is that complicated, frustrating, messy guy in relationships,' she said. 'We came at the song from different angles. It was just so cool to get in a room and write with him, because he really is an incredible writer.' Taylor's evocation of 2 a.m. arguments and screaming in the rain are vivid.

Rain is a favoured element in Taylor's songwriting, and it appears yet again in 'Forever & Always'. This upbeat track was a very late addition to the album. Just as the collection was ready to be mastered, Taylor suddenly became determined to add the song. She phoned the label and initially met with some resistance to her idea for a late change. So she 'absolutely begged' them to change their minds and let her include the song. Some industry figures are terrified by such last-minute changes to an album. They like the process to be calm and ordered. Taylor, however, gets excited about changing things around. 'I think it's fun, knowing that two days before you're scheduled to have the last master in and everything finished and they're ready to print up the booklets, I can write something, call my producer, we can get in the studio, put a rush on it, get an overnight mix and that can be a last-minute addition to the record.'

As for the song itself, it is about a sad, inexorable decline in love. 'It's about when I was in a relationship with someone and I was just watching him slowly slip away,' she said. 'I didn't know why, because I wasn't doing anything different. I didn't do anything wrong. He was just fading. It's about the confusion and frustration of wondering why. What changed? When did it change? What did I do wrong? In this case, the guy I wrote it about ended up breaking up with me for another girl.' As for the music itself, it has, as she told the *LA Times*, a 'pretty melody', yet by the end the intensity of it all has risen. 'In the end, I'm basically screaming it because I'm so mad. I'm really proud of that.'

'The Best Day', as we have already seen, is one of the album's sweetest moments and, indeed, arguably the most heart-warming song Taylor wrote for any of her first four albums. Her vocals here are notably, and deliberately, gentler than elsewhere on *Fearless*. As she is singing about her childhood, she wants to sound younger than her years. Although some of the lyrics, such as those about the trees changing colour in 'the Fall', could be accused of being clichéd by a cold heart, this is a song of warmth. Its sweetness and vulnerability are what make it so potent.

Not that the song is whitewashing or deluded. After the bliss of the first verse and chorus, in the second verse Taylor turns to the tribulations life throws at teenagers. She focuses on the day she was rejected and then humiliated when she suggested a day at the mall to some girls she considered her friends. She gives Andrea credit for easing her out of the pain of that episode, and others similar. She then sings about her 'excellent' dad and how God smiles on her brother Austin who is, she sings, 'better than I am'. Taylor's maturity mounts throughout the song and, by the end, some of life's mysteries have been solved for her, thanks to her mother.

The track itself was a very sweet Christmas surprise from Taylor to her mother. The girl who grew up surrounded by Christmas trees chose just that festival to show her mother how much she loved her and appreciated all her efforts. Andrea told the story of how Taylor unveiled it to her during a television interview. 'The first time that she played "The Best Day" for me was Christmas Eve,' she told TV show *Dateline*. 'She had made this edited music video. I'm looking on the TV and this video comes up with this voice that sounds exactly like Taylor's. And I looked over at her and she said, "I wrote it for you, Mom." And that's when I lost it. And I've lost it pretty much every time I've heard that song since.' Such tears are understandable. Even for a dispassionate listener, this song is touching. For Andrea it must be like an emotional juggernaut.

Where 'The Best Day' was all gentleness and vulnerability, 'Change' sees Taylor's tough side come to the fore – but in the best of ways. A motivational call to arms, this is a wonderfully fierce tune. With its stadium-rock production and punchy lyrics, the song details how hard she had to work when she signed for a brand-new independent label, having passed on the chance to tie herself to an unsatisfactory agreement with a more established industry giant. It is pertinent that, here, Taylor does not cast herself as the sole hero, overcoming the odds alone, as many a rock and pop diva has done.

However, when Taylor sings about how 'we' made it work, there is a more encompassing triumph at play. 'There were times I was working so hard that I didn't realise that every single day our numbers were getting bigger,' she said. 'Every single day, our fanbase was growing. Every single day, the work that we were doing was paying off.' After she won the Horizon Award at the CMAs, she suddenly realised how much had changed. 'I looked over and saw the president of my record label crying. Walking up those stairs, it just occurred to me that that was the night things changed.' She added: 'It changed everything.' Scott Borchetta noted that it was one of the first songs she wrote that wasn't about love. 'Live, it's becoming this tour de force. It's almost like a U2 moment now. So the maturation process is amazing, because she's found a different place where the songs are getting even more important. But it's still her.' Still her indeed – but what would the world make of *Fearless*?

Oftentimes, a young artist who has received plentiful praise for their debut album then receives something of a critical pasting when they release album number two. It is the backlash syndrome. This comes about for two reasons. The first is that the critical bar is set enormously high by a successful debut. The second factor is that reviewers are keen to make their name with a counter-intuitive write-up. Therefore, there was reason for Taylor to feel anxious as she awaited the media's verdict on *Fearless*. After hearing the album, *Rolling Stone* magazine was moved to describe Taylor as 'a songwriting savant with an intuitive gift for verse-chorus-bridge architecture'. To emphasise how strongly the magazine felt that songwriting was among Taylor's arsenal of talents, it added: 'If she ever tires of stardom, she could retire to Sweden and make a fine living churning out hits for Kelly Clarkson and Katy Perry.'

However, the *Guardian* felt that Taylor's lyrics have been overrated. Star reviewer Alexis Petridis declared: 'Back home, comparisons have been made to Randy Newman, Hank Williams and Elvis Costello, which turns out to be setting the bar perhaps a tad higher than Swift can reach.' He also complained that Taylor showed 'a tendency to use the same images over and over again'. He added that Taylor was 'fantastically good at regarding teenage life with a kind of wistful, sepia-toned nostalgia'.

Many of the reviewers singled out 'Fifteen', particularly the chorus's observation that, at the age of 15, if someone tells you that they love you, you are going to believe them. The *Boston Globe* said the song's message showed that 'hindsight apparently comes early for Swift'. The *Washington Post* also lapped up the song, describing it as 'a wistful cautionary tale'. Its reviewer Chris Richards concluded: 'And that makes Swift's most obvious precedents the legendary girl groups of yore. Like the Shangri-Las, Crystals and Ronettes before her, Swift has found a way to swathe the fun in profundity.' *Billboard* preferred to contrast rather than compare, arguing that 'aside from sharing, possibly, a box of Clairol, there is nothing remotely Britney- or Christina-esque about Swift'.

Probably the harshest verdict came from *Slant* magazine. Not content with declaring Taylor a 'terrible singer', Jonathan Keefe also couched his review with cynicism, more interested in crediting the collection to purely commercial decisions made by 'Swift and her management' team, rather than to Taylor the artist. 'There's simply no risk to these songwriting choices, with easy images that seem chosen primarily because they will evoke a desired response from an audience of primarily very young listeners, not because they show any real spark or creativity or work cohesively to build larger themes,' he complained.

Taylor rejected this image of long, clinical summits in which every syllable of each song was weighed up for its market potential by money-driven men. Indeed, the way she described the creation of the album was rich with the spark that *Slant* felt she lacked. 'Most of the time, songs that I write end up being finished in 30 minutes or less,' she said, during an interview with *Time* magazine. She said that 'Love Story' had been written in 20 minutes as she lay on her bedroom floor. 'When I get on a roll with something, it's really hard for me to put it down unfinished.' Perhaps the best way to try to reconcile *Slant*'s view of her songwriting and Taylor's own description of it is to wonder: would it be wrong even if *Slant* had called it accurately? Writing for one's audience is surely better than writing *against* them.

Offering her own assessment of the album, Taylor said that *Fearless* was 'the same' as *Taylor Swift* – 'just two years older'. She agreed the album had 'crossover appeal', but preferred to refer to this as 'spillover, because I'm a country artist and I write country songs, and I'm lucky enough to have them played on pop radio'. The album was released on 11 November 2008. As midnight struck on the previous evening, she made a promotional appearance at her local Walmart store in Hendersonville. She signed albums and thanked her delighted fans for their support. She also appeared on *Good Morning America* on the day of release, the same show she had rolled up to on the launch day of her debut album. For her, the album was a significant step up. 'I've never been more proud of anything in my life,' she told US newspaper *Newsday*. 'I wrote every song on it. I co-produced it. So to have people go out and actually buy it, it's wonderful.'

People were indeed going out and actually buying it. The first-week sales were a step up from her debut: in the first seven days it was on the shelves it sold over 10 times the number that its predecessor did in the same period. It reached number one in the *Billboard* 200 in doing so. Taylor was showing that her previous successes were no freaks and that she was not a gimmicky artist. Here, she was setting down the roots that hold strong to this day. She was in it for the long haul.

Yet her brand was not above being exploited commercially. That same month, as her album was hitting the store shelves, Taylor herself did so, too – in the form of a plastic doll. The product was released with her approval. Citing the 'great connection' that 'tweens' felt with Taylor, the manufacturers launched a range of figurines, including one that brandished Taylor's signature crystal guitar. 'When I was a little girl, I dreamed of becoming a country music star and having my very own fashion doll line,' gushed Taylor in the promotional blurb. 'Now it's come true! I can't wait to see little girls play with my doll and rock out with my crystal guitar!' It felt cheap.

In truth, Taylor felt a deeper sense of pride and excitement when she received awards – and a fresh shower of honours rained down on her in November. She landed no less than three BMI Country Awards, including 'Teardrops On My Guitar' being named Country Song of the Year. Hank Williams Jr, who was honoured as a 'music icon' on the same night, gave Taylor a thumbs-up as she walked to the stage to accept the gong. Later, Kenny Chesney texted his congratulations and to tell Taylor he loved her. At the Country Music Awards, she finished the evening trophyless for the first time in three successive ceremonies. However, she still made her mark with a theatrical re-enactment of the video for 'Love Story', with Justin Gaston taking the male lead on the night, as he had in the video itself.

The month's next ceremony was the American Music Awards (AMAs). Here, there was a reverse of her CMA experience – having never previously won an AMA, this time she did. The category of Favourite Female Country Artist was a clear fit for her and she duly lifted the prize, writing later on her blog that she was unable to express how 'thankful/amazed/excited/ecstatic/overjoyed/blown away' she was. She added that it was the fact it was a 'fan-voted award' that made it so special to her.

The press continued to crave a real-life romance for her. Like a young princess watched by an expectant nation, Taylor seemed to have romantic happiness being wished upon her. Although she sang about her private life, Taylor had thus far managed to keep it out of the media. When she began to date a famous pop heart-throb, though, that was bound to change – and it did. Joe Jonas was one-third of sibling boy band the Jonas Brothers. Between 2005 and 2013, the trio from New Jersey enjoyed enormous commercial success. Thanks to a tie-in with the

Disney Channel network, they adopted a clean-cut image, which was carefully maintained by their management. It was partly due to the requirements of that image – that the three brothers appear to their fans to be not only available but virginal – that Joe's relationship with Taylor was such a complicated affair, and one destined for failure.

They met in the summer of 2008 and, as whispers circulated about them, the press began to speculate that they were romantically involved. With both parties regularly granting interviews to the media, questions were soon asked of them both. In retrospect, their first and curiously similar public statements on the matter seem carefully coordinated. Taylor told *MTV News*: 'He's an amazing guy, and anyone would be lucky to be dating him.' Then, asked if he was dating Taylor, Jonas said: 'She's a great girl. I think anybody would love to go on a date with her.' Yet Taylor had recently stated that she wanted to date someone from the showbiz world, ideally a celebrity who would understand the pressures on her. She saw the advantage of getting together with someone 'who gets what you do and gets that you're not going to be around a lot'.

Jonas, who had been famous since he was in his early teens, fitted the bill perfectly. The fact that he was very cute only added to his allure. They were spotted snacking on ice cream together near her home, and then he was reported to have been backstage at one of Taylor's concerts. Radio disc jockey Mishelle Rivera told the media she had spotted Jonas, who was trying to be incognito. She said: 'He was trying to hide from the crowds by kicking in between a few people – he was wearing a baseball cap and real casual dress so he wouldn't stand out.' The broadcaster then explained how Jonas crept backstage to join Taylor after her performance, but claimed he 'hid' when he realised people had recognised him. 'It was real obvious he didn't want people to know he was there to see Taylor,' she said.

Taylor was left with a curious paradox: she had wanted to go out with someone famous who would understand the pressures of celebrity, yet it was the very nature of Jonas's fame that meant they had to be so secretive – something Taylor was uncomfortable with. 'When someone's not allowed to go out with me in public, that's an issue,' she said later. This tiptoeing around sat uneasily with Taylor's upbringing, in which she had been encouraged always to be honest. As long as one is truthful in life, she was taught, one should have nothing to fear.

While both artists were being encouraged to present a wholesome image to the public, it was Jonas who was under the most pressure to play his every move in a squeaky-clean style. He wore a 'purity ring'; this is an item of jewellery sometimes known as a 'promise ring'. He and his brothers were champions of teenage abstinence, and their rings were as much a symbol of their image as cyclist Lance Armstrong's yellow wristband was, once upon a time, a reflection of his. For Taylor, the issue was not necessarily chastity so much as the restrictions that Jonas's fame put on their day-to-day life together.

But he left an impact on her creatively. Indeed, it is widely believed that her song 'Love Story' was, in fact, about Jonas. Despite her previous insistence that she did not want to write songs 'about being on the road and being in hotels and missing your family and missing your friends' – or being, in other words, a pop star – it seemed she had done just that in 'Love Story'. In doing so, she went against her 14- or 15-year-old self, who would say 'Ugh, skip' when she heard such themes on the albums of other artists.

Speaking later, she joined the various dots. 'I was dating a guy who wasn't exactly the popular choice,' she said. 'His situation was a little complicated, but I didn't care. When I wrote the ending to this song, I felt like it was the ending every girl wants to go with her love story. It's the ending I want. You want a guy who doesn't care what anyone thinks, what anyone says.' It was subsequently rumoured that what had actually caused Taylor and Jonas to break up was that he was seeing someone else – Camilla Belle, an actress. 'They've been together for months,' Taylor told the press. 'That's why we broke up.'

As news of their split spread, Taylor received a crash course in how a celebrity story can take on a life of its own. One rumour had it that she had fallen pregnant. This was an incendiary piece of gossip: it threatened both parties' public images. Taylor knew she had to jump on it without equivocation. 'I read a very creative rumour saying I'm pregnant, which is the most impossible thing on the planet,' she said. 'Take my word for it – impossible!'

With that rumour stamped upon, another one took its place. Yet far from being a victim of this one, Taylor was the person driving it. The story of how Jonas had ended their relationship was tailor-made for headlines. It had it all: the girl of the romance as the injured party, the man as the cold villain and a dramatic figure in the mix, too. It all started when Taylor explained how they had parted ways. 'He broke up with me over the phone,' she said. 'I looked at the call log – it was, like, 27 seconds. That's got to be a record.'

It made for a memorable tale and it quickly became legend. Later, she posted a video diary onto her MySpace page in which she mocked Jonas further over the phone call. She held a plastic Joe Jonas doll during the video and joked that it came complete with a phone, which the doll could use to 'break up with other dolls'. In an online posting, Jonas addressed the subject, although he never mentioned Taylor directly by name. 'This blog is not an attack of anyone,' his missive begins. 'Anytime you are in a relationship for any length of time, there are going to be issues. Sometimes they resolve; other times they lead to a change of heart. This was the case recently.' Jonas was also cryptic. He has insisted he 'never cheated on a girl-friend', adding, 'Maybe there were reasons for a break-up. Maybe the heart moved on.'

Naturally, he had to address the 27-second dimension of the story. He did not dispute the length of the call, but he did challenge Taylor's memory of which of them terminated it. 'For those who have expressed concern over the '27-second' phone call … I called to discuss feelings with the other person,' he wrote. 'Those feelings were obviously not well received. I did not end the conversation. Someone else did. Phone calls can only last as long as the person on the other end of the line is willing to talk. A phone call can be pretty short when someone else ends the call. The only difference in this conversation was that I shared something the other person did not want to hear. There were later attempts at communication that had no response.'

Her romance with Jonas and its aftermath had been an eye-opening experience for Taylor. It meant that as well as being written about for her music, she was now also the subject of stories about her personal life. If that did not feel invasive enough, there was the added layer that by definition Taylor had 50 per cent less control over stories involving a partner. She would, in time, find a serenity of sorts in the powerlessness she felt amid the media sagas. Back then, though, it cut deep.

She had to focus on her music to remind herself what made it all worthwhile. Soon, it was time to get out on the road and promote the new album. She had taken the deliberate decision not to rush into a headlining arena tour. When acts move too soon into arenas they are sometimes forced to curtain off some sections of the venue to make up for seats that were not sold. This can be a demeaning experience. 'I never wanted to go into an arena and have to downsize it so there were only 5,000 or 4,000 people there,' she said. 'So we waited a long time to make sure the headlining tour was everything I wanted a headlining tour to be.'

This was not going to be a problem for Taylor. When her tour went on sale, fans eagerly snapped up the tickets within minutes. Even the huge Madison Square Garden, with its 40,000 seats, sold out within 60 seconds. Her appearance at the huge LA venue the Staples Center was booked out within two minutes. She was delighted. Moments before the tour went on sale, the concert promoter had called her to let her know that the tickets were about to be made available. 'Okay,' replied Taylor, 'well, let me know tonight how we're doing.' Just three minutes later, the promoter was back on the phone. 'You sold out,' he told her. That, she later reflected, was the moment she realised she was 'having a good year'.

She had never realistically expected such demand. When she had imagined touring one day, she had thought that worries over ticket sales would be part of the experience. 'I look at things from a very practical place and a very realistic place. I've always had crazy dreams, but I've never expected them to come true.' On the tour she would harness all she had observed and learned during her time supporting other established acts on the road. The likes of Rascal Flatts, Brad Paisley and others had given her several ideas. 'Some things have blown me away, and I've taken away some things that I really want to incorporate,' she said. She had been opening for other acts since she was 16, so she had spent many hours sitting on the tour bus in the evening imagining what she would do if she did her own tour.

Taylor put into context what it meant to her to be finally the top billing on the road. 'Headlining my own tour is a dream come true,' she said. 'This way I can play more music every night than I ever have before. Having written my own songs, they are all stories in my head, and my goal for this tour is to bring these stories to life.' It was a high standard to set herself. Attention to detail was a principle that was clearly at the heart of the tour, from onstage choreography to the backstage areas. And it was Taylor herself who was calling the shots. She dictated that images be projected onto the stage itself, so the evening would be a non-stop visual extravaganza. And there would be numerous costume changes, including one midway through each evening's opening track – 'You Belong With Me'. Taylor's suggestions were readily accepted by the crew. 'Anything Taylor wants to happen, happens onstage,' said the tour's bassist Amos Heller.

She also had directives for what should go on backstage. 'It looks nothing like backstage,' she wrote. 'It looks like your living room. The walls are covered in magenta/maroon/gold/purple draped fabric, and the floors are carpeted with oriental rugs on top. There are lanterns hanging from the ceiling and candles everywhere.' For Taylor, this meticulousness was well worth it, because the experience of live performance was something that always made her come alive. 'When I hear that high-pitched sound of all those people screaming together, it's like I want to get onstage right now,' she has said. 'I love being onstage. It's one of my favourite things in the world.' For her, the planning in and of itself was something to get excited about. 'I'm in heaven right now,' she wrote on her blog. 'Constantly having meetings with the video crew and the lighting guys and the carpenters and the band and running through things over and over and over again.' With everything agreed, she could not wait for the tour to start.

The opening night was at a venue in Evansville, in Indiana. Before the show, Taylor, her musicians and crew all gathered in a huddle. She told those assembled that she had never had a senior class or a sorority and that she saw them as her equivalent to that. She told them they were the people helping her to become 'the person I'm going to be'.

The show was a success, prompting its star to say, 'The energy was just incredible. The people were, like, freaking out, losing their minds.' Yet even as she left the stage to thunderous applause and cheers at the end of the night, she had in mind some changes to the 'lighting and stuff' for the remainder of the tour.

Taylor had high standards for her work, whether in the studio or onstage. Yet she tried to balance that with courtesy. She wanted to be demanding, but not a diva. 'There are times when you get frustrated, but the one thing you always focus on is treating people well. You just cannot storm off and freak out. People don't take you seriously if you scream, if you raise your voice – especially when you're a 19-year-old girl.' By the end of the tour, she was delighted with what she and her band mates had achieved. She described them as her 'one true love'. Whether it was her biological relatives or her adoptive musical soul mates, somehow or other it was always about family for Taylor.

Chapter Five

Misbehaviour at pop award ceremonies can quickly conjure up a media storm. They have been the scenes of raucous, attention-grabbing behaviour for many years. As far back as 1984, Madonna took to the stage at the MTV Video Music Awards (sometimes known as the VMAs) wearing a white wedding dress, only to roll and writhe around on the stage as she sang her hit 'Like a Virgin'. In the comparatively demure 1980s, this behaviour from Madge was enough to raise eyebrows around the globe. It prompted almost as much outrage and publicity as she hoped it would.

She inspired dozens of copycats. In 1996, Jarvis Cocker, lead singer with indie band Pulp, ran onstage at the BRIT Awards to interrupt Michael Jackson's messianic performance of 'Earth Song'. The bespectacled Brit-popper clowned around, pointed his (clothed) backside at Jackson and was then removed from the stage. Later, he explained: 'My actions were a form of protest at the way Michael Jackson sees himself as some kind of Christ-like figure with the power of healing. The music industry allows him to indulge his fantasies because of his wealth and power.'

Other shocking moments – all of which took place at the ever-controversial MTV VMAs bashes – include the lesbian kiss shared by Britney Spears and Madonna in 2003, Prince's ass-revealing trousers in 1991 and Lady Gaga's simulated suicide in 2009. The allure for publicity-hungry artists to make a bid for the top headlines at these parties remains strong for good reason. Ask Miley Cyrus. At the 2013 MTV VMAs, her duet with Robin Thicke was the talk of the night. The young singer stripped down to a skimpy, skin-coloured latex outfit and pointed a huge foam finger at Thicke's crotch area. Then she twerked enthusiastically against his genital area, with a hugely mischievous and excited expression on her face.

In the days and weeks after the ceremony, Cyrus's twerking was widely and endlessly discussed. Among the adjectives the media used to describe it were 'crass'; they even referred to it as a 'train wreck'. The *Hollywood Reporter* said it was 'reminiscent of a bad acid trip'. Social networks were awash with comments about what she had done. At the peak of these discussions, Twitter users were generating 360,000 tweets per minute. Soon, it felt like Cyrus's twerking stunt was being discussed from a countless number of angles. Feminists were up in arms. Was what Cyrus had done in some way racist, asked some, who felt she was mocking 'ratchet culture'? Irish song-stress Sinéad O'Connor then entered the debate with a widely shared open letter in which she said the young

Cyrus was being pimped. As for Cyrus herself, she later brushed off the controversy, saying of her critics, 'They're overthinking it. You're thinking about it more than I thought about it when I did it.' In truth, people were thinking about it at least as much as Cyrus hoped they would. Indeed, just a few months later, she was courting controversy at the 2013 MTV Europe Music Awards (EMAs). She arrived in a skimpy outfit and later lit what appeared to be a spliff. Cue a renewed wave of publicity for the singer.

The moral of the story is that headline-grabbing behaviour at awards ceremonies can prompt a considerable amount of media coverage. Cyrus's conduct at awards bashes in the second half of 2013 is the benchmark for how to ride that tiger. Yet, for all the discussion of her twerking, she cannot boast as prestigious a contributor to the debate as Taylor can when it comes to her own high-profile ceremony moment. When Taylor unwittingly hit the headlines for an incident at a bash in 2009, President Barack Obama himself, no less, joined in the subsequent discussion.

It all began at that scene of numerous scandals – the MTV VMAs. Held at the Radio City Music Hall in Manhattan, it was an exciting evening. Michael Jackson, who had died earlier that year, was the subject of a special tribute, before the awards proper began to be handed out. Taylor, who was wearing a KaufmanFranco dress, was the first to get a gong on the night. She won the Best Female Video category. In doing so, she had beaten off competition from the likes of Pink (for 'So What'), Lady Gaga (for 'Poker Face') and Beyoncé (for 'Single Ladies – Put a Ring On It').

When she was announced as the winner, Taylor walked to the stage expecting to receive the trophy, make a brief acceptance speech in which she would thank key people, then return to her seat, the subject of rapturous applause. Well, that was the plan. Thanks to a bizarre interruption from another star on the night, she scarcely got through one sentence of her speech. She said: 'I always wondered what it would be like to maybe win one of these some day, but never actually thought it would happen ...'

Everything was going according to plan, but then the rapper Kanye West appeared, having decided that what the world needed was for him to intervene on behalf of runner-up Beyoncé. He grabbed the microphone from Taylor's clutches and said: 'Yo, Tay, I'm really happy for you and I'm gonna let you finish, but Beyoncé had one of the best videos of all time. One of the best videos of all time!' Taylor was stunned and the shocked expression on her face cut the carefully controlled atmosphere of the event to ribbons.

Much of the audience was similarly shocked. And confused, too. What was West *doing* there? Was this just a joke, or a gimmick that had been pre-arranged with the hosts? In time, though, people realised exactly what West was doing. Elliott Wilson, the chief executive officer of *Rap Radar*, observed the awkward spectacle firsthand. 'You could feel everybody being nervous and not knowing if it was a prank or something,' he told CNN. 'Then people started booing him really loud. The reaction to his tantrum was so strong … and what happened was he gave everyone the finger.'

Could it be that West was drunk? He had, according to the *Daily Mail*, been spotted 'swigging Hennessy cognac on the red carpet earlier in the night'. (In 2006, when he disrupted the MTV EMAs after missing out on the Best Video award for 'Touch the Sky' to Simian, he had admitted to having a 'sippy sippy' earlier in the evening.) Beyoncé looked shocked and embarrassed as she sat in the audience. There was nothing in her reaction to suggest that she endorsed what the rapper was saying on her behalf. Later in the evening, she won the Best Choreography award for 'Single Ladies'. She took the opportunity to give Taylor the moment in the spotlight that West had denied her.

Beyoncé told the audience how much her first VMA, which she had won as a teenager with Destiny's Child, had meant to her. Having put into context what an exciting moment it can be for a teen to win such an award, she invited Taylor onto the stage to continue the speech that had been so rudely interrupted. Taylor accepted the invitation and stood at the microphone. 'Maybe we could try this again,' she said. The audience showed its approval with a standing ovation. Then, she finally got to deliver her speech. 'I would really like to thank Roman White, who directed the video, and Lucas Till for being in it. I would like to thank all the fans on Twitter and MySpace and everyone that came out to my shows this summer.

And I would like to thank my little brother's high school for letting us shoot there.'

Taylor was just relieved to have her time in the spotlight, and she was enormously grateful to Beyoncé for the gesture. 'It was just so wonderful and so incredibly classy of her and just gracious and wonderful to let me say something,' said Taylor later. 'She's just been my hero and one of my idols ever since I was little ... She's always been a great person before anything else ... I thought I couldn't love Beyoncé more tonight, then tonight happened and it was just wonderful.'

The shadow that West had cast over Taylor's big night came with a considerable and obvious silver lining: the episode had focused colossal attention and significant sympathy onto Taylor. Millions of people around the world who had never heard of Taylor previously were made aware of her existence by the headlines the incident generated the following day. Thanks to the hunger and scale of the twenty-first-century media, those headlines continued for weeks afterwards. All of them cast Taylor as the hero of the piece. Her dignity played well with the media as well as its readers and viewers. Her manager, Scott Borchetta, acknowledged explicitly that the drama ended up being 'positive in her career in terms of name recognition'.

West, though, struggled to change his position as the villain of the piece. As pressure grew for him to apologise, he did just that in a blog post. Much of the post was written in capital letters and it included liberal use of exclamation marks. This only seemed to lessen the sincerity of it. He wrote: 'I'm sooooo sorry to Taylor Swift and her fans and her mom.' He also took a moment to praise Swift, and wrote that he likes 'the lyrics about being a cheerleader and she's in the bleachers'.

'I'm in the wrong for going onstage and taking away from her moment!' Although he insisted that Beyoncé's video remained 'the best of the decade', he apologised to his fans and to his 'friends at MTV', and promised to 'apologise to Taylor 2MRW'. He continued: 'Everybody wanna boooo me but I'm a fan of real pop culture!!! ... I gave my awards to OutKast when they deserved it over me ... that's what it is.' He added, 'I'm still happy for Taylor!!!!!' and told her she is 'very, very talented!!!' In conclusion, he wrote: 'I really feel bad for Taylor and I'm sincerely sorry!!! Much respect!!!'

It was too late to save his credibility in the eyes of many of his industry colleagues. Pink was disgusted. She said: 'Kanye West is the biggest piece of s**t on Earth. Quote me. My heart goes out to Taylor Swift. She is a sweet and talented girl and deserved her moment. She should know we all love her. Beyoncé is a classy lady. I feel for her, too. It's not her fault at all, and her and Taylor did their thing. And douche bag got kicked out.' Kelly Clarkson wondered if West got 'hugged enough' as a child. Joel Madden, of the rock band Good Charlotte, described the rapper as 'a bully on that one'. Katy Perry was more succinct, saying simply, 'F**k you, Kanye.' She likened his actions to stepping on a kitten.

Angry words, then, from a variety of pop royalty, yet they were about to be upstaged when US President Barack Obama weighed in. During an interview with CNBC, he was asked whether his daughters had been upset by West's interruption of Taylor. 'I thought that was really inappropriate,' he said. 'You know what, it was like, she was getting an award and, what, are you butting in? The young lady seems like a perfectly nice person, she's getting her award and what's he doing up there? He's a jackass.'

Later, West apologised more sincerely during an appearance on *The Jay Leno Show*, in tones that were nearly those of a therapist's client. 'It's been extremely difficult, just dealing with the fact that I hurt someone or took anything away, you know, from a talented artist — or from anyone,' he said. 'My entire life, I've only wanted to give and do something that I felt was right. And I immediately knew in this situation that it was wrong and it wasn't a spectacle. It was actually someone's emotions that I stepped on.' He added: 'It was rude, period. And, you know, I'd like to be able to apologise to her in person.'

Some 48 hours later, Taylor herself appeared on US talk show *The View* to give her account of what it's like when your speech at an awards do is hijacked by another artist's ego. She said: 'Well, I think my overall thought process was something like: wow, I can't believe I won, this is awesome, don't trip or fall. I'm gonna get to thank the fans, this is so cool. Oh, Kanye West is here. Cool haircut. What are you doing here? And then: ouch. And then: I guess I'm not gonna get to thank the fans.' She admitted she was 'rattled' by the incident.

Yet she did not want it to be blown any further out of proportion. 'He was very sincere in his apology and I accepted that apology. I'm just honestly trying not to make it into a bigger deal than it already is. It's become more of a big deal than I ever thought it would be. It happened on TV, so everybody saw [it]. I would just like to move on.' In a further attempt to bring some perspective to the table, she said: 'I've had a few days – and everyone has them – when you feel humiliated or you're shocked by something or something knocks you down a few pegs. But in those moments, I've been very quick to realise and remind myself that there are people out there with real problems. To get hung up on any bad moment that happened this year would be unfair to all the good moments I've had this year.'

All seemed peaceful, but within months West was seemingly retracting his apology and then firing borderline insults at Taylor. 'I made a mistake,' he told Hot 97, a New York radio station. 'My timing was definitely extremely off and the bigger plans, the bigger fight – how do you go about it? How do you go about getting it done?' Having seemingly revealed that all he regretted was his timing, rather than what he had actually done, he then suggested that Taylor should have done more to defend him.

As the interview wore on, he spoke more about the incident. He denied there was anything arrogant about what he did, arguing instead that it was 'completely selfless'. Indeed, he even compared his intervention to 'jumping in front of a bullet', adding that he had 'lost an arm' in the course of it. This portrayal of himself as a selfless man who had been not just wronged but injured by what he had done was one that sat uneasily with the perceptions of many observers. It was an inversion that won him few admirers.

For Taylor, a quiet dignity on the matter had served her well. In November, she was given the chance to exorcise the embarrassment when she attended the Country Music Awards, where she was up for glory in four separate categories: Music Video of the Year, Female Vocalist of the Year, Album of the Year and the biggie, Entertainer of the Year. Taylor, decked out in a long gown, arrived at the Nashville Sommet Center looking splendid and then opened the evening with an attention-grabbing performance of 'Forever & Always'.

Then, it was time for the winners to be announced. She won the Video gong for 'Love Story' and then returned to the stage to take Album of the Year for *Fearless*. For Taylor, this was important. 'I'd have to say that was the most mind-blowing experience, hearing my name called and winning that award,' she said later. 'That is an award I had placed in an unattainable spot in my head. To be the youngest to win it makes me love country music even more. We wished for this, my parents and I, every single day, without actually believing it would come true.'

Then she was back onstage as the winner of Female Vocalist of the Year. This time, she made light of Westgate when she thanked 'every single person here for not running up on to the stage during my speech'. There were further jokes about West from hosts Brad Paisley and Carrie Underwood. Country music veteran Little Jimmy Dickens even chipped in with one of his own. Taylor's musical family was letting her know they had her back.

She felt even more valued when she won the Entertainer of the Year award. There to present it to Taylor were Tim McGraw and Faith Hill. It was time to put the joking aside and for Taylor to explain why she was so deeply touched by this approval of her work. 'I'll never forget this moment, because in this moment everything that I could ever have wanted has just happened to me,' she said. 'You guys, this album is my diary, and so to all the people who voted for this: thank you for saying you love my diary, because that's the nicest compliment.'

At the American Music Awards in December she won five separate honours, including Favourite Pop/Rock Artist of the Year, a category in which she was up against none other than the recently deceased pop legend Michael Jackson. She said it was an 'unimaginable honour' to win this award in the circumstances. 'Music has never been ultimately about competition,' she added. Maybe not, but it is always nice to win, isn't it?

Being cast as a victim has a certain appeal for a celebrity, but as the West controversy rolled on, it was clear that Taylor needed to reassert herself. She wanted the world to remember that she was a fun and happy character, rather than the wronged soul she had been cast as in recent times. She got the chance to do just that when she guest-hosted *Saturday Night Live (SNL)*. A legendary US television show, *SNL* began in the mid 1970s. It steadily built a reputation as a beacon of live sketch comedy and variety performances. It began its thirty-ninth series in the autumn of 2013, making it one of the longest-running shows in American broadcasting history.

Taylor even wrote her opening monologue herself. She delivered it in the form of a self-deprecating tune, which she called 'Monologue Song'. Naturally, it referenced the West saga, but did so wittily. It was a big ask for someone as young as Taylor to enter the sharp, sometimes even sour, lion's den of *SNL*. She seemed to please most commentators. *Entertainment Weekly* said of her: 'Whether shrewdly letting her Kate Gosselin wig do most of the acting during a typically pungent parody of *The View*, or gleefully screeching while wearing braces in a public-service commercial satirising texting-while-driving, Swift was always up for the challenge, seemed to be having fun and helped the rest of the cast nail the punchlines.'

As far as Taylor was concerned, *SNL* was a natural challenge for her. She was, she said, 'a theatre kid' when she started in performance. So for her, the slot was the natural culmination of that. She said the experience did take her out of her 'comfort zone'. Yet she was soon acting on the small screen again when she appeared in an episode of *CSI*. Since it launched in the autumn of 2000, the

American crime drama series has become hugely popular. The programme is now an internationally loved franchise, and Taylor had wanted to appear on it for some time. 'I've always joked around with my record label and my mom and everybody,' she said. 'All my friends know that my dream is to die on *CSI*. I've always wanted to be one of the characters on there that they're trying to figure out what happened to.'

Producer Carol Mendelsohn said she 'reached out' to Taylor after hearing from a CBS executive that she was a fan. 'So Taylor came in to meet me and we talked about the character, but I said: "It's a very edgy part – this may not be what you want."' In the first of many comments about what she will tell her grandchildren, Taylor cited her *CSI* appearance as the source of some pride. 'When I'm really old and can only remember one story about my life to go back and relive and tell over and over and over again to the point where my grandchildren roll their eyes and leave the room – that's the story,' she wrote on MySpace.

Her love life was back in the limelight, too, when she became involved with another famous young pin-up. The moment she was linked to the actor Taylor Lautner, the media could hardly believe its luck. Here was a romance between two Taylors: a gym-pumped pin-up from a generation-defining film series and a clean-cut country singer. They met when they were cast in the same film – the rom-com *Valentine's Day*. Swift was excited to make the move from the small screen to the big screen. She had landed the job following a call from a crew member. 'I got a phone call from Garry Marshall saying, "Taylor, I want to have lunch or breakfast with you. I really want you to be in this movie. Will you? Will you let me write a part for you?" And I could not believe it. I couldn't believe it; because I didn't have the time to be a big role in this movie, Garry was going to write a small part for me. It blew my mind.'

Cast as boyfriend and girlfriend – Lautner played Willy, Taylor played Felicia – their characters agreed that they would remain chaste until 14 February. The filming was quite an experience for both Taylors. Although Lautner was more accustomed to making movies than Swift, filming at a real-life school was a challenge. 'We're walking into school and it's interesting because we shot this scene in an active high school. Active. As in, school is in session while we're filming,' said Swift. 'Every 30 minutes, there would be a bell that would ring and hundreds of students were pouring out, exactly where we were, and there were loads of people screaming out of windows and groups of kids gathering together chanting things. It was definitely an interesting and very exciting day. For me to step outside my immediate comfort zone and try comedy, and to have one of the coolest directors – a legendary director – laughing that hard at my first scene, it was really wonderful.'

Their characters kiss in the movie – and Taylor made sure she gave sufficiently enthusiastic statements about the experience to the media. Females linked to male teen heart-throbs can become the focus of intense envy. So she had to make sure she was not seen to be taking the experience lightly. She said the experience changed her life. 'I love him, he's so cute,' she said. As for Lautner, he added that his pretty blonde co-star was certainly his 'type'.

He appreciated her personality, too. 'We get along great, we instantly clicked,' he told *Rolling Stone*. 'And she's – she's an amazing girl. Aside from being beautiful, she's extremely funny, charismatic and fun to be around, and so we definitely get along. We're close.' Luvvies traditionally gush over how wonderful their co-stars are, but were these merely two thespians pouring theatrical platitudes over one another? Or was something serious afoot? They were spotted together during the autumn of 2009, dining out at romantic restaurants, watching basketball and hockey games and hanging out in the Beverly Wilshire Hotel. Lautner also showed up at a few of Taylor's concerts and they were spotted on a frozen-yoghurt date, chaperoned by Andrea.

Questions were soon asked about whether they were involved romantically. How the media craved an official confirmation from either party! As with Jonas, Taylor seemed to prefer being slightly coy. She never denied the relationship, but at first only hinted at it. 'I don't know, he's an amazing guy and we're really close and … ah, yep … and we're in a movie together and I'm really excited about seeing it.'

For the media, there was by now enough evidence that the pair were an item. They were duly nicknamed 'Tay

Tay'. This might not roll off the tongue as elegantly as, say, 'Brangelina', but it looked great on the page. After just three months together, however, the couple went their separate ways. A source close to Taylor reportedly told *Us Weekly* magazine: 'There was no chemistry and it felt contrived … He liked her more than she liked him. He went everywhere he could to see her, but she didn't travel much to see him. They plan to stay friends.'

Taylor took lessons from the experience, which she outlined in *Girl's Life* magazine. 'However hard and painful they are, you will learn something from a break-up. That is the most contrived, you've-heard-it-a-million-times lesson, but I really do feel like everything is put in your life to teach you something – even if it is terrible or hard.' She has a knack of repeating well-worn clichés in a way that lends them a degree of self-awareness and a sense of originality. For her younger fans, these were fresh sentiments.

She had, by this stage, bought her own home – a huge moment in the life of any young lady. But Taylor's first home was not typical. In the fall of 2009 she moved into a penthouse apartment in Nashville. Now, she felt, as she paced around her own pad, she had really arrived in the city she had dreamed of as a child. It was a plush 4,062-square-foot apartment – and a property she immediately set about imposing her own identity upon. With the same sort of inspired eye for detail with which she had designed aspects of her tours, she made the apartment her own. She took her guiding principle from the fact that when she first looked around the place, she had said to herself: 'The view is amazing – let's change every-thing else.'

So Taylor did just that. She installed a pond, which she filled with koi, and a birdcage. She chose some beautiful antiques and picked bright colours to bring the place to life. 'I love more of an old-world, eclectic feel, with mismatched chairs and a different knob on every cabinet,' she told Oprah Winfrey. She felt the property had a 'whimsical' feel to it and she gave it a new moniker to reflect this: 'The Imaginarium'. It was not – thank good-ness – indulgence on the scale of some rock and pop stars' houses. It was never going to rival Michael Jackson's gawdy Neverland, for instance. She also preferred to keep her presence there low key, as opposed to, say, the high-profile 'Supernova Heights' house Noel Gallagher took in north London at the height of Oasis's fame. But it did allow her, and her inner artist, some fun.

Most of all, however, her new pad made her feel *mature*. She positively revelled in her newfound inde-pendence. 'Living alone, you can do so many fantastic things,' she said. 'You can walk around and have conver-sations with yourself and, like, sing your thoughts … I think I'm the only one who does that.' How fascinating it would be to hear some of those impromptu songs and spoken streams of consciousness. For Taylor, though, this privacy – where she was free to express herself – was precious. Performing in front of tens of thousands of concert-goers or millions of television viewers was one thing. While she loved those experiences, and worked hard for them, there was also something beautiful in her being able to hold these private performances for an audience of just one – Taylor Swift. It was a rare joy for her to be able to perform – and even exist – in such serenity and solitude. Her life was getting more frantic all the time, and she was beginning to feel like all eyes were upon her.

Chapter Six

During 2010, the gossip circuit linked Taylor to three famous men: John Mayer, *Glee* star Cory Monteith and her 'Mine' video co-star Toby Hemingway. However, the most discussed rumour was that surrounding her relationship with a Hollywood heart-throb. After successfully co-hosting *Saturday Night Live*, Taylor returned to the studio for a subsequent episode to support her friend Emma Stone, who was herself appearing on the show. While she was there, Taylor met one of Hollywood's most famous young men of recent times. They agreed to meet up again for a date. The relationship that developed between her and Jake Gyllenhaal would be quite an experience for Taylor, and the break-up would inspire some of her best-known songs.

You could say Gyllenhaal was put on this earth to act. He was born in Los Angeles in 1980, the son of a director father and screenwriter mother. He began acting at the age of 10, but it was not until his late teens and early twenties that he hit the big time. In 1999 he took a lead role in the coming-of-age story *October Sky*. Two years later he made himself cult royalty when he starred in the indie flick *Donnie Darko*. More recently, he has carved out a place for himself as a versatile talent, appearing in further indie flicks – such as *The Good Girl* – as well as mainstream blockbusters like *The Day After Tomorrow* and powerful, critically acclaimed dramas such as *Brokeback Mountain*. He has been nominated for an Academy Award and won a BAFTA.

As well as his thespian activity, he has been much discussed for his good looks and his love life. Gyllenhaal has dated actresses Kirsten Dunst and Reese Witherspoon. He was named one of *People* magazine's '50 Most Beautiful People' in 2006 and listed as one of the same journal's 'Hottest Bachelors' in the same year. He has also been voted top of several major 'fanciable male' polls by gay men. Gyllenhaal had split from Witherspoon ten months before he met Taylor. When Taylor ran into him backstage at *SNL* she was very familiar with his story. A surprisingly cautious 'source' was quoted in *People* as saying the two 'were careful not to be seen too close' as they 'walked around together backstage'. The source concluded: 'It was hard to tell if they were together.' There was a considerable age gap between Taylor and Jake: he is nine years older than her. That, and the differing natures of their fame, would become an issue for them as the heady early days drifted into the reality of greater familiarity, with all the challenges that can entail.

After meeting at the television studios, they were seen together in Brooklyn, near his sister Maggie's home.

They then stopped for lunch at the Al Di La restaurant, with Emma Stone joining them to eat. Tongues were wagging and it was only to be a matter of time before Taylor was asked about the rumours. When she appeared on *The Ellen DeGeneres Show*, the host asked her how optimistic she was about her love life. 'I'm always optimistic about love,' said Taylor. 'Yes, always, sometimes.' Ellen was in a particularly impish mood and replied: 'Especially if your boyfriend is Jake Gyllenhaal, because he's very handsome.'

Later in November, Taylor and the actor were seen at the luxury Post Ranch Inn in Big Sur, California. Taylor reportedly 'laughed at everything Jake said' as they ate ice cream and yoghurt together. Taylor had yoghurt with rainbow sprinkles, while Gyllenhaal opted for Swiss chocolate chip. She also stood on tiptoes and measured her height against Jake's. Witnesses said the couple 'smiled a ton' and were 'happy' and 'friendly'. Things seemed to be going well.

Actress Gwyneth Paltrow, wife of Coldplay frontman Chris Martin, had been a friend of both Jake and – through Martin – Taylor for some time. She told *USA Today* that she had hosted a dinner for the young couple in London. Everything seemed to be going so well. So smitten were they that Taylor reportedly changed her Thanksgiving plans at the last moment and chose to spend it with the Gyllenhaals rather than with the Swifts. During the festival in New York, she met his family – a sure sign that a relationship is getting serious. The visit seemed to be a success, with Jake's sister Maggie telling *Us Weekly* it had all gone 'great'.

Then came the now-famous photographs of the couple sipping maple-syrup lattes from Gorilla Coffee in Brooklyn – the very epitome of the Fall-loving American young adult. Then, having flown to Nashville, they were seen on romantic strolls and taking further pit stops for coffee and a late breakfast. Among the cafés the caffeine-keen couple popped into were Frothy Monkey, Crema and Fido. Their relationship had, it seemed, quite a buzz to it on several levels – if the photographic evidence was anything to go by, the pair must have been caffeined up to the gills.

As with previous relationships of hers, including the one with Jonas, Taylor was evasive when the press questioned her. When MTV asked her if she was dating Gyllenhaal, she said: 'I write in great detail about my personal life, but I don't talk about it.' Yet sources kept cropping up in the press. One, in *Us Weekly*, said Taylor was 'smitten' by Gyllenhaal. 'She loves how nice and affectionate he is. Jake likes that Taylor is sweet, low key and very easy to be around.'

When he reportedly flew her to Britain, where he was deep in promotional junkets for his latest film, to spend a weekend with her, it looked serious. Some media claimed he spent £100,000 to whisk her by private jet across the Atlantic so they could spend just 48 hours together in his plush suite at The Dorchester hotel on the capital's posh Park Lane. This made the relationship seem quite intense.

Some even speculated that the couple would marry. Things were certainly moving very fast.

As Taylor was celebrating her twenty-first birthday, there were conflicting signals over where she stood with the Hollywood hunk. Some new stories had it that he had spent $11,000 on a vintage Gretsch guitar for Taylor. Others said he had spent £100,000 on a golden bracelet, which came with dozens of diamonds. To complete the reported gifts there was a coffee grinder and coffee maker, complete with Kona coffee beans. Such generosity, if the reports were true, hinted at a firm relationship with the two parties seeing a long-term future together.

However, when she joined 70 specially invited guests for a birthday party, Gyllenhaal was not among them. While work commitments could have explained his absence, it was notable that she spent Christmas with relatives rather than ditching them for Jake, as she had at Thanksgiving. Soon, it became clear the two had parted ways. 'He said he wasn't feeling it any more and was uncomfortable with all the attention they got,' a source told *Us Weekly*. 'He also said he could feel the age difference. Taylor is really upset. We told her not to move so fast with this, but she didn't listen.'

Where had it all gone wrong? It seemed that the escalation in media attention he received as a result of being linked to Taylor had revolted Gyllenhaal and made him feel uncomfortable. He was no stranger to the press, of course, but he cherished his self-image as a credible actor who focused on indie films. Many actors like to aspire, at least in part, to the lifestyle and image of reclusive, mysterious thespians such as Robert De Niro. The more teeny, poppy image of Taylor, and the nature of the press coverage she consequently attracted, made him feel uncool.

Taylor noted his objections, but felt he was being oversensitive about the press. She told *Vogue*: 'Also, I can't deal with someone who's obsessed with privacy. People kind of care if there are two famous people dating – but no one cares that much. If you care about privacy to the point where we need to dig a tunnel under this restaurant so that we can leave? I can't do that.' She would do more talking about what they went through together, but that would be done on her next album.

In the meantime, there were yet more awards to put on her sideboard. At the 2010 Grammys, she won Best Female Vocal Performance, for 'White Horse'. This was a landmark moment in her career. 'This is my first Grammy, you guys! This is a Grammy!' She also won other gongs, including Album of the Year. She added: 'All of us, when we're 80 years old and we are telling the same stories over and over again to our grandkids, and they're so annoyed with us, this is the story we're going to be telling over and over again – in 2010, we got to win Album of the Year at the Grammys.'

An added benefit of the evening was that she was uninterrupted as she expressed her gratitude. But just as she exorcised one awards-show demon, another popped up to take its place. It was her performance with country legend Stevie Nicks that became the most talked-about element of the evening this time. It brought on Taylor's head the most hurtful criticism of her career to date. She sang a medley of 'You Belong With Me' and 'Today Was a Fairytale' alone and also performed a duet with Nicks on a cover of 'Rhiannon', the Fleetwood Mac track. Unfortunately, due to some technical issues, she was unable to hear her vocals as she delivered them. As she is used to having this as a guide, her voice lost its key and pitch.

Ironically, just weeks earlier she had spoken about how, to her, emotion was more important than perfection when it came to her vocals. She told the *Los Angeles Times*: 'It's really more about portraying the song in a way that gets the feeling across, rather than every phrase being exactly perfect.' She added that, as a songwriter as well as a singer, she was more 'obsessed' with the meaning of her lyrics than the 'vocal technique' with which she delivered them. 'Overthinking vocals and stuff – I never want to get to that point.'

This was a sentient point to make. In the era of the reality-television singing contest, the technical quality of vocal delivery has become an overrated beast. Hopefuls on shows such as *The Voice* and *The X Factor* are performing tracks written by other artists in order to please judges and the voting public. They can therefore focus too much on hitting every note perfectly, rather than connecting with the meaning behind the lyrics, which after all they did not write themselves.

However, the media was considering none of this as it reacted to Taylor's Grammy performance. The *Los Angeles*

Times said she had given a 'strikingly bad vocal performance', which was 'tinny and rhythmically flat-footed'. *Entertainment Weekly* said she was 'badly off key'.

Among online and less mainstream publications, the voices were even harsher on Taylor. Scott Borchetta leaped to her defence. He said: 'Maybe she's not the best technical singer, but she is the best emotional singer, because everybody else who gets up there and is technically perfect, people don't seem to want more of it.' He added: 'No one is perfect on any given day. Maybe in that moment we didn't have the best night, but in the same breath, maybe we did. She's a very intelligent girl. She's going to keep addressing it and keep getting better.'

For her, the criticism had been painful. Later, she felt she could be vulnerable enough to open up to radio network NPR. She admitted the incident had thrown her. 'Absolutely,' she said. 'My confidence is easy to shake. I am very well aware of all of my flaws. I am aware of all the insecurities that I have. I have a lot of voices in my head constantly telling me I can't do it. I've dealt with that my whole life. And getting up there onstage thousands of times, you're going to have off nights. And when you have an off night in front of that many people, and it's pointed out in such a public way, yeah, that gets to you. I feel like, as a songwriter, I can't develop thick skin. I cannot put up protective walls, because it's my job to feel things.'

Yet there were some positive observations. As Alan Light of *SPIN* magazine wrote: 'The fact that it's not perfect, in some ways, has been an asset. That makes it all the more believable to a certain point.' But more importantly, perhaps, was the fact that she had won her first Grammy awards. As a Grammy-decorated act, Taylor was now among the most legendary artists in musical history. Not bad for a girl who 'cannot sing'.

Success and recognition can dampen the enthusiasm of some musical artists. Once they have been bathed in those two elusive experiences, they often find that the incentive that once drove them has been placated. They therefore lose some of their motivation and go to ground temporarily, or even permanently. Workhorse Taylor is different. Success only drove her on all the more. 'The second that I put out *Fearless*, the moment that album came out and I was done with it, I started writing for my next album,' she said. 'I love to plan 20 steps ahead of myself.'

She worked again with Nathan Chapman on this album, returning to her roots in that sense. They recorded most of the songs in Chapman's basement. 'A lot of times we got a magical first-take vocal and we would keep it,' she said. As for the producer, he noted changes in Taylor and was the first to see how she had changed since *Fearless*. 'She's left home, she's living on her own now and she's seeing the world in a different way after growing up a bit.'

The album, *Speak Now*, had a broad and big sound to it. It opens with 'Mine'. This song, she said, 'is about my tendency to run from love'; a tendency, she said, that was a 'recent' development. The song is about 'finding the exception' to the temporary nature of her experiences with love up until then, she added. 'I saw the entire relationship flash before my eyes, almost like some weird science-fiction movie,' she told Yahoo! As Borchetta explained, it had been an exciting song for her and her crew to nail. 'We probably played that song four or five times,' he said. 'I'm jumping around playing air guitar, she's singing the song back to me, and it was just one of those crazy, fun, Taylor teenage moments.'

We can only speculate as to whom the song is about, but whoever it is, Taylor has said that the day the song was released he emailed her, having recognised that it was about him. 'I had no idea,' he wrote. 'I realise I've been naive.' He stands in a long list of men who have listened to Taylor albums only to realise one of the songs is about them.

Then we turn to 'Sparks Fly'. This was a song that had been sitting on Taylor's shelf for some years. It was only when she received positive feedback after live performances of it that she was drawn to record it. The album's first big, slow epic is 'Back to December'. 'This is about a person who was incredible to me, just perfect to me in a relationship, and I was really careless with him.' It seems likely this song is about Taylor Lautner. The physical descriptions in the song match the *Twilight* hunk neatly. She has also dedicated it onstage to 'the boy from Michigan' – his hometown.

In the titular 'Speak Now', Taylor sings about how she found out that her high-school crush had married someone who was treating him badly. 'He had met this other girl who was a horrible person. She made him stop talking to his friends, cut off his family ties and made him so isolated. And, randomly, I was, like, "Oh, are you going to speak now?"' This was in reference to the moment in a wedding ceremony when guests are invited to reveal if there is any reason why the wedding should not go ahead. 'I've always been fascinated by that moment in a wedding, because I think it's a metaphor for a lot of the times in our life when we're just about to lose something, and that's when we realise we have to speak up.'

The likely subject of 'Dear John' is country singer John Mayer, who had been linked with Taylor. A slow heartbreaker of a song, it is a ballad that grieves. 'A lot of times when people's relationships end, they write an email to that person and say everything that they wish they would have said,' she explained. 'A lot of times they don't push send. That was a tough one to write and I guess putting it on the album was pushing send.' Mayer was unimpressed by the perceived link to him. 'It made me feel terrible – because I didn't deserve it,' he said. 'I'm pretty good at taking accountability now, and I never did anything to deserve that. It was a really lousy thing to do.' He described the move as 'cheap songwriting'. When Taylor was confronted with his words on Katie Couric's talk show *Katie*, she rolled her eyes and sighed, 'Oh, come *on*.'

'Mean' is Taylor's musical response to the criticism she received for *that* Grammys performance. 'It's a song I wrote on a really, really bad day, but it has produced so many happy days for me since,' she said. As she explained, the Grammys fallout had reminded her of when she was abused by fellow pupils at school. '"Mean" is about bullying at a different stage in my life,' she said. 'I'm not at school and I still know what it feels like.'

Yet there was something beautiful about how she turned the experience on its head, as she acknowledged to NPR. 'The kind of magical way that criticism has helped me is that that's another thing that I put into my music. I ended up writing a song called "Mean" about that experience, and about this one particular guy who would not get off my case about it. To stand up at the Grammys two years later, to sing that song and get a standing ovation for it, and to win two Grammys for that particular song, I think was the most gratifying experience I've ever had in my life.' Just as she had previously found a bright side to the bullying she had received at school, so too did she find a positive from the Grammys horror.

With this song casting Taylor as the victim, she was anxious to address perceptions that she was oversensitive. She separated constructive, work-focused criticism from unpleasant personal attacks. The latter, she said, were 'mean'. She added: 'There are different kinds of ways to criticise someone.' In any case, sensitive or not, her musical responses to bad experiences made for fruitful creative inspiration.

'The Story of Us' was a landmark track in the construction of the album. 'After I finished that one, I knew I was done,' she said. It was the last song she wrote for the album, and at that stage, she and Chapman danced around the room in celebration. However, the song itself is about a less festive feeling. '[It] is about running into someone I had been in a relationship with at an awards show, and we were a few seats away from each other. I just wanted to say to him, "Is this killing you? Because it's killing me."' They never had that conversation, she explained, 'because we both had these silent shields up'.

As we have seen, when Taylor moved into her first apartment she relished the freedom it gave her to speak and sing out loud as she wandered around it. It clearly made for a fertile environment, as we see in 'Never Grow Up'. Taylor has explained: 'I walked into this apartment after I bought it and thought: oh man, this is real now. We're all getting older, and soon my parents are going to be older, and then I have to think about grown-up things.'

Again, we see Taylor as the elder sibling here. Or is she actually feeling cluckier than that and having pangs of yearning for motherhood? 'Every once in a while I look down and I see a little girl who is seven or eight, and I wish I could tell her all of this. There she is, becoming who she is going to be and forming her thoughts and dreams and opinions. I wrote this song for those little girls.'

One day in New York, Taylor met someone who really grabbed her attention. She was so moved by the encounter that she returned to her hotel suite and wrote a song that summed up how she felt. It was called 'Enchanted'.

'Meeting him, it was this overwhelming feeling of: I really hope that you're not in love with somebody. And the whole entire way home, I remember the glittery New York City buildings passing by, and then just sitting there thinking: am I ever going to talk to this person again? And that pining away for a romance that may never happen … but all you have is this hope that it could, and the fear that it never will.'

The song itself is very mature – and almost cinematic in its gravitas. It is believed that the man who so struck her in this way was electronica artist Adam Young. He once wrote an open letter to her on his website. Its conclusion hinted strongly that he was the subject of this track. 'Everything about you is lovely. You're an immensely charming girl with a beautiful heart and more grace and elegance than I know how to describe. You are a true princess from a dreamy fairytale, and above all I just want you to know … I was enchanted to meet you, too.'

If you enjoy angry Taylor, then you will have loved her furious songs, such as 'Picture to Burn'. That ire rises again in 'Better Than Revenge', in which she hurls insults at a woman who had, Taylor believed, been the other party when one of her boyfriends had cheated on her. The lyrics are petulant and unflinching, yet the metaphors about someone stealing other children's toys in the playground have a certain wit to them.

In 'Innocent', she addresses the Kanye West drama. 'That was a huge, intense thing in my life that resonated for a long time,' she said. Even though she was asked about the incident wherever she went, she chose to keep her silence on the matter for some time. When she was ready to 'speak' about it, she chose to sing about it instead. She later explained: 'Even then, I didn't talk about it and I still don't really talk about it. I just thought it was very important for me to sing about it.' The song explains how everyone has the chance to reinvent themselves. 'Nothing is going to go exactly the way you plan it to,' she said. 'Just because you make a good plan, doesn't mean that's gonna happen.'

'Haunted', said Taylor, is about 'being really strung out on a relationship and wishing you had it back, and being tormented by it'. Again, it has a big-screen feel to it – this could easily be on the soundtrack of a *Twilight*-esque 'tween' movie. 'I wanted the music and the orchestration to reflect the intensity of the emotion the song is about, so we recorded strings with Paul Buckmaster at Capitol Studios in Los Angeles. It was an amazing experience – recording this entire big, live string section that I think in the end really captured the intense, chaotic feeling of confusion I was looking for.'

'Last Kiss' is a ballad that attempts to capture the moment when you fully connect with the sadness you feel over a lost love. This is not, as with many break-up songs, about the initial drama of a split, but more about a feeling further down the line. 'Going through a break-up, you feel all of these different things,' she explained. 'You feel anger, and you feel confusion and frustration. Then there is the absolute sadness of losing this person, losing all the memories and the hopes you had for the future.'

There is so much gloom in *Speak Now*, yet the album finishes on an upbeat note. She was inspired to write the catchy melody for the final track during a concert. In between the main chunk of her performance and the subsequent encore, she was in the dressing room when a tune came into her head. She made a quick note of it and then returned to her adoring audience. Later, she revisited the melody and the result was 'Long Live'.

Suitably, given the location of its genesis, she turned the song into a tribute to those who work with her. 'Sort of the first love song that I've written to my team,' was how she described it. Listening to it, you want to be on – and in – Taylor's team. There is just the right level of pride, and plentiful courage. *Rolling Stone* compared it to Bon Jovi, and rightfully so – this is another Taylor song that is made for big arenas.

That *Rolling Stone* comment was emblematic of the praise *Speak Now* got from the critics. The music monthly said the album stood within a steady progression of Taylor's talent. It declared that the album 'is roughly twice as good as 2008's *Fearless*, which was roughly twice as good as her 2006 debut'. The *Guardian* gave *Speak Now* four out of five stars and said it was 'mostly' a 'triumph'. It praised the courage of 'Never Grow Up', which its reviewer found 'devastating and genuinely uncomfortable'.

While the BBC website found Taylor was progressing at a 'stately' pace, it also felt that the album was too long.

'When you've heard half a dozen perky laments you've heard, well, quite a lot,' it said. The *Washington Post* made a similar point about length, complaining of the album's '14 wordy, stretched-thin, occasionally repetitive songs, all written entirely by her'. But at least the same reviewer was moved to say that *Speak Now* was a 'captivating exercise in woo pitching, flame tending and score settling'.

The *New York Times*, meanwhile, described *Speak Now* as 'a bravura work of nontransparent transparency'. Yet it was Ann Powers of the *Los Angeles Times* who got closest to the heart of the appeal of the album, and of Taylor in general. Wrote Powers: 'Much of mainstream pop music now sounds like advertising jingles and football chants, with melodic earworms the size of tapeworms and itchily irresistible beats. Outrageous personalities complement these pushy sounds. Swift reminds us that there's another way to hook in listeners. Not surprisingly, coming from someone so focused on childhood imagery, it's a trick parents often use with their kids: use a soft tone. Focus everything inward. Make the one you're addressing feel like you and she are the only ones in the world.'

The tour to promote the album began in February 2011. It would take in 17 countries, with her playing 100 tour dates over a year. It was the most lucrative tour of 2011 according to *Billboard*, which estimated that she made $123.7 million. Yet it was not easy work. 'Going through these performances, it's like an athletic marathon,' she told Katie Couric. 'When I'm underneath the stage and then it pops me up like a toaster, and then I'm like six feet in the air, and I'm like, "Made it through that ... did the banjo song ... okay ... onto this next blocking ... change clothes ... flying above the crowd – awesome ..."'

Alongside the careful planning, Taylor aimed to keep much of the evening 'in the moment'. She wanted a blend of preparation and spontaneity. She said: 'One of my favourite things about this tour – although it's a very theatrical show, and it really reminds me a lot of my favourite musical theatre productions in its scenery, costumes and production – there are lots of moments in the show that are very spontaneous.'

The freedom of that spontaneity was something that Taylor would occasionally look back on in the future and question whether it had disappeared from her life. The perspective one eventually gets on a lost relationship, as Taylor explored in 'Last Kiss', was something she would also find with regards to her career. Her fame was about to rocket to new heights. And while enjoying much of the ride, Taylor would at times look back and wonder where some of the fun had gone.

Chapter Seven

What is the difference between a star and a superstar? We each have our own instinctive idea of what each term means, but the difference is not entirely tangible. However, Taylor went a long way towards discovering the answer to this question during 2012, as her fame took on ever-greater intensity. She found herself in a vortex of recognition. Increased media stature is both a driver and signpost of newfound fame. Celebrity is a phenomenon that feeds itself: the more you get the more you get. Taylor was about to get plenty.

The February 2012 edition of *Vogue* magazine featured her on its front cover. *Billboard* named her its 'Woman of the Year', making her the youngest artist to receive the honour. With all this recognition came considerable fortune for her. She came top of *Billboard*'s 'Top 40 Money Makers in Music' list and was named by *Forbes* as the highest-earning star under 30. Among the other magazines to feature her on their front covers were *Elle* and *Rolling Stone* – which added her to its list of 'Women Who Rock', lauding her as a 'genuine' rock star with 'a flawless ear for what makes a song click'. She was gaining recognition and respect across a wide range of media. Serious music magazines paid tribute to the country roots of her craftsmanship, women's monthlies saw her as an inspiring and intriguing character, while teen and celeb weeklies knew she was of interest to their younger, poppier readership.

This gave her enormous currency and delighted her record label no end. As far as the public relations department was concerned, Taylor was a dream act to promote: everyone was only too happy to promote her latest releases. With some artists, such departments have their work cut out trying to get stories or reviews printed. Yet Taylor was sweeping the board, appearing in every publication her label could reasonably wish to see her in.

Britain's broadsheet paper the *Guardian*, which prides itself on its discerning relationship with the arts, published an in-depth interview with her. In it, she attempted to explain why her songs connected so strongly with her listeners, particularly young females who were facing the emotional and physical hydra that is adolescence. 'There are so many emotions that you're feeling, you can get stifled by them if you're feeling them all at once,' she told them. 'What I try to do is take one moment – one simple, simple feeling – and expand it into three and a half minutes.' The interviewer, Alex Macpherson, was impressed. He reflected: 'In Swift, the traditions of storytelling and confessionalism are intertwined, held together by an instinct for the universal.'

Yet for all the respect Taylor was attracting from high-brow publications, there was still plentiful fascination with her love life among the more gossipy corners of the media. When she co-starred with *High School Musical* hunk Zac Efron in the animated Dr Seuss film *The Lorax*, there was a sense of inevitability to the speculation that they had become an item off screen. Yet Taylor shot the rumours down. 'We are not a couple,' she told Ellen DeGeneres. 'He's awesome; we are not a couple, though. You hear people get together when they're shooting movies, co-stars. But not like animated co-stars. You know what I'm saying? Oh my god, as we were recording our voiceovers on separate coasts, we really connected.'

The next famous man she was accurately linked to was not an actor, but a member of a well-known political clan. Cute Conor Kennedy is the grandson of Robert F. Kennedy. He had a three-month summer romance with Taylor in 2012. They were first spotted in July. They were lunching at a pizza restaurant in Mount Kisco, New York. Within days they were spotted at the Kennedy compound in Hyannis Port, Massachusetts. They were seen together there many times, holding hands on occasion. Another time, baby-faced Conor was seen kissing Taylor. Things seemed serious: she was also reportedly considering buying property in the area.

She was accused of being a 'wedding crasher' when she and Conor rolled up at a family ceremony. Taylor's representatives denied she had turned up without being asked. There was more family stuff going on when she accompanied Conor for a visit to the grave of his mother, who had hanged herself only months earlier. She helped remove some overgrown vegetation from the site. Although things seemed serious between them, they soon split up. A close friend told *Us Weekly*: 'They quietly parted ways a while ago. It was just a distance thing. No hard feelings. They're fine.' Another relationship had gone by the wayside. More lessons learned for Taylor and, most importantly, new inspiration for her songs.

However, her fling with Kennedy would be dwarfed when compared to her next relationship – with another international teen pin-up. As far as the celebrity press was concerned, *here* was a romance made in show-business heaven: a beautiful, blonde singer with a history of heartbreak, and a baby-faced boy-band studlet with a reputation as a player. Between them, the two had many millions of fans around the world who were already fascinated by their every move. Together, they were gold and guaranteed to generate many miles of column inches. Indeed, the connection between Taylor and Harry Styles was so convenient that the question was asked how deep their relationship really was.

Before he had ever met Taylor, Styles's love life was already a mainstay in the media. While all of the members of his pop band, One Direction, were of interest to the press, Styles had jumped out of the pack. It all started when he was linked with *Xtra Factor* presenter Caroline Flack, who was 14 years older than him. The age gap alone made the story a veritable bombshell: One Direction fans were as furious as the tabloid press was excited. Flack received death threats from jealous 1D fans and lots of people had an opinion on the rumoured dalliance. Eventually the pair went their separate ways, but the fling had made Styles one of the media's central targets.

Reporters followed him everywhere and tried to link him to a chain of people. Most of the stories were fabricated. Even the Radio 1 host Nick Grimshaw, a close friend of Harry's, was alleged to be romantically involved with the young singer – something they both deny. At one point, Harry was moved to say he felt as if he had '7,000 girlfriends' – according to the media, at least. As for Taylor, we have seen that she, too, had considerable media currency, albeit from a more wholesome place. There were few celebrity magazine editors who did not covet juicy gossip involving her. So when whispers began to circulate that the two young stars had become an item, it was bound to be a big story.

They reportedly met for the first time at an awards night in 2012. It was March and the Nickelodeon Kids' Choice Awards was in full swing. Taylor was spotted dancing during One Direction's performance. Next to her was her friend Selena Gomez, but it was Taylor who caught the most attention. The reporters present quickly sensed the opportunity for a story and later, after the two singers had chatted, Styles was asked if he had anything to report. With a smile, he described Taylor as 'nice'.

With the intense scrutiny paid to his words, Styles had grown accustomed to weighing his every syllable carefully, particularly when speaking about his private life. Therefore, he was extremely measured in what he said about Taylor.

Even when he spoke about her to *Seventeen*, he sounded more like a politician than a pop star. He said: 'She honestly couldn't be a sweeter person. She's genuinely nice and extremely talented and she deserves everything she has.' Few teenage boys choose their words so cautiously or speak with such nuance when discussing attractive ladies.

That nuance meant the guessing game had to carry on. In fact, the first people to hint that the pair had become an item were neither Taylor nor Styles, but other celebrities. The prince of pop Justin Bieber teased the media with a deliberately cryptic allusion to them. 'I already know one of the biggest artists in the world thinks Harry is so hot, but I have been sworn to secrecy,' he said. Styles's One Direction bandmates were also seen teasing him about the gossip, including at the MTV VMAs.

Then, after Taylor appeared on the final of the US *X Factor*, the show's anchor Mario Lopez offered the press what he called 'a little inside scoop'. He said: 'During the rehearsals, Harry from One Direction came and slapped me on the back and said: "Hey, Mario, how ya doing?" And I said, "What are you doing here?" And he sort of pointed toward Taylor.' Lopez said they left holding hands. The show's official Twitter feed also bumped up the story, saying the two had eaten cheeseburgers together.

This was enough to convince the world that the pair were an item, and soon they were dubbed 'Haylor'. Lopez would surely not have touched with a barge pole any unsubstantiated rumour about One Direction, seeing as they were the beloved product of his own employer, Simon Cowell. Although stories are frequently placed in the media by the *X Factor* team, those stories are all carefully controlled at the source. While the Lopez quote was revealing, as the media jumped on the story, the one thing reporters were still lacking was a 'smoking gun' – in other words, solid proof.

Styles continued to be coy when he was asked about his love life. For instance, he told *Cosmopolitan* magazine: 'There's someone I like ... but this girl ... isn't my "type". It's more about the person. How they act, their body language, if they can laugh at themselves.' This could have been anyone, so the media settled for speculation. They wondered whether Taylor was trying to buy a house in London so she could be near Harry. This cast the relationship as moving very quickly, yet nobody knew for sure if such a relationship was even in place.

The clues kept coming. Taylor was seen wearing a silver airplane chain, identical to one owned by Styles. She also hinted that she was now interested in relationships with 'bad boys'. While to older readers the concept of baby-faced Styles as such a creature may seem odd, for younger people, he has a reputation as a heartbreaker. 'There's a really interesting charisma involved,' said Taylor. 'They usually have a lot to say, and even if they don't, they know how to look at you to say it all. I think every girl's dream is to find a bad boy at the right time, when he wants to not be bad any more.'

Talk of the relationship gained more currency when Harry's close friend Nick Grimshaw spoke publicly about it. This was the first time anyone in the inner circle of either Taylor or Styles had officially spoken about them being involved. 'Harry really likes Taylor, he's fallen for her in a big way,' he said. 'At first, I wasn't sure if the relationship was a real one, but I talk to him a lot and it seems to be that she's the one for him – for now, anyway.'

He explained that Taylor's wit was a big factor in her appeal. 'Harry likes people who make him laugh. I talk to Harry a lot on the phone while he's away touring and he talks about her a lot. He is very happy with her. I like her a lot, too; she came on my show recently and we had a really fun time.' This talk of Taylor's wit tied in with what Styles had said previously about the importance of humour in finding someone attractive.

In December 2012, the media got the sort of photographic evidence it had been after when Taylor and Harry visited Central Park Zoo together. Photographs of their time in the zoo were splashed everywhere. After that date, the two reportedly spent two evenings together at Taylor's Manhattan hotel. Then they were seen at the after party of a 1D gig at Madison Square Garden. They left at 4 a.m. and retired to the same hotel, then emerged shortly after one another the next morning. During the holiday season, both Taylor and One Direction had a series of appearances and performances to honour on America's East Coast.

In the New Year, she reportedly flew Harry to Britain to help her celebrate her twenty-third birthday. They ate at the George & Dragon pub in Great Budworth, Cheshire. 'He's amazing,' Taylor was reported to have said of the much-coveted Styles. They also went for a walk in the Peak District and dined with Styles's sister at the Rising Sun Inn. Harry reportedly introduced Taylor to the goofy UK teen comedy *The Inbetweeners* while she was in Britain. An American version of the series has been made since, but it is said that Taylor was tickled by the original.

As well as learning things about British humour, Taylor was learning a great deal about the nature of fame. When she dated Jake Gyllenhaal, he had been the one who had been uncomfortable with the increased whirlwind of media scrutiny. However, with Styles it was Taylor's turn to be shocked. 'I don't know necessarily how much privacy I'm entitled to, but I know I don't get much out of it. At the same time, I asked for this. I could be playing in a coffee house. I'd be happy doing that, but not as happy, probably.' She said that knowing masses of people would hear her music was 'the most amazing feeling', but added that the presence of 'dudes' with cameras 'hiding in the bushes' is a 'less awesome feeling'.

It was said that the already much-inked Harry had got yet another tattoo that referenced his feelings for Taylor, while she was said to be splashing £50,000 on Beatles memorabilia for him. At the final of the US *X Factor*, where One Direction performed their single 'Kiss You', Harry was asked about Taylor. 'She's good,' he replied. Hardly a world-changing comment in itself, yet in the context of this story it was treated as if it were media gold.

Then Taylor jetted off to Australia on a promotional jaunt. She was amused at the prospect of spending the run-up to Christmas Day in the heat of the Aussie summer. 'It's going to be non-stop sun,' she said. 'So it will be weird to have a tan around Christmas, but I'm really excited about it.' She was back in the US for New Year's Eve, where she was booked to perform for *Dick Clark's New Year's Rockin' Eve* in Times Square. She sang 'I Knew You Were Trouble' and 'We Are Never Ever Getting Back Together'. According to a fan on Twitter, Taylor and Harry 'made out' in an elevator afterwards.

As with Gyllenhaal, it seemed her relationship with Styles was beginning to accelerate. Unnamed 'insiders' were telling the press that Taylor and Styles were planning to marry. It was at this stage that, according to reports, her father Scott intervened and took Styles to one side to tell him to 'slow down and take things easy'. While Scott was, according to the reports, not seeking to split the couple up, he was arguing strongly that they should not rush into anything.

However, early in 2013 Taylor and Harry were flying off in search of the sun. They jetted to the British Virgin Islands. Photographs were snapped of them eating alongside some fans at a restaurant in Virgin Gorda. It was a blissful scene and one worth pausing on for a moment, as within hours the scene would change. When Taylor was later spotted alone on a boat while Styles continued to party elsewhere, it seemed that their love was on the rocks.

During an alleged row, she had reportedly told him he was 'lucky' to be with her. With their relationship seemingly a thing of the past all of a sudden, the media moved to question whether it had ever genuinely existed. American tabloid the *National Enquirer* even suggested that Taylor was unaware of the truth herself. It claimed: 'Little does Taylor know that Harry's handlers went to great lengths to put the two together because she's such a huge star.' The *Guardian* said it was 'inevitable' that they would have dated, 'seeing as, between them, they have allegedly dated every single person on the planet'. With cynicism at the fore, it added that 'the fact this relationship happened to bookend Swift releasing an album and One Direction announcing a tour is just one of those coincidences that often accompanies celebrity relationships'. Lest any reader had not picked up on the implication, it added that 'some of their dates might have had the suspicious smack of PR exercises'.

Taylor's fling with Harry had indeed felt a little too convenient at times. Yet there is not a celebrity coupling in history that could not be subject to a similarly cynical reading. While many famous couples have got together to boost their respective profiles, there are many stars who date other stars simply because they want to be with someone who understands the pressures of celebrity. As for Taylor, she was left on her own again. This is one of her deepest fears, as she has admitted. 'I think the one thing I'm really afraid of is that the magic doesn't last,' she has said. 'The butterflies and daydreams and love, all these things I hold so dear, are going to leave some day.' Meanwhile, she had a new album to promote.

After *Red* was released in October 2012, Taylor opened up during an interview with radio network NPR about how her relationships have inspired her songs and why she writes so openly about them. With several high-profile relationships in her recent past, the words on her new release were going to be more closely scrutinised than ever. 'The first thing that I think about when I'm writing my lyrics is directly communicating with the person the song is about,' she said. 'I think what I've learned recently is that it's not ... heartbreak that inspires my songs. It's not love that inspires my songs. It's individual people that come into my life. I've had relationships with people that were really substantial and meant a lot to me, but I couldn't write a song about that person for some reason. Then again, you'll meet someone that comes into your life for two weeks and you write an entire record about them.'

However, for Taylor, the music itself matters at least as much as the lyrics and their perceived themes. For *Red*, she had drawn on the widest range of styles yet. 'I'm inspired by all kinds of different sounds,' she told *Rolling*

Stone, 'and I don't think I'd ever be someone who would say, "I will never make a song that sounds a certain way, I will never branch outside of genres," because I think that genres are sort of unnecessary walls.'

She had been working hard on new material for her next album – and one of the first tracks she composed in these sessions would be called 'State of Grace'. In its final form, this song turned into something bigger than any previous Taylor track. Never before had a song of hers been so rich and heavy. The opening bars hint at a stadium-rock tune, the likes of which U2 or REM would have been keen for. It would also be a song that was all the richer for its paradoxes and contradictions – and it kicked off her epic 16-track album with powerful confidence.

While Taylor sounds assured here, there is at the same time an additional layer of vulnerability. Her voice seems too gentle to compete with such a fulsome backing track, and the way she draws out the syllables of the final words in each line of the bridge only adds to this tantalising dichotomy. Yet in the middle eight, she goes all sassy on us, confidently and wisely delivering her verdict on the story. He was never a saint, she sings, while she loved in shades 'of wrong'. Her repetition of the words 'never' and 'ever' hints at a later track still to come on *Red*.

Overall, the lyrics deliver a message of mature pragmatism when it comes to love and romance. She neither celebrates them as perfect forces, nor slams them as the source of all heartbreak. Instead, she knowingly reflects on the happy and unhappy aspects of each. Making love work is a 'fight', she sings, but a 'worthwhile' one. When it works, a state of grace – that most Christian of concepts – is found. Indeed, the lyrics of the chorus are straight out of the U2 textbook, and one can easily imagine the band's Christian lead singer Bono appreciating and singing them.

In recording 'State of Grace', Taylor aimed for 'a really big sound' – and she got one. The melody and production are, in fact, euphoric at times. Although starting with an almost Stone Roses feel, the reverb-heavy guitars build and build. The drums crash throughout. She achieved what she set out to do, which was to represent 'the feeling of falling in love in an epic way'. At her concerts this song would prove a fists-in-the-air favourite, just perfect for the large arenas she now commanded on the live circuit. Again, it is the contradiction that gives the song its power: the lyrics, which thousands bawl along to at concerts, are among her most intimate and vulnerable. She sings of her and her love alone in their room, with their slates clean.

The lyrics imply that the song was inspired by her romance with Jake Gyllenhaal. The lines about the lovers having 'twin fire signs' and 'four blue eyes' would suggest as much: both Taylor and Gyllenhaal were born under the fire sign of Sagittarius and they both have blue eyes. Dedicated de-coders of Taylor's lyrics, of whom there is a growing number, found this song straightforward to analyse.

Then comes the album's title track. It starts with a banjo line, bringing the country sound straight back after the album's rocky opener. In the verses she lists a series of similes that comes closer to a checklist of irony than Alanis Morissette's 'Ironic' ever did. The song then goes all soft-rock up-tempo on us in the chorus, in which she deploys colours simply and deftly to express the emotions of loss and love. Loving him was, she concludes, red. Later in the song she clarifies that she means a burning red. A stabbed keyboard repeats naggingly after each chorus, creating a catchy looped motif.

Speaking on *Good Morning America*, Taylor would later explain the concept behind the track. 'I wrote this song about the fact that some things are just hard to forget,' she said, 'because the emotions involved with them were so intense and, to me, intense emotion is red.' The song divided opinion among critics; some felt she had attempted too many genres in one song, leading to a spoiled broth. Yet the website Taste of Country more than welcomed 'Red', saying, 'It's a songwriting spotlight for Swift, who toys with colours like a skilled artist, and this song is her Sistine Chapel.'

It was a tricky song for Taylor to complete. She left it to marinate for a while, only returning to finish it once she had a clear idea of what overall direction the album, and her career, would take. This song, too, seems to be about Gyllenhaal. Her secret code for the song was 'SAG', and this could again be a reference to her and Gyllenhaal's shared star sign. Some argue that it is the acronym for the

Screen Actors Guild. This seems an outlandish theory, but if accurate it again points to Gyllenhaal.

If you want to write the best song, you turn to the best songwriter to collaborate with. For track three on *Red*, 'Treacherous', Taylor turned to Dan Wilson, the frontman of Semisonic and the man who co-wrote one of the biggest hits of the twenty-first century so far: 'Someone Like You' by Adele. Taylor told Wilson that she wanted to create a song on the concept of treachery. She had a melody in mind but wanted to work with him to turn it into something special. As they worked, they thought they had finished the track, but then they decided it would benefit from a heavier dimension. So they added the rockier chorus, which proved powerful in its own right and also provided a fine contrast to the gentle, almost whispered verses. Those verses were described well by *Billboard*, which wrote of their 'hushed, confessional beauty'.

Wilson was heartily impressed with Taylor having worked with her in the studio. 'An interesting quality, objectively speaking, was how on fire she was, the clarity she had,' he said. 'She was so open and excited about the things I would add. She works at a very high level of positivity, and that is rare.' Yet the track itself is no inanely jolly effort. In common with several of *Red*'s tracks, it presents a more knowing, almost jaded view of love. Taylor seems to have grown up so fast – too fast, some would say. As Taylor told *USA Today*, the song details a relationship that could only 'end in fiery, burning wreckage', but that nevertheless has a 'magnetic draw that doesn't really let up – you walk toward it anyway'.

Overall, the track is reminiscent in sound of Taylor's previous album *Speak Now*. It forms a gentle bridge between 'Red' and the album's stand-out track, 'I Knew You Were Trouble'. When she met up with her co-writer and producer for this track, she told them that she wanted the song to explode after the chorus into something 'crazy', adding: 'I want it to be really chaotic.' She got her wish. An almost punk-rock feel is added to a dubstep track already rich with a mesmerising collision of genres, paces and moods. Here, we have punk-pop reminiscent of Busted, reggae sounds, including dubstep and dancehall, R&B and the aforementioned punk rock. Yet they blend together in Taylor's hands into a country-fused feast. She has shown she can jump between genres easily by doing so wholeheartedly in this track.

It has been widely suggested that this song was written about One Direction heart-throb Harry Styles. An unnamed source was quoted across the world's celebrity media stating: '"I Knew You Were Trouble" is 100 per cent about Harry.' This perception was only strengthened when Taylor discussed performing the song at the BRIT Awards, a ceremony that Styles was due to attend, along with thousands of others. 'Well, it's not hard to access that emotion when the person the song is directed at is standing by the side of the stage watching,' she said.

The rumours proved a useful publicity tool for the song, for Taylor and, as if he needed any more of the spotlight, Styles himself. Yet the timing of the track's appearance on the airwaves makes it tricky for it to have been about Styles. The song was previewed in the early autumn of 2012, but Taylor had been working on *Red* for nearly two years before that, and the couple's split seemingly came months after it. In all, she wrote 30 songs for *Red*, only around half of which made the final cut. Generally, the songwriting for a major-release album is completed many months ahead of its release, or sometimes as much as a year or more before.

When she unveiled the song, she explained its genesis to MTV. 'I had just gone through an experience that made me write this song, about knowing the second you see someone, like, "Oh, this is going to be interesting. It's going to be dangerous, but look at me going in there anyway,"' she said. Taylor added that the song had a similar theme to 'Treacherous', in that it detailed a scenario she entered despite knowing the clear dangers involved. She reasoned that the chances of regret would be greater by avoiding such a relationship, rather than giving it a go. Having dived in, she found that there was indeed trouble. So much so that she hypnotically repeats the word after each chorus – trouble, trouble, trouble. The song was such a success that it brought Taylor the very opposite of trouble. Among its fans is none other than Justin Bieber, who reportedly told Taylor that he believed it to be 'the best song ever'.

The anger and power chords of 'I Knew You Were Trouble' are nowhere to be found in the song's successor.

'All Too Well' is a vivid, terribly sad song of reminiscence for a broken relationship. It is a bittersweet affair: the weary, resigned tone of the vocals is offset by the beauty and richness of Taylor's memories. She recalls dances in the kitchen illuminated by the fridge light, road trips with the wind in her hair, autumn leaves dancing in the air. Every listener can picture the scenes and most can relate to the underlying emotions they induce. The lyrics are, as with 'I Knew You Were Trouble', defiantly melo-dramatic. In that previous song she was lying on 'the cold hard ground', whereas here she is a 'crumpled-up piece of paper'.

The song was, for Taylor, her lifeline out of a period of creative block that had lasted as long as six months. 'I was going through something that was so hard it was almost stifling, and so I wrote all these verses about everything from beginning to end of this relationship, and it ended up being, like, a 10-minute song.' The song was completed in collaboration with songwriter Liz Rose, prompted by Taylor's call to her to say: 'Come over, we've gotta filter this down.' Together, they edited the epic song into a final cut that, though still lengthy at five minutes and 29 seconds, was of a more palatable length for the commercial market.

Pertinently, 'All Too Well' throws *Red*, and Taylor herself, straight back into country-music territory after her flirtations with other genres. Indeed, just like 'Treacherous', musically it would not seem out of place on *Speak Now*, though its jaded view of love and life make it quite at home on *Red*. As *Billboard* put it: 'Just like that, Swift snaps back to her core demographic: "All Too Well" is sumptuous country, with Swift dancing "around the kitchen in the refrigerator light" in the memory of a romance that has seemingly been buried in time.' The PopCrush website felt that it was a 'melancholic, confessional ballad'.

There is ample evidence that 'All Too Well' is also about Jake Gyllenhaal. The symbolic scarf, which is mentioned throughout the song, is surely the one that she was sporting in several of the photographs of the couple together. As we have seen, they spent time at Gyllenhaal's sister Maggie's place in Brooklyn, and autumn was a particularly strong time for their relationship. These images are dropped deftly into the lyrics of this heartbreak ballad, which remains one of Taylor's most impressive compositions to date. The motif of the couple dancing around the kitchen in the refrigerator light shows Taylor at her songwriting best.

The lyrics for that song have not been without their controversy. Matt Nathanson, a folk singer, claimed that some of them seemed to have been lifted almost directly from a song of his own, called 'I Saw'. 'She's definitely a fan … and now she's a thief,' Nathanson wrote on Twitter about the allegation. Taylor is indeed a fan of Nathanson and it remains possible that she unintentionally borrowed his lyrics having found them in the back of her mind and not recognised where they were from. It's also possible that the similarity is entirely coincidental.

Having navigated grace, anger and heartbreak, in '22' Taylor turns playful with some pure pop. A romp of a tune, here she celebrates what she considered when she wrote the song to be the best age of her life. This song is pure hedonism and euphoria. For once, she is not looking back or forwards, instead she is simply enjoying the moment: partying and clowning around all evening with her friends. For Taylor, being 22 seemed the ideal age, blending as it did a sense of maturity and wisdom with a remaining spirit of youth and frivolity. 'You're old enough to start planning your life, but you're young enough to know that there are so many unanswered questions,' she said. She found this combination heady, bringing about in her a 'carefree feeling'.

She was inspired to write the song during a plane journey, yet the enclosed, claustrophobic atmosphere of air travel is not one that has any place in this song. It is the sound of Taylor and her friends letting loose and celebrating the good in their lives, while poking fun at the sadder aspects of it. She worked with Max Martin on the song and said she was 'fascinated' by how he 'can just land a chorus'. She added: 'He comes at you and hits you and it's a chorus – all caps, with exclamation points.' This song is brimful of both, and its frothy hedonism is a much-needed lift after the anger and heartache of its predecessors. If it recalls any other artist of the moment it would be Katy Perry, yet even Perry would have struggled to lend it quite the playtime quality that Taylor pulls off. Her chant of 'Twenty-two-ooh-ooh' is as catchy as pop came in 2012.

'I Almost Do' is back-to-basics acoustic country fare. It is as if she is taking a break from the experimental forays into more commercial territory, to show us her grounding in tradition and her credibility. The mood immediately becomes considerably quieter and more sombre, though amid the heartache of the song there is an element of redemption and healing. Here, she sings about the moment in the aftermath of a break-up when the heartbroken party considers taking her ex-lover back, but just knows that such a move is ill judged. 'Writing the song was what I did instead of picking up the phone,' said Taylor, explaining just how precisely the song reflects her real life. The 'never, ever' refrain makes its second appearance on the album, prefacing its starring role in the following song.

Which is 'We Are Never Ever Getting Back Together'. It is said that the best form of revenge is to live well. Another good form of revenge is to write a song that will drive your ex-lover crazy on several levels. This is, according to Taylor, the theme of this song. She was working in the studio with Shellback and Max Martin when a friend of her ex appeared and said he had heard that the estranged couple were getting back together. Taylor was furious, and when the man left she fumed out loud. She told her studio colleagues that, actually, she and her ex were never, ever, ever getting back together.

There could be a song in that, Martin had said. Less than half an hour later, they had created the basic structure of that song, which would go on to break records. At first, when Taylor set her 'never, ever, ever' rant to a guitar background, she wondered if it was too 'obvious' to just chant those words. But she was encouraged to keep exploring the notion and liked what she found. 'It came from a very real place and it came from a very spontaneous situation,' she said.

The line about the man's 'indie' music, which is so much 'cooler' than Taylor's, is for her a pivotal part of the song. She said it reflected her experience of feeling 'critiqued and subpar' during the relationship. Her ex-partner would deliberately listen to obscure music and would 'drop' any act the moment he realised that any of his friends had heard of it. 'I felt that was a strange way to be a music fan,' she said.

However, this gave her a tantalising idea: why not create a pop song that referenced him and did so in the most proudly uncool style she could muster? She set out, she said, to make a song 'that I knew would absolutely drive him crazy when he heard it on the radio'. If the song became the hit she hoped it would, he would find it hard to escape. The fact that it would be 'the opposite of the kind of music that he was trying to make me feel inferior to' only added to her hand-rubbing glee.

It is indeed a song that any indie-loving music snob would hate – and is all the better for it. It is not a song to stroke your beard to. Instead, it is a clipped, bubblegum-pop romp to dance along to with confidence, festivity and sassiness – a stadium-friendly song of girl power indeed. The choral chant of 'never, ever, ever' sticks in the head like glue – almost cruelly so. The way she adds, in spoken voice, the 'Like … ever' only adds to the defiant tone. It's all wonderfully snarky. The overall song has been compared with those of Avril Lavigne, and certainly it would have struggled to fit in with any previous Taylor long-player. *Rolling Stone* described it well as 'a perfect three-minute teen tantrum'.

Gyllenhaal is, once more, the lead suspect for the song's character. The promotional video starred actor Noah Mills as the ex-lover. He bears a reasonably strong resemblance to Gyllenhaal. The video also features humans dressed as animals, which has been widely read as a reference to the human rabbit in Gyllenhaal's film *Donnie Darko*. However, it is the scarf she waves in the video that most connects the song with him. The scarf had become a central motif of their relationship, and Taylor would not have let it within a mile of the video without knowing the conclusions people would draw.

With so much heartbreak and indignation on *Red*, it is 'Stay, Stay, Stay' that lightens the mood both musically and thematically. In contrast to previous tracks in which the finality of the message is clear, here she sings about how, despite imperfections, some relationships are worth sticking with and fighting for. She has hinted that this is a fantasy relationship, as opposed to one she has experienced. It is another of the album's nods back to Taylor's past releases, particularly the single 'Ours'. She has stated that it was a relief to exit the 'really dark places' that she had to go to emotionally elsewhere on *Red*. Yet even in this fun, light tune, she cannot help hurling a passing jibe at the 'self-indulgent takers' she had previously dated, who took their worries out on her. For some listeners, this brief outburst of bitterness almost ruins the song, yet her subsequent giggle as she sings about her new man carrying her groceries goes some way to redressing the balance.

In 'The Last Time' she duets with Gary Lightbody, whom she met through Ed Sheeran. Lightbody is the lead vocalist of the band Snow Patrol, best known for their hits 'Chasing Cars' and 'Run'. When the two sat down to work together, Lightbody had a melody and Taylor had an idea for lyrics. Out of that combination came 'The Last Time'. The track is her musical representation of the moment a man asks a woman for yet another last chance. It is a hypnotic tune, its repetitive format an intentional motif to represent the scenario. It could, suitably enough, have been on a Snow Patrol album.

'Holy Ground', a percussive track, takes the mood upwards again. She was inspired to write it after bumping into an ex-boyfriend. It is believed that the ex was either Lautner or Jonas. She wrote 'Sad Beautiful Tragic' while sat on her tour bus. She recorded it the same day and preserved the first-take vocals for the final polished version. She wanted that authenticity to reign in the album version. Her gentle vocals attempt to evoke the 'cloudy recollection' of a lost fling. The reference to the relationship having been on 'New York time' is a nod to it being about Gyllenhaal.

In 'The Lucky One', Taylor opens up a little about the elements of her privileged lifestyle that make her feel uncomfortable. Although she is believed to be hooking the experiences she describes onto Joni Mitchell, there is no doubt that Taylor is also singing about herself here. 'Everything Has Changed' is not short on cliché, but the presence of Ed Sheeran gives it a lift. There was a pleasant coincidence to their meeting. 'I fell in love with his music and I couldn't believe we hadn't had his album come out in the US yet,' she said. When she contacted his 'people' about a possible collaboration, she was amused to learn that he had just asked them to reach out to her for the same reason. They met, sat on a trampoline in Taylor's garden and wrote this song together. It is about how meeting the right person romantically can change your perspective on everything.

There are just two songs left on this epic album. 'Starlight' was born in the moment Taylor saw a photograph of Ethel and Robert F. Kennedy at a ball in the 1940s. 'They look like they're having the best night,' she told the *Wall Street Journal*. The joy she saw in them was the starting point for this song. It is one of *Red*'s lightest and most fun tunes.

The album closes with its most country-flavoured track. 'Begin Again' is Taylor reflecting on how, even after a bitter break-up, there is that moment when you spot someone across a crowded room and 'it clicks and, bam, you're there – in love again'. With its softer production, violin and banjo, this song also sounds more like it comes from earlier Swift albums. Country fans will have been relieved to hear the strains of this song after the rock- and pop-infused tracks that precede it. All listeners will, one hopes, be encouraged by the optimistic feeling the album leaves behind.

'When she's really on, her songs are like tattoos,' said *Rolling Stone*. The *Los Angeles Times* said: 'By setting rural music alongside more "urban" sounds of the moment, Swift is arguably just responding to a pop world in which country singles might please her base, but certainly doesn't expand it.' *Slant* magazine, noting how long the album is, said that while songs like 'All Too Well' 'prove how adept Swift is at expressing genuine insights into complex relationship dynamics, there are also a handful of songs that lack her usual spark'. AllMusic, though, praised her album's 'pristine pop confections', while the 4Music website said the album included 'a large serving of soul and tenderness alongside a huge dollop of talent'.

The *Guardian* said: '*Red* is another chapter in one of the finest fantasies pop music has ever constructed.' Tackling the rogues' gallery of damned males, it added: 'Men will always be drippy, emasculated partners who exist to serve her needs.' *Billboard* said: '*Red* is her most interesting full-length to date, but it probably won't be when all is said and done in her career.' Praise for the present and hope for the future: this was just the sort of verdict that would be music to Taylor's ears.

Perhaps the verdict she had been waiting for most anxiously was that of Jake Gyllenhaal. Although she was characteristically vague about whom she was talking about, it seems that, during an interview with the *New Yorker*, she revealed that the actor had spoken favourably to her about *Red*. 'I heard from the guy that most of *Red* is about,' she said. 'He was like, "I just listened to the album, and that was a really bittersweet experience for me. It was like going through a photo album." That was nice. Nicer than, like, the ranting, crazy emails I got from this one dude.' (The 'dude' was widely believed to be John Mayer.)

Yet with such a longstanding and high-profile résumé of heartbreak on her CV, some wondered whether she was destined always to be unhappy. With characteristic perspective and maturity, Taylor explained why she was not worried. 'That's the thing with love: it's going to be wrong until it's right,' she said. 'So you experience these different shades of wrong, and you miss the good things about those people, and you regret not seeing the red flags for the bad things about those people, but it's all a learning process. And being 22, you're kind of in a crash course with love and life and lessons and learning the hard way, and thankfully, I've been able to write about those emotions as they've affected me.'

As for those who paint her as a serially heartbroken, vengeful lady, she shrugs off their perception of her. 'I mean, they can say that all they want,' she told the *New Yorker*. 'Those are real feelings that every single person goes through. I think that it's okay to be mad at someone who hurt you. This isn't about, like, the pageantry of trying to seem like nothing affects you. I'm a songwriter. Everything affects me.'

Perhaps the biggest creative legacy of *Red* was that it saw Taylor drop the country twang in her vocal style. Since her debut album, she had delivered her lyrics with a Nashville tone, which seemed to be exaggerated. That vocal slant had slowly eased ever since, and in *Red* it is virtually absent. It worked – the album was a commercial smash from the start. In its first week on sale, *Red* sold an amazing 1,208 million copies – more than any album has sold in a single week since 2002. It became only the eighteenth album to sell a million units in a single week since SoundScan started tracking sales in 1991. As of the autumn of 2013, it had sold over six million copies worldwide.

Having dated A-list teen heart-throbs and released such a successful album, Taylor's stature had never been higher than it was in the second half of 2012. She had achieved so much. Nevertheless, her rocketing fame brought with it a degree of pressure she had previously been unaware of. It certainly took her far beyond the life experiences of most other 22-year-olds. 'I do think about it,' she told radio network NPR. 'There's not really one day that goes by that my life isn't documented some-where. I live in a world where I know for a fact that my grandkids will get to Google what I wore today. It's a strange dilemma, because it puts an amount of pressure on your every move that other 22-year-olds don't neces-sarily have to think about. In the grand scheme of things,

I'm living a life … I know I'm going to make mistakes. I'm just going to try to handle those mistakes as a good person. The perception of you is going to change daily when you do what I do, but I just want to end up knowing in my heart that I did that right thing and tried my best, and if you mess up, hopefully it teaches you something.'

As such a famous face, she was invited to express her opinion on every issue going. For instance, as the presidential election of 2012 approached, she was encouraged to make a clear statement about which candidate she would vote for: Barack Obama or Mitt Romney. 'A lot of people tell me that when they were 22, they thought they had it all figured out, but they didn't,' she explained. 'Just when I start to think that I know how I feel about something, I learn something else that changes my mind. I just feel like I don't have enough wisdom about myself as a person yet to go out there and say to 20 million followers on Twitter, and these people on Facebook, and whoever else is reading whatever interview I do, "Vote for this person." I know who I'm going to vote for, but I don't think that it's important for me to say it, because it will influence people one way or another. And I just want to make sure that every public decision I make is an educated one.'

Taylor was again in a position of some paradox. She was at once a wise elder sister to her fanbase and a younger sibling to much of the pop-music industry. To many of her country-music heroes she was young enough to be a daughter. To only confuse the picture further, she was simultaneously a music artist and a gossip-page princess. All these contradictions were just fine by her, as they made her day-to-day life more interesting. 'I've kind of realised that I have no idea where I'm going to be next year, or in six months, or in two months; I have no idea where I'm going to be mentally, emotionally, dreams, goals, wishes, hopes.' She loves to daydream, but she knows that planning for the future can never be a precise art. Something will always come along and throw you off course.

Chapter Eight

What did a typical day in the life of Taylor Swift look like in 2013? According to the lady herself, it was a blend of anxiety, confidence, terror and – ultimately – creativity. It sounds as if she has a typical artist's temperament. 'I worry about everything,' she told the *New Yorker* late in 2013. 'Some days I wake up in a mind-set of, like, "Okay, it's been a good run." By afternoon, I could have a change of mood and feel like anything is possible and I can't wait to make this kind of music I've never made before. And then by evening, I could be terrified of the whole thing again. And then at night, I'll write a song before bed.'

This rollercoaster of emotions she describes will be familiar to many creative souls. Elsewhere, Taylor has defined the difference that successful creative activity can have on her mood. 'If I've just written a song, I'm the happiest you'll ever see me,' she said. 'But if I haven't written a song in a week and a half, I am more stressed than you will ever, ever see me at any point.' For mood to be so dependent on one's creative output seems, on the face of it, to be an almost captive state of affairs. However, when the result of such tension is songs like 'State of Grace', 'I'm Only Me When I'm With You' and 'I Knew You Were Trouble', the pay-off seems fairer.

As Taylor's fame and popularity soared, there was a very real danger she could lose any sense of who she was as a person and a performer. As she prepared to embark on the Australian leg of her world tour to promote *Red*, she was asked whether she now considered herself to be in the same bracket as pop icon Madonna. She must have felt tempted to agree to the comparison, but she could not do it. She insisted that she was something smaller and more grounded than the likes of Madonna, with her huge stage productions. 'I would never see myself that way,' she said. 'I see myself as this girl who writes songs in her bedroom. You can kind of dress it up all you want and you can put together an amazing theatrical production, you can become a better performer as time goes by, and you can try to excite people, but I'm always going to be a girl who writes songs in her bedroom in my own personal perception of myself.'

The *Red* tour was, in all senses of the word, colossal. The North American leg of the tour alone was seven months long, and its shows included a raft of eye-catching features, including LED lights, multi-level stages and Jumbotron screens. Joining her on the road were 15 dancers, four back-up singers and a seven-piece band. There were hydraulics, confetti showers and more costume changes than anyone could remember. Most importantly, though, there were thousands and thousands of screaming fans who went home delighted by the show they had witnessed.

The North American leg ended with Taylor feeling under the weather. At her final concert, in Nashville, she was suffering from a cold. 'It was a struggle,' she told the *New Yorker*. 'I found it a little bit easier to sing than to talk, which was, like, a miracle.' When she was about to sing 'Sparks Fly', she suddenly realised she had to leave the stage to take care of something. 'I'm sorry, guys, but I just really have to blow my nose,' she told the fans. 'I swear I'm gonna do this really fast, can you please scream to fill the awkward silence, please?' The 14,000-strong crowd obliged with a loud scream, and when she returned she continued the performance in style.

Throughout the tour, Taylor had shown her class. This applied away from the stage as much as on it. A seven-year-old fan called Grace Markel was caught in a traffic accident as she journeyed to Taylor's concert in Columbia in August 2013. As she and her father Will stepped out of a taxi at the venue, Grace was hit by a speeding SUV driven by an uninsured driver on a suspended licence. It was a nasty accident: young Grace suffered skull fractures, a left orbital fracture, numerous head lacerations, a severe concussion and road rash over her face and body. She spent two days at Children's Mercy Hospital before she was allowed home. Naturally, she had missed the concert and was enormously upset.

The following month, she got to see Taylor at a subsequent concert – and the singer made it an even better experience when she agreed to meet Grace backstage just before the show. Grace's mother, Amy, was impressed with the star's attitude. 'Taylor greeted Grace by her name and immediately knelt down and hugged her,' she told *People* magazine. 'She told Grace she had a cold and asked Grace to sing extra loud to help her out.' Taylor also autographed the sleeve of the girl's Taylor Swift shirt with "I heart Grace! Taylor." A classy piece of public relations from the Swift camp, yet those closest to Taylor are adamant that her charitable endeavours come from the heart.

Meanwhile, the awards just kept on coming. She faced a humorous 'repeat episode' of the much-discussed Kanye West incident at the Peoples' Choice Awards in 2013. She looked very sleek in a plunging white gown as she walked to the stage to collect her award in the Favourite Country Artist category. But then the host, Olivia Munn, jokingly fought Taylor for the gong, pretending that the song 'We Are Never Ever Getting Back Together' was written about her. As tension mounted in the hall, Taylor did her best to smile through the incident. She said: 'This always happens to me … God!' Munn told her to get used to it, saying, 'This is your lot in life now, Taylor.'

Eventually, Munn relinquished the award and allowed Taylor her moment in the spotlight. She said: 'I want to thank the fans, because this is a fan-voted award and I absolutely love you with all of my heart. I want to thank radio and I want to thank the fans for calling radio and being, like, "Play her music" – thank you for doing that.'

She continued: 'You guys have blown my mind with what you've done for this album *Red* and I just want to thank you for caring about my music and for caring about me. Thank you so much you guys, I love you.' She also presented an award herself at the ceremony, handing over the gong for Favourite Movie, which went to *The Hunger Games*. As awards season gathered pace, she was excited to be nominated for a Golden Globe, but watched as the British star Adele was named as the winner instead.

In February she was awarded a Grammy for 'Safe & Sound', a song written for *The Hunger Games* soundtrack. She had opened the ceremony with a lively performance of 'We Are Never Ever Getting Back Together'. All night she was on form, eschewing the industry-cool behaviour of so many attendees and instead dancing and celebrating wildly as other acts performed or received their own gongs. Alongside her friend Claire Kislinger, she made for quite a merry sight. Eagle-eyed viewers might have spotted the diamond bracelet she was sporting. It was made by a pediatric cancer patient called Jaimin, who designed it especially for Taylor. It was given a bright and sparkling look because, said the designer, 'Taylor sparkles'.

Which she surely does: as the gong season rolled on, she flew to Britain to perform at the BRIT Awards, where she was also up for an award, namely the hotly contested International Female Solo Artist. The annual ceremony has been the scene of many huge production performances in recent years from the likes of Take That and Lady Gaga. However, the appearance that made the biggest indent on musical minds was that of Adele in 2011, when she sang 'Someone Like You' accompanied by nothing more than a single pianist. This approach then became the style to emulate.

Therefore it is a brave artist who turns back to the pyrotechnics at the BRITS. Taylor appeared in a wedding-dress-style floor-length gown but reduced it to a more revealing outfit mid-performance. Surrounded by dancers and visual effects, she danced more suggestively than usual. Later, she partied with the actress Carey Mulligan and her husband Marcus Mumford of the award-winning band Mumford & Sons. She also danced with Rizzle Kicks singer Jordan Stephens.

In October 2013, she set a record when she won a prestigious country music industry award for the sixth time. The Nashville Songwriters Association International named her Songwriter/Artist of the Year for the sixth year running. Previously, the only artists to equal her were the five-time winners Alan Jackson and Vince Gill. Her exceptional standing is heightened by the fact that she is the youngest artist ever to win the award.

She was thrilled by the honour and took the opportunity to announce that she would open her own school. The Taylor Swift Education Center will open at the Country Music Hall of Fame and Museum in Nashville. The establishment will be spread across two floors and three classrooms. It has come into being as the result of a generous $4 million donation that she gave back in 2012. Through the school, she hopes children will be given a better chance than her to nurture their musical roots. 'In school, I was taught a certain amount about music, a certain amount about theatre, and that interest sparked something in me. It made me look elsewhere to learn much more about it,' said Taylor. 'I think, for me, it's just going to be so interesting to see Nashville continue to be this hub for music, and this hub for music education.'

Taylor has also become something of an ambassador for Nashville. She has even convinced Ed Sheeran of its charms. 'Oh, I definitely did,' she told news agency Associated Press. 'Ed loves Nashville. You know, so many people live here now. It's really exciting, because nobody who comes here ... doesn't like it, and it just makes me proud to live here and it makes me proud to make music here and I love it. I just love it becoming such an exciting place to live.' She sometimes has to pinch herself to remember the days before she first visited Nashville, when she was waging a campaign to persuade her parents to take her there so she could have a crack at building just the sort of career she now enjoys.

Taylor had won so many awards over the years that an internet joke had been created on the matter. Photographs of her looking – or at least trying to look – shocked as her name was announced at various ceremonies became an internet 'meme', loosely titled 'Taylor Swift's surprised face'. However, while awards bashes are enjoyable and receiving honours at them a thrill, there is always a sense that industry politics might be behind some of the selections. Artists measure their success in many different ways, but an authentic yardstick remains the number of records sold. In January 2013, Taylor became the first artist since The Beatles to spend six weeks or more at number one in the *Billboard* charts with three consecutive studio albums. There was – and can be – no arguing with such a fact.

Another important sales stat came days later when the Recording Industry Association of America (RIAA) released its figures for 2012. The data revealed that Taylor had earned the year's highest album certification, scoring triple-platinum certification for 'We Are Never Ever Getting Back Together', with several other singles hitting platinum status.

She released a single called 'Sweeter Than Fiction' in the autumn of 2013. It was taken from the movie soundtrack for the film *One Chance*. The track has a levity and a dreamy tone that makes it feel like a throwback to her earlier years. The film is based on the life of *Britain's Got Talent* winner Paul Potts, and Taylor said she has been inspired by Potts. 'Getting to see the struggles and triumphs of someone who never stopped chasing what he was after really inspired me,' she said. 'It's a beautiful movie and I just wanted to share it with everybody.'

Her income for 2013 was set to be higher than the $60 million she is reported to have made in 2012 – a figure which equalled the income of Beatles legend Sir Paul McCartney for the same year. What an exciting 12 months it was for Taylor. Throughout the year, she must have paused whenever she could to try to make sense of where she had come from. It is tempting to consider that the process which took her to fame was some sort of master plan, with Taylor and her parents treading a carefully considered path and pooling their respective talents: Taylor's creativity; her father's business nous; her mother's poise and determination. Yet, while there is truth to such a narrative, Taylor and the Swifts were, to a large extent, busking it. Asked by NPR whether she had always been convinced she would make it, Taylor replied: 'No, actually.' She added: 'I was never convinced I was going to make it. And I look back – my mom and I reminisce about this all the time, because we had no idea what we were doing. My parents bought books on what the music industry was like. They had no idea what the music industry entailed and what was involved with it.'

Some of Taylor's greatest admirers in the industry argue that her songwriting is her richest talent. Many composers, particularly in the country music world, have found that their ability improves as they grow older. Life experience can wither a songwriter's connection with the youth-driven world of pop. In the wise, knowing sphere of country music, experience only enriches the craft. In the future, Taylor wants to draw more on her creativity than her performance. 'When I'm 40 and nobody wants to see me in a sparkly dress any more, I'll be like: "Cool, I'll just go in the studio and write songs for kids." It's looking like a good pension plan.'

Chapter Nine

Taylor Swift's fifth album, *1989*, was the album that no one expected her to make – and also the album she was absolutely, inevitably going to make. It marked a positively revolutionary shift in style and tone, but this should not have surprised people as much as it did. Most artists are different in their mid-twenties compared to their mid-teens, simply because most *people* are different in their mid-twenties compared to their mid-teens. And while the nuts and bolts of her music had changed, the underlying Swiftian philosophy remained the same. The new album was simply about how Taylor's life looked in that moment, as she, her music and her vibe moved from Nashville to New York, where she had dropped $19.9 million on a pair of penthouses in Manhattan's Tribeca neighbourhood.

Most of the new album was written during the 2013–14 *Red* tour, as Taylor enjoyed a flush of creativity on the road. She stored the demos on her phone in a folder she cutely entitled 'Sailor Twips'. The new material that built up in that nautical folder saw Swift shift from the awkward teen and heartbroken twentysomething the world knew and loved to a new identity: an infinitely more self-aware young woman, delighting in impishly toying with the media and public perception of her. She had been transformed from 'America's sweetheart' to a young woman whose more visible dating history had earned her a quite different reputation in the public psyche. No longer the girl next door, she had become the woman on the front pages.

Musically, the overall sound was also so different: banjos were replaced with beats, the Southernness was replaced with sass, and the violins with electro. It was a 'farewell to twang', as one critic put it, and for Swift this was an evolution she needed to make. She had noticed a difference in how female and male artists were able to stay in the game for the long run. Male artists were allowed to continue showing up with much the same image and sound from album to album, but female artists were expected to continually reinvent themselves if they wanted to retain the adoring gaze of the media and public.

Also, Taylor wanted to challenge herself musically, which meant she had to explore new sounds. 'I know that I don't have the option of making music that sounds just like what I've done before,' she told PopCrush. 'People will call me out on it. They'll see right through it. They'll see that I was lazy,' she added. 'So with this album I definitely changed things up and I think I changed them for the better.'

The record's genesis came from a moment of despair. *Red* was nominated for Album of the Year at the 2014 Grammys and Taylor had felt it stood a good chance of winning. When it didn't, upset, she went home, ate burgers and fries with her friends, had a good cry and went to bed. Waking up the next morning Taylor felt galvanised and ready to work on a new album that would capture the attention of the world.

Swift explained that oftentimes the best songs are the ones that 'just kind of come from some *crazy* sparks of creativity'. She said: 'A lot of the songs on the album that I'm most proud of are ones that I got an idea and just kind of rolled with it and went with it, and 20 minutes later I had most of the song done.' She worked on the maxim that if she got a '*really* crazy lightning-bolt idea, then that's the one you should chase and the one that you should follow'. Songs where she found it 'a bit harder to get into the groove' were sometimes left by the wayside; the abandoned babies of Swift's creative energy.

For any artist, knowing which tracks to pick and which to drop for an albumn is a difficult task, but Swift found that a good measure of whether a song deserved to make the cut was wanting to keep returning to her recording, and to listen to it 'over and over and over', rather than losing interest in it after a few months. 'So I write for two years, and usually most of the stuff that I write in the first six months to a year gets thrown out,' she explained. 'This Love' and 'Out of the Woods' were two such tracks that she kept going back to, which is why the world got to hear them on *1989*.

The songs that were most directly about Taylor's life were often the ones that stuck around long enough to be taken forward. When she's asked why she has never put pen to paper to write a celebrity memoir, Swift wonders why she would even need to, given that her lyrics are so nakedly autobiographical. One of her finest skills is telling her own story anywhere other than on the page of a book, whether it is in a song or in her carefully crafted social media posts, or sometimes even her clothes.

Swift is a star who has liberated herself from dependency on traditional media routes. By 2014, over 11 years into her career, Taylor hadn't granted a traditional magazine profile for some time, preferring to make statements via social media rather than sitting down with a trusted – or perhaps not so trusted – celebrity reporter. Unlike less influential artists, Taylor is not dependent on the media for a voice.

Until her fifth album, a lot of Swift's lyrics were about her love life. Its presence in her material was part of her very brand, but that was about to change as her focus widened. The Taylor of this era wanted to dig a bit deeper. 'This album is not about boys,' she said. 'It's not about something trivial; it's not about revenge or break-ups. It's about what my life looks like now.'

Swift had always dreamt hard of an exciting future, but she didn't get carried away with the idea that those hopes would definitely come true. So when her life turned out to be a lot like she'd hoped for, she was both surprised and unsurprised. 'I think my dream looked a lot like this, but my expectations were kind of … I thought that, you know, I'd still be looking for what I want to do with my life, which is completely normal for 25,' she said.

She was a young woman on the move. She cut her hair, moved from country music to pop music, and from Nashville to New York. Life in the Big Apple was certainly exciting for her, but the spotlight on her life brought challenges with it, too. In Nashville, Taylor could wear the same shoes two days running – a simple thing that most people wouldn't have to think twice about. But in New York, she quickly learned, she 'should not repeat outfits because that will be very loudly pointed out to me', she told *Nashville* magazine, so there were 'very interesting dynamic changes from city to city, and yet I'm used to all of them, strangely'. She was also acutely aware that this was just one of the pressures that female artists face to which male celebrities are blissfully immune.

But while much had changed in Taylor's life, some things stayed the same, and even with her new neighbourhood and fresh sound, Swift was not about to reach out for the 'cool' demographic anytime soon. 'I still don't feel like it's a priority for me to be cool, edgy or sexy,' she said. Noting that, for girls, those three themes 'are so obnoxiously thrust upon them through the media', she said she hoped she could encourage her young female fans to be 'imaginative, intelligent, hardworking, strong, smart, quick-witted, charming' instead. Swift's role as an unofficial big sister to a generation was standing strong, and she was taking that responsibility seriously, however weightily it rested upon her young shoulders.

That said, the new album would emerge as a much cooler collection than anything she had released before. For *1989*, Swift wanted a tight unit around her. Recorded in LA, New York, Sweden and London, with the likes of Max Martin, Johan 'Shellback' Schuster, Imogen Heap, and Jack Antonoff alongside her to help, the new album had a slimmer, trimmer team. She had consciously narrowed down the list, as she was driving to create a 'sonically cohesive record', rather than spreading herself too thin.

Where she had once put out albums with a touch of sheepishness, the Taylor of album five was a much brasher artist. She chose a suitably totemic site to announce *1989*: a fan gathering at the Empire State Building, in New York, which was streamed live online, showing from the start that the album would receive a full-on marketing campaign. She described the release as her 'very first documented, official pop album' and partnered with brands including Diet Coke and Target to take the hype to new and evermore lucrative levels.

Swift was stepping away from her roots, but she was quite straightforward about it. She thought a lot about what the musical community she sprang from would feel about her new material. Country had been a springboard for Swift, so there was bound to be sensitivity over her leap into the pastures of pop, and it was important for her to handle the transition sensitively. 'I think that the country community wasn't surprised that I made a pop album,' she told the *National Post*. 'I think they were surprised when I was honest about it.'

When she appeared at an ACM (Academy of Country Music) gala, she paid tribute to the musical family from which she had emerged. 'You truly see who a person is when you give them news that they weren't expecting,' she told them. 'And so, to the country community, when I told you that I'd made a pop album and that I wanted to go explore other genres, you showed me who you are with the grace that you accepted that with.'

Her new material would get next to no play on country music radio stations, but there were still some supportive noises from those parts. 'Taylor is one of us, one of our children,' said Mark Razz, the music director at WXTU-FM, a country music station in Philadelphia. 'You're there for them along the way, and then they need to go to what they are going to do. She's gotten to where she is through country music, and if she goes on to be the next pop sensation around the world, we are behind her 100 per cent.' In other words, just because country stations weren't interested in her new sound because it was inappropriate for their listeners' taste buds, that didn't mean they didn't wish her well.

The good feeling was mutual. While Taylor's style was evolving, she was not trying to rewrite history. Indeed, she brushed aside any suggestions that she regretted or felt embarrassed by her wholesome persona. 'I'm not going to sit there and say, "Oh, I wish I hadn't had corkscrew-curly hair and worn cowboy boots and sundresses to awards shows when I was 17; I wish I hadn't gone through that fairy-tale phase where I just wanted to wear princess dresses to awards shows every single time,"' she told *Elle*. 'Because I made those choices. I did that. It was part of me growing up.'

But what did the grown-up Taylor actually sound like? Where *Red* had been an album of gentle evolution, with her previously country-focused sound allowing in just some early hints of pop and rock to create a new blend, *1989* was more centrally focused on pop, with synth-pop being a strong feature. Swift didn't want to try to please two musical masters; she was ready to dig for gold in just one area. As she explained in an interview with *Rolling Stone*, she didn't want to blend this time because 'if you chase two rabbits, you lose them both'. It was good logic.

Although the influence of the Big Apple is very obvious in the album's opener, 'Welcome to New York', it's also found throughout the collection. The overall feel of *1989* echoes the famous city's vibrancy, diversity and dynamism. It also reflected her love of the place. She was so thrilled by the fact that she could, on occasion, blend in to the city in temporary anonymity; it was a real tonic. Yet this opener is one of the city's finest musical tributes of recent years, as well as a song of vivid imagery, such as putting your broken heart away into a drawer. To borrow her lyrical refrain, it felt as if New York had indeed been waiting for her.

She hoped to capture and convey the optimism that Manhattan's energy had flushed her with. 'My friends and people who know me have commented that I'm physically different since being here,' she told NYC radio station WKTU. She added that 'Welcome to New York' is 'about the endless hopefulness and endless possibilities that New York seems to present'.

While moving to New York was one major change, she explained, perhaps more pertinent was the change in her mood around her love life. She was single and she was surprised by how happy she felt to be single. 'I never thought I would be so happy being completely unattached to anyone romantically,' she said. She added that she thought it 'healthy for everyone to go a few years without dating, just because you need to get to know who you are'. On her own, she was doing more 'thinking and examining and figuring out how to cope with things'. Part of her reason for stopping dating was that she had a point to prove. 'It meant a lot to me to set the record straight – that I do not need some guy around in order to get inspiration, in order to make a great record, in order to live my life, in order to feel okay about myself,' she explained.

'I feel like watching my dating life has become a bit of a national pastime,' she told *Rolling Stone*. She added that she was no longer 'comfortable providing that kind of entertainment' because she didn't like seeing media 'slide shows' of men she was rumoured to have dated, and she didn't want to give comedians 'the opportunity to make jokes about me at awards shows'.

'Blank Space' moves further still from country music. In fact, it might be the most *1989* track on *1989*, embodying the overall change in direction more clearly than its album mates. An electropop track with a hip-hop flavour, it was inspired by the decade of the album's title. The 1980s were soundtracked by synth-pop made with synthesisers, drum pads and overlapped vocals.

For the casual listener, it was a very catchy pop track, but to the more attuned ear the satirical punch was clear. Its lyrics poke fun at her image: she told *GQ* that it was a nod to her image as a 'girl who's crazy but seductive but glamorous but nuts but manipulative'. The song played on the media's obsessive portrayal of her as a woman who moved casually from one relationship to another. 'Some of the things I write about on a song like "Blank Space" are satire,' she said to *GQ*. 'You take your creative license and create things that are larger than life.' She realised that the joke would go straight over the head of some people, and she was okay with that. 'I knew some people would hear "Blank Space" and say, *See? We were right about her*,' she said. 'And at that point, I just figure if you don't get the joke, you don't deserve to get the joke.'

With this track, she took the cheap media caricature and played it to such an extreme level that its absurdity became obvious.

Like all the greatest artists, Taylor could find the creative silver lining in most of life's clouds. She told Grammy Museum that the media had had a 'wonderful fixation on painting me as the psycho serial dater girl' and 'every article was like, "Here's Taylor Swift standing near some guy. WATCH OUT GUY!"' At first she thought this trend was a 'bummer', she added. 'But my second reaction was, "Hey, that's actually a really interesting character they're writing about: she jet-sets around the world collecting men – and she can get any of them, but she's so clingy that they leave and she cries in her marble bathtub surrounded by pearls." I was like, "I can use this."'

Its message – that a relationship was either going to be forever or go down in flames – was so relatable for her younger fans. With 'Blank Space' she had grabbed herself a new army of listeners, who loved this pure pop sass.

'Style' saw a departure for her: Taylor was stating an admission of fault. 'I would never have said anything like that on a previous album,' she told Ryan Seacrest. 'My previous albums have always been, "I was right, you were wrong." What happens when you grow up is you realise that the rules in a relationship are very blurred.' The play on the name of Harry Styles met with much approval. 'Naming a song that you will never explicitly say is about your ex with a literal variation of that ex's name is next level,' said *Cosmopolitan*, 'but then to have that song be maybe the best one on your album' is 'positively inspirational', it added.

The incident mentioned in the bridge of 'Out of the Woods' was inspired by a snowmobile accident that she and an ex-partner had endured, but it can also be seen as a metaphor for the fragility of relationships. When the media realised that 'Out of the Woods' was a true story, Taylor delighted in the fact that it showed they couldn't know everything about her private life. 'It was almost like this very strange, subtle clue to the media that they don't know everything that happened in that relationship, and I can have something really major and traumatic happen to me and they don't know about it,' she told NPR. Musically, it reminded some listeners of the rhythmic vocals of *The Lion King* soundtrack, and as far as Taylor was concerned, it was the quintessential *1989* track.

'All You Had to Do Was Stay' came to her in a dream where her ex turned up at the door and, instead of giving him a piece of her mind, all that came out was a high-pitched plea to 'stay'. 'Shake It Off' was the last song recorded for *1989*, and it came to life when Swift arrived at the studio one day with a challenge for her co-writers and producers Max Martin and Shellback: 'We need drums that make even the person who's having a terrible night at the wedding [go], "Oh, it's my song!"' The result was her iconic repost to celebrity takedown culture, with her listing the accusations thrown at her by the press and shaking it off.

'Shake It Off' touched on her relationship with both the media and social media, but in a way that empowered her fans; you don't need to be a celebrity to have had a hurtful comment directed at you online, but perhaps Swift's song will help you to get past the hurt. For 'Shake It Off', she wrote the lyrics and composed the melody with Martin and Shellback. The up-tempo pop banger could easily have been quite different: her label asked her to add a violin. She gave them a 'firm no', she remembered. The song was the obvious choice for the lead single.

'I Wish You Would' sees Swift pining for an ex, and even driving down their street and wishing she'd never hung up the phone or ended their relationship. Curiously, she told *Rolling Stone* that the true story was the other way round: the song was 'about an ex who bought a house two blocks from hers'. A hidden message in the CD booklet said: 'He drove past her street each night.' This was one of the 'bridge tracks' of the album, in the sense that it could just as easily have sat on *Red*.

Swift hinted in a *Rolling Stone* interview that 'Bad Blood' was about a very famous female musician, saying the person did something 'so horrible' that it made them 'straight-up enemies'. It is widely believed that Katy Perry is the subject, and musically the track sounds not unlike Perry's style. Perhaps this was a sass too far, because, musically, it's far from Swift's finest hour and came in last place in *Rolling Stone*'s 2023 ranking of all 243 Taylor Swift songs.

In the Lana Del Rey-influenced song 'Wildest Dreams' she imagines the end of a relationship before it's officially begun. 'How You Get the Girl' is 'kind of a tutorial', she told Radio.com. 'If you follow the directions in this song, chances are things will work out … Or you may get a restraining order.' 'This Love' acts as a hint of the paths she would take on *Folklore* and *Evermore*. Speaking to Scholastic book club, she said this song originally started out as a poem in her journal, 'then all of a sudden in my head, I started hearing this melody – and that's when I realised it was going to be a song'. Along with 'Style', 'Wildest Dreams' touched on the idea of fleeting romances and the impermanence of all relationships. Capturing moments and memories, the lyrics acknowledge the transient nature of it all, in a reprise of one of the themes of 'Out of the Woods'.

In 'I Know Places', Taylor laid bare her worries about how she could hold down a relationship with the harsh gaze of the celebrity spotlight trained on it. 'I decided to write a love song [about] what would I say if I met someone really awesome and they were like, "Hey, I'm worried about all this attention you get,"' she told Grammy Museum. 'So I wrote this song about, "Hey, I know all these places we could hide. We can outrun them."' It made clear her struggles with fame and the invasive presence of the paparazzi culture, likening herself to a fox being hunted.

Although she transitioned to a more mainstream pop vibe, Swift jealously guarded the authenticity that had taken her to this point. The stories in her songs remained deeply personal and symbolic. The album's closer, 'Clean', was more than a cheap break-up song (believed by fans to be about Harry Styles): it encouraged personal growth, inspiration and a sense of liberation after a chapter of despair, and features a beautiful bridge.

Ultimately, *1989* is more than an album: it is a craftily curated diary of the recent period of Swift's journey through life. Every song, video and lyric is rich with the narratives, emotions and memories that offer a glimpse into her world. Listeners could dive in deeply, or not, as they liked. The songs stood on their own strength and would connect with fanatical Swifties and passing radio listeners alike.

One of the very first listeners was Swift's friend Ella, also known as Lorde. 'She's one of my favourite people to kind of bounce ideas off of,' explained Swift, because 'she gives really good advice'. Another early listener of the complete work was Ed Sheeran. 'Having friends where who [sic] I completely respect their musical opinion is really helpful because they all have their different favourites and stuff, and their different favourites definitely reflect them as musicians, for sure.' Ella's favourite on the new album was 'Welcome to New York', and Sheeran's favourite was the divisive 'Bad Blood'.

Where the influences on her previous albums had included a galaxy of country stars, including some veterans, Taylor took inspiration from the pop world for *1989*. Even then, though, the stand-out influencers were of yesteryear. She was inspired by Annie Lennox, the Eurythmics' lead singer, saying 'the way she conveys a thought, there's something really intense about it', and Peter Gabriel, who she described as 'an artist who has such incredible taste' and 'such an incredible finger on the pulse of what would excite people, musically'. It was fitting that these two inspirations produced their own best material in the 1980s, the decade of the album's title.

But while the media often distilled the album down to her switch to pop music, for Swift's fans there was a much wider shift going on. This was not just in a musical sense, but in a thematic, aesthetic and personal way. The titular year, 1989, was symbolic of starting fresh, as she shed her old image and emerged as quite a new artist. The front-cover Polaroid image not only evokes the 1980s, but also rejects the slickness of her past art. The muted, pastel aesthetics and the nostalgic vibe reflected moments in time and celebrated the change that time inevitably brings. Packaging like this on a Taylor album would have been simply unimaginable just a few years earlier.

Swift explored new pastures through her promotion, too. Her Secret Sessions essentially built a 'safe space' with her fans. Bypassing the media filters, she could share her music more directly and intimately, selecting who would attend these parties by looking at social media accounts. 'I would go online and I would look at their Instagram pages, or their Twitter or their Tumblr or whatever, and I just kind of watched them for months and months,' she told the BBC.

These were more than simple promotional events. Held at five of her homes across the world, 89 carefully selected fans were only told they were attending some sort of secret event, with no precise details of what was in store for them. Although the events were supposed to stay hushed up, it was rumoured that Swift's special guests got to meet and carry one of her cats, Olivia Benson, see her various American Music Awards and Grammy Awards and eat pumpkin chocolate-chip cookies made by Taylor herself. In a behind-the-scenes clip, an apron-clad Swift can be seen whipping up some batter in her kitchen. This was a surprising level of access for a star of Swift's status to offer into her private territory; it is hard to imagine Beyoncé or Adele agreeing to the same opportunity.

Anticipation for the album soared and soared before it was finally released on 27 October 2014, and it wasn't just the fans who were excited – Taylor was buzzing too. 'It's so exciting to unveil who you've been for the last two years,' she told *Esquire* magazine, adding that her life had 'changed drastically in the last year and a half'.

The release of *1989* was not without controversy or drama. Swift took on two mighty corporations: first Spotify and then Apple, claiming she could stand up for all artists as she did so. Those watching closely would have noticed that the groundwork for the battle had been laid sometime earlier. Four months before the release of *1989*, she penned an op-ed for the *Wall Street Journal*, setting out her manifesto. 'The value of an album is, and will continue to be, based on the amount of heart and soul an artist has bled into a body of work, and the financial value that artists (and their labels) place on their music when it goes out into the marketplace,' she wrote. 'It's my opinion that music should not be free, and my prediction is that individual artists and their labels will someday decide what an album's price point is. I hope they don't underestimate themselves or under-value their art.'

Some doubted the extent to which she was standing up for other artists. After all, as one of the globe's leading pop stars, she stood to make millions of dollars from streaming no matter what happened with them. She also benefited from recommendation algorithms, featured playlists, paid exclusives and other advantages retained for the famous. So the issues with streaming did not apply equally across the board. From Swift's point of view this privilege was irrelevant: she was taking a stand in the hope that any breakthroughs she made could be enjoyed by everyone.

After refusing to allow *1989* to be streamed on Spotify, she laid down a line saying that she objected to her music being made available for free. Speaking to Yahoo, Taylor explained that 'everything new, like Spotify, all feels to me a bit like a grand experiment' and she was not willing to 'contribute my life's work to an experiment that I don't feel fairly compensates the writers, producers, artists, and creators of this music'. Whether streaming services really felt like an experiment to her in 2014 is open to debate, but, seven years on, it's clear that there's nothing experimental about the medium. It is here to stay.

She then criticised Apple's decision not to pay royalties to artists in the consumers' trial period of three months when signing up to Apple Music. Writing on Tumblr, Taylor explained that her stance was 'about the new artist or band that has just released their first single and will not be paid for its success' and 'the young songwriter who just got his or her first cut and thought that the royalties from that would get them out of debt'.

To the surprise of many, Apple's Senior VP, Eddy Cue, yielded to Swift's pressure within 24 hours. Peace had broken out quickly, and Taylor took to Twitter to say that 'after the events of this week, I've decided to put *1989* on Apple Music ... and happily so'. Her music was also returned to Spotify after a three-year boycott. But it was a landmark moment in music history when Swift successfully took on such huge, powerful companies. As artists across the globe worried about the detrimental effect that streaming was having on their revenue, Swift was widely seen to be standing up for them all, and *1989*, with its spikier and bolder vibe, was just the right release for her to take a strong stance with.

When the album was released, the reaction of the critics was of more interest than usual to her camp, and because she had gone out on a limb with a new sound and image, more was at stake. The reviews were positively purring, with many noting that this was the album that most reflected the artist herself. The new collection put Taylor 'leagues ahead of the teen-pop competition', said the *Guardian*, adding that 'the really striking thing about *1989*' is 'how completely' Swift, rather than any producer, 'dominates the album'. *Rolling Stone* said it was 'deeply weird, feverishly emotional, wildly enthusiastic', and sounded 'exactly like Taylor Swift, even when it sounds like nothing she's ever tried before'. *NME* put it alongside a historic classic, calling it no less than 'a new generation's answer to *Thriller*'.

The *New York Times* said Swift was 'aiming somewhere even higher, a mode of timelessness that few true pop stars ... even bother aspiring to'. However, the *Los Angeles Times* felt it had a 'slightly juiceless quality', describing it as a 'would-be tell-all bleached of the detailed insight she's trained us to expect from her'. *Slant Magazine* was also not fully convinced, concluding that 'Swift is still in the process of finding her own voice as a pop artist'. *Entertainment Weekly* offered not so much a review as a warning, saying that 'if she ditches what makes her special to get there, then she's doing a huge disservice to her fans – and an even bigger one to herself'.

For Taylor, her ultimate verdict on the album was one of overall satisfaction. As she often does, she used a rich metaphor to explain how she felt. 'I feel like we gave the entire metaphorical house I built a complete renovation, and it made me love the house even more,' she told *Elle*, 'but still keeping the foundation of what I've always been.'

The *1989* world tour took seven months to plan and three months to rehearse. The evening's setlists would begin with 'Welcome to New York', and included much of the new album, plus a generous sprinkling of older tracks. Taylor was loving being back on the road, as she told a journalist mid-tour. 'I was thinking about this yesterday and it hit me: I don't want this tour to end. Ever,' she told the *NME*. 'And that's never happened to me before.' She was also buzzing when *1989* won Album of the Year at the Grammys in 2016, exorcising her heartbreak at *Red* missing out, and vindicating the creative starting point that had spawned its successor.

As well as promoting the album, the tour was a huge earner in its own right, taking in $250 million. It made the gamble she had taken with the album seem worthwhile. 'Taking the easy way would have been 100 per cent good enough,' said *Rolling Stone*, continuing, 'It just wasn't what she wanted to do. Instead, she wanted to push a little harder and make a gloriously epic pop mess like this.' The magazine later included the *1989* world tour in its list of the 50 Greatest Concerts of the Last 50 Years.

Album five spawned three number-one hits on the *Billboard* Hot 100: 'Bad Blood' featuring Kendrick Lamar, 'Shake It Off' and 'Blank Space'. Other tracks like 'Style' and 'Wildest Dreams' made it to the Top 10 following the album's release. Her successful night at the Grammy Awards made her the first female solo artist to win twice for Album of the Year. Like many Swiftian achievements, she has since bettered this.

But the move into a new sound and image was not without its critics. Promotional videos for two of the album's tracks drew an unfamiliar scale of criticism for Swift. In the video for 'Shake It Off', she is seen dancing with a variety of movers, including ballerinas, cheerleaders and b-boys. There are also hip-hop dancers, several of whom are Black, and she is seen giggling as she crawls under their disembodied, twerking behinds. The rapper Earl Sweatshirt accused the video of 'perpetuating Black stereotypes'.

Then came a storm about her video for 'Wildest Dreams', which has a mostly white cast, despite being filmed in Africa. The *Guardian* described the video as 'colonialist-fantasy', the *Huffington Post* accused it of 'channeling white colonialism' and the *Daily Dot* said it had a 'major race problem'. Swift's team pointed to the message at the end of the video, which told viewers that 'all of Taylor's proceeds from this video will be donated to wild conservation efforts through the African Parks Foundation of America'.

Commercially, she had never doubted that *1989* would sell one million copies in its first week, but she was warned that she might be being overly optimistic. But it did shift in big numbers: it sold 1.29 million copies in its first week, and 'all of a sudden, I didn't look so naive anymore', she said. It is worth noting that the album was released into a tricky industry. Downloads were now a slumping format, as CDs had been before them, making the initial sales even more remarkable.

1989 has since gone on to sell more than 10 million copies and has become, said *Billboard*, a 'kind of cultural omnipresence that's rare for a 2010s album'. Her record label boss was chastened but thrilled. 'I learned a long time ago: don't ever doubt the power of Taylor Swift,' he said. It's a lesson that a lot of people have had cause to learn.

With more remarkable sales came an evermore remarkable stature. In October 2014, Taylor was named *Billboard*'s Woman of the Year, making her the first artist to receive the award twice. The accolade goes to the female artist who 'has shaped and inspired the music industry with her success, leadership and innovation' over the previous 12 months. 'Over the course of her career, she's charted 60 entries on the *Billboard* Hot 100 – the most of any female artist since her debut in 2006,' said Janice Min, of *Billboard*.

There was an awkward moment during Swift's acceptance speech when a joke she had prepared fell flat. Describing the gong as an 'amazing early birthday present', she said: 'I turn 25 at midnight tonight, and I fully intend to celebrate like it's 1989.' After only a smattering of polite laughter, she added: 'I knew it was a bad joke when I wrote it, and I just did it anyway!'

This was a period of Taylor just doing it anyway. For an artist of 25, she had already achieved so much. The scale of her achievements became clear when she was compared to other acts at the same age. At a quarter of a century, Madonna was only beginning to kickstart what would become her meteoric rise. Beyoncé was still transitioning from her success with Destiny's Child and had yet to properly establish herself as the force that she has become.

Whitney Houston and Britney Spears are examples of female artists who had achieved at lot at 25, yet Swift's ascent had been steadier and she had more albums under her belt than they did by that age. Adele's experience at

25 was more similar to Swift's: she had released four albums by that age. She had also, like Swift, maintained a consistent rhythm of releases and accumulated many sideboards' worth of awards.

Swift stood tall in her songwriting pedigree and her evolving sound. Swift was able to draw on the foundation of her early and consistent success to evolve, while retaining her intimate connection with her fans. Her reinvention had been a bold and risky move. It was so gratifying for her to make a success of it.

Away from the music, Taylor's love life continued to fascinate and thrill the public as she moved away from her singleton period. In 2015, she started dating Calvin Harris, the Scottish DJ, record producer, singer and songwriter. They first met backstage at the *Elle* Style Awards after being introduced by their mutual friend, Ellie Goulding. They quickly hit it off and met up the following day at the BRIT Awards and again the day after that. After becoming 'Instagram official' thanks to a post Harris made of Swift's cats, they stepped out formally together for the first time at the 2015 *Billboard* Music Awards in May.

In March 2016, they celebrated their one-year anniversary with a romantic getaway to a tropical location. It is thought that this was the longest relationship she had been in up until this point in her life. The two posted romantic photos from their respective Instagram accounts. 'I'm in a magical relationship right now,' she told *Vogue*, but within months the magic had fizzled out. Remembering how he and Swift broke up, Harris said that 'for both of us, it was the wrong situation' and 'clearly wasn't right, so it ended'.

Many had hoped that the lovers would also become regular musical collaborators, but they teamed up only once, when they collaborated as co-writers on the track 'This Is What You Came For', recorded by Rihanna. The relationship ended unpleasantly, and the aftermath was also painful, with Harris reacting badly when the papers reported that Swift had written the smash-hit single. In a series of since-deleted tweets, he told her that 'if you're happy in your new relationship you should focus on that instead of trying to tear your ex bf down for something to do'.

There was a new wave of excitement when Swift and the actor Tom Hiddleston were photographed kissing, holding hands and cuddling in Rhode Island just two weeks after her split from Harris went public. The two had had a dance-off the previous month at the 2016 Met Gala while Swift was still dating Harris.

There were many public sightings of the new couple, now known as 'Hiddleswift', with accounts of them in the US, Europe and Australia over the summer of 2016. They were snapped together in Nashville, England and Rome. She held her annual Fourth of July party at her Rhode Island home, with Hiddleston seen cuddling up to her in the water and having fun as they slid down a giant water slide.

When they split after three months, there were suggestions that the entire relationship had been a media stunt. Hiddleston later denied this, saying during an interview with *GQ*, 'Taylor is an amazing woman. She's generous and kind and lovely, and we had the best time. Of course it was real.' According to reports, they broke up because she and Hiddleston had a disagreement on how high profile their relationship should be: he wanted it more public but she wasn't so keen. There were no hard feelings on his side, though.

Taylor said it had been 'interesting' to 'have gone through so many phases in front of the entire world'. She had spent a lot of time reflecting on her highs and lows, her good decisions and her bad mistakes. She wouldn't change a thing, though. 'Even though you know where you could've made a better decision or you could've said a better thing, or something like that, I just think I wouldn't change anything because I think being a songwriter, every experience you have ... and your experience shapes your work,' she said. 'So even the times where I've felt terrible emotions like regret or humiliation or embarrassment or failure, I took those emotions and kind of turned them into the next batch of songs,' she said.

There was so much to celebrate as she reached a quarter-century, but there was trouble ahead, with one inadvertent foreshadowing of the next chapter of her life. When she gave an interview to the BBC, she spoke about what it was like to be so high profile. 'I don't really have anything to hide at this point,' she told Fearne Cotton. 'It's sort of understood that anything I do is going to be discussed and dissected and debated and I'm used to that dynamic now.' The inevitability of her fifth album was reflected in its essentially sunny mood. There were clouds in her sky, but not many. She was more confident and was wearing it well within and outside of her music. Wasn't it just like life, then, when clouds suddenly filled her sky and a storm like no other arrived in Taylor's world?

Chapter Ten

Rarely have the opening bars of an album been more symbolic of the album itself and the place from which it emerged. The start of '… Ready For It?' is dark, serious and iconic – and with good reason. Album six was where things became darker for Swift. She was a changed woman and a changed artist from who she had been as she had approached album five. The experience of *1989* had transformed her from pop star to pop icon. This brought lots of nice things: more money, more fame and more recognition.

But the flipside of this is that it also increased the pressure on her. So, the anticipation for her latest album simply dwarfed anything that came before. Although it was album six, this release had something of the pressure of the 'difficult second album' about it, because it was the second pop album of Taylor's career and also the second album that a new army of fans, who had only arrived since *1989*, would buy.

This also meant that every time she was featured prominently in the media, a few more people would feel they'd heard enough of her. This trend had been growing for some time. As far back as March 2013, the *New York Times* mentioned that 'her ubiquity, not to mention her dating history, has begun to stir what feels like the beginning of a backlash'. By the time *Reputation* was simmering in the background, that backlash had moved from beginning to formulation. Of course, millions and millions still loved Taylor, but the army of Swift cynics was growing steadily.

Meanwhile, Taylor was feeling as if life itself was giving her a kick in the teeth. In 2015, her mother Andrea found out she had cancer. Writing to her fans on Tumblr, Swift said she was writing with 'an update I wish I wasn't giving you, but it's important and I'm used to sharing important events in my life with you'. She explained that she had asked her mother for the 'gift' of her visiting the doctor to 'get screened for any health issues, just to ease some worries of mine'.

Andrea agreed to go, but the news was not good. Although her mother felt fine, explained Swift, 'the results came in, and I'm saddened to tell you that my mom has been diagnosed with cancer'. She added that her mother wanted the fans to know 'because your parents may be too busy juggling everything they've got going on to go to the doctor, and maybe you reminding them to go get checked for cancer could possibly lead to an early diagnosis and an easier battle'. Following her treatment, Andrea went into remission, but that would not be the end of the story.

Another challenge came Swift's way as a longstanding issue came to a head legally. She faced a civil case against a former DJ who she said put his hand under her skirt in 2013. Swift had said that David Mueller had assaulted her by grabbing her bottom as a photo was taken after he, then a host on KYGO, had been invited to meet Swift before a show.

She said nothing like this had ever happened to her before. She considered herself 'really lucky', but 'that was one of the reasons it was so traumatising', she said. 'I just didn't know that could happen. It was really brazen, in front of seven people.' She complained to KYGO and the station duly fired Mueller two days later. This could have been the end of the story, but what he did next put paid to that.

The incident only became public two years later, when Mueller had originally tried to sue Swift, saying that her allegations had cost him his livelihood. That lawsuit was thrown out by a judge.

After Mueller had forced the matter into the open, Swift counter-sued him for battery and sexual assault, seeking a symbolic $1 (77p) in damages. The trial lasted one week and saw Swift behave inspirationally in the witness stand. She was strong and determined in court, refusing to let Mueller's representatives intimidate her. When she rejected an accusation that she had misidentified Mueller, she said: 'I'm not going to allow you or your client to say I am to blame.' When asked why a photo taken at the time of the incident does not show the front of her skirt ruffled, she responded: 'Because my ass is located on the back of my body.'

During another exchange, she said: 'I know exactly who did this. It is not alleged. It is a fact.' She added: 'You can ask me a million questions about it and I'm never going to say anything different.' When the lawyer asked if Swift was critical of her bodyguard for not interfering if Mueller really had reached under her skirt, she responded, 'I'm critical of your client sticking his hand under my skirt and grabbing my ass.'

Later, she explained to *Time* magazine why she was so direct during her testimony. 'I had already been in court all week and had to watch this man's attorney bully, badger and harass my team, including my mother, over inane details and ridiculous minutiae, accusing them, and me, of lying,' she said. She was 'angry', she continued, so she 'decided to forgo any courtroom formalities and just answer the questions the way it happened'. She added that although she had been advised to use the term 'rear end', she preferred 'ass' and had been told 'it was the most amount of times the word "ass" has ever been said in Colorado federal court'. The jury ruled in Swift's favour and ordered Mueller to pay her $1.

For those present, it was electrifying to see her stand up so bravely to a courtroom full of men. No wonder one journalist described Swift's testimony as 'sharp, gutsy and satisfying'. Her courtroom defiance earned her a place on *Time*'s Person of the Year cover, as one of 2017's 'silence breakers' who spoke out during the year's cultural reckoning surrounding sexual harassment and abuse. The magazine said her 'clear-eyed testimony marked one of several major milestones in the conversation around sexual harassment this year'.

Swift said she asked only for a symbolic $1 in damages from Mueller because she did not want to bankrupt him, but rather use the case to send a message to all women that 'they will decide what will be tolerated with their body'. In a statement, Taylor said: 'I acknowledge the privilege that I benefit from in life, in society and in my ability to shoulder the enormous cost of defending myself in a trial like this.' Later, when on stage, she offered her love and support to anyone who had been too scared to speak up about abuse, or who had spoken up and had not been believed. Swift admitted that she didn't know what she would have done had she been disbelieved. She added that her hope was 'to help those whose voices should also be heard' and that she would be 'making donations in the near future to multiple organisations that help sexual assault victims defend themselves'.

Another consequence of the saga came closer to home. Swift has had security cameras installed at every meet-and-greet since, pointedly trained at her lower half. 'If something happens again, we can prove it with video footage from every angle,' she told the *Guardian*.

But when asked by *Elle*, she denied that she had ever experienced sexual mistreatment from anyone else. The question had come up quite organically, because this was a time of reckoning for several predators in the showbusiness sector. Most pertinently, widespread allegations of sexual assault about the Hollywood producer Harvey Weinstein came out soon after her case. Although she had crossed paths with the producer, Swift said he had never mistreated her. He had asked her to write a song for the romantic comedy *One Chance*, which earned her a second Golden Globe nomination. He also got her a supporting role in the 2014 sci-fi movie *The Giver*, and he attended the launch party for *1989*.

But there was no contact beyond these professional interactions. 'I absolutely never hung out,' she told the *Guardian*. 'I believe women who come forward, I believe victims who come forward, I believe men who come forward,' she added, noting that it seemed to her that Weinstein's abuse was a 'power thing' and that he picked on women who were vulnerable. 'So, to me, that doesn't say anything – that I wasn't in that situation,' she said.

The symbolic victory of the courtroom battle had been a moment of light in a dark period for Taylor. There had been ongoing criticism from Calvin Harris fans after she was seen as acting badly after their break-up, and from Kanye West fans after she was said to have been less than honest in her online spats with the rapper. Earlier in 2016, Swift fell out with West after he referenced her in his song 'Famous', which included a lyric about him thinking he and 'Taylor' might 'still have sex' and bragging that he 'made that bitch famous'. The latter was a less-than-subtle reference to the moment when Kanye cut Taylor off during her MTV VMAs acceptance speech in

2009, declaring that Beyoncé was the better artist. The next day Twitter was alight with support for 19-year-old Taylor and condemnation of West's ungracious behaviour, which in turn boosted her profile. For 'Famous', West insisted he had had Swift's approval for the line ahead of releasing the song. She denied this, saying West had actually asked her to promote the track. Things didn't get any calmer when West then released the video to the song, which depicted naked wax model celebrities in a bed – one of whom was Swift.

The two episodes sparked several critical hashtags on social media, including #TaylorSwiftIsASnake and #TaylorSwiftIsCanceled. Kim Kardashian West tweeted about National Snake Day, which some interpreted as a comment aimed at Swift.

Speaking to *Vogue* magazine, Swift attempted to put into perspective how this felt. 'A mass public shaming, with millions of people saying you are quote-unquote cancelled, is a very isolating experience,' she said. 'I don't think there are that many people who can actually understand what it's like to have millions of people hate you very loudly.' She added that this messaging could even be perceived as a call for her to take her own life.

Swift faced yet more criticism via her so-called 'girl squad'. This was her collection of supermodel, actress and pop-star friends who became even more famous thanks to Swift's closely watched Instagram feed. Much like Swift herself, they were universally loved at first but then turned against. Where they were once seen as a potent expression of female solidarity and a feminist force, now they were regarded as impossibly beautiful women flaunting unattainably perfect and elitist lives.

Some of this change of heart came from within the squad. When she was invited on stage next to Swift, Lily Aldridge, Gigi Hadid and Hailee Steinfeld at a concert in New Jersey, Lena Dunham said that she felt 'chubby' and short in comparison to the other women. 'I was so thrilled to support my friend and so displeased to learn about the truth of my own height,' she said at a talk hosted by the Film Society of Lincoln Center. 'I've been feeling pretty tall, feeling pretty sturdy, and it was amazing to me, like, "Oh, I'm not tall, I'm chubby."'

The criticism kept coming. During the 2016 presidential election campaign, as Hillary Clinton battled with Donald Trump for the White House, Swift declined to throw her weight behind either of the candidates. She did encourage Americans to vote – she just didn't say which way they should vote. This caused annoyance within and beyond her fanbase. People wondered why an outspoken advocate for women's rights would not publicly support the first female candidate for president, particularly against a candidate such as Trump, who had made so many distasteful remarks about women.

At this stage, it would be understandable if she thought that, whatever she did, she would be damned by someone. This is a frustration that many stars feel when they reach the upper echelons of fame, particularly in the modern era, when social media gives celebrities the chance to comment instantly on every issue – and the chance to be condemned when they choose not to comment. They quickly feel that they cannot win – and Swift has certainly felt that.

Later, Taylor gave *Vogue* her side of the story over her political silence. She pointed out that, the summer before that election, 'all people were saying was "She's calculated. She's manipulative. She's not what she seems. She's a snake. She's a liar."' These were, she added, 'the same exact insults people were hurling at Hillary', so 'would I be an endorsement or would I be a liability?' She imagined people thinking that 'snakes of a feather flock together' and 'two lying women' and 'two nasty women' might become a reason not to vote Democrat. 'Literally millions of people were telling me to disappear,' she told *Vogue*, 'so I disappeared – in many senses.'

When stars are used to almost universal praise, the moment these accolades begin to be tempered by criticism, it can feel as if the level of criticism is as strong as the praise previously had been. It was from this feeling that Swift's next album emerged. The album was recorded at two studios in Los Angeles, and at other studios in Stockholm, Brooklyn, Portland and Atlanta. For her, she was working on more than an album: it was as if Swift wrote *Reputation* as a 'defence mechanism' against the media attacks and as a way of processing the hurt it caused in her mind. One of her producers, Jack Antonoff, told *Entertainment Weekly* that he wanted to capture where she was now, in the face of public criticism. He wanted to render musically how 'in the course of a day

– in the course of two minutes – you can feel like you can conquer the world, or you can feel like the biggest piece of garbage that ever existed'.

The album would certainly reflect that. The promotional campaign would be unlike anything she had undertaken before. On 18 August 2017, Swift suddenly vanished from the internet. She disappeared across her Facebook, Twitter, Instagram and Tumblr accounts, deleting all of her social media posts, unfollowing everyone she had previously been following and leaving her accounts empty of any content.

But it was not just a digital clear-out that was underway: she was also erasing every part of her image that she and her team had worked on so hard since she was 11 years of age. 'I realised I needed to restructure my life because it felt completely out of control,' she explained. 'I knew immediately I needed to make music about it because I knew it was the only way I could survive it. It was the only way I could preserve my mental health and also tell the story of what it's like to go through something so humiliating.'

Misunderstandings had been conjured by the darkness of the initial publicity campaign, which featured moody, silent, black-and-white videos of CGI snakes on social media. 'When it first came out everyone thought it was just going to be angry,' she told *Entertainment Weekly*, but 'upon listening to the whole thing they realised it's actually about love and friendship, and finding out what your priorities are.'

Another change was her decision not to give any promotional interviews for *Reputation*. Later, speaking to Zane Lowe on Beats 1 for Apple Music, she explained why. 'At the very beginning of the album I was pretty proud of coining the term, "There will be no explanation. There will just be *Reputation*,"' she said. 'And so that was what I decided was going to be the album,' she explained. 'And I stuck with it. I didn't go back on it. I didn't try to explain the album because I didn't feel that I owed that to anyone.'

The first track was called '… Ready For It?' Few were. Pumping with electropop melodies, bold synthesisers and a fast-paced tempo, the verses were not like anything that had come before. The almost industrial noise subsides for a while in the chorus, but then it's quickly back to the new sound, via a post-chorus bridge of beat drops. 'End Game', a collaboration with Ed Sheeran, was one of the album's other divisive tracks: its disjointed verses and rap-trap beats were confusing for a lot of her fans. But the emotionally open and impishly self-aware vibe is familiar Swift territory, even if the music is less 'her'.

Track three, 'I Did Something Bad', was a much more unifying effort. Its unapologetic tone carried spite in a way that was much more familiar to her fanbase. And the opening line, where she declares that she never trusts a narcissist but they love her, was trademark Swift sass. It also featured her most explicit lyrical moment to date, when she said that if a man 'talks shit' then she owes him nothing. Musically, it has shades of 'We Are Never Ever Getting Back Together'.

'Don't Blame Me' starts with an almost gospel vibe, but the chorus gets more ominous, complete with her comparison of love with a drug, which she will use for the rest of her life. 'Delicate' sees the first explicit namecheck for the theme of the album, where she admits that her reputation 'has never been worse'. The music is subdued but the message is clear: this is Taylor playing with the public's perception of her.

'Look What You Made Me Do' develops the theme of 'Don't Blame Me'. It sees Swift deny responsibility for grief. Dealing with various episodes that had sullied her reputation over an electroclash, dance-pop and electropop soundtrack, it explains that she has a list of names and the individual being addressed has hers underlined in red. The nightmarish vibe had barely been seen so directly before in her music. It made 'Bad Blood' seem like a child's lullaby. Similarly, where 'Blank Space' was a fun and upbeat self-satire, here the vibe was darker.

In 'Look What You Made Me Do', she declared that 'the Old Taylor [is] dead', and added that she trusts no one and no one trusts her in return. Anyone who thought that she had shed her old image with *1989* had not seen anything: here, she was truly scraping away the wholesome persona that had taken her to pop's peak, in favour of a bold new tone and a more openly vengeful image.

She said that her sixth album's 'split' between exploring 'vengeance' and finding 'something sacred through the battle cries' was influenced by *Game of Thrones*. 'Look What You Made Me Do' is literally Arya Stark's 'kill list', she told *Entertainment Weekly*. The latter track saw Swift present herself more darkly: even her trademark red cupid's bow had turned black. Swift said it was 'interesting' because she'd 'never before had an album that wasn't fully understood until it was seen live'.

When Swift said the 'old Taylor' couldn't come to the phone because she's 'dead', it stood as a potent symbol for her change of image. For some UK observers, it was eerily reminiscent of a similar quip made by Amy Winehouse. Appearing on the pop panel show *Never Mind the Buzzcocks*, Winehouse had been asked what had happened to the more fresh-faced, healthy version of herself that she had presented in her early years. 'She's dead!' joked Amy, though the joke didn't seem so funny in the end. Not everyone was a fan of the track itself, either. 'The songs Swift is borrowing from are superior to "Look What You Made Me Do",' said the *Guardian*.

Other stand-out tracks include 'This Is Why We Can't Have Nice Things', a sibling track to 'Look What You Made Me Do', and 'Call It What You Want', which is the most familiarly Swift moment on *Reputation*. The tone turns around completely on 'New Year's Day'. Here, a single piano line provides a stripped-back, gentle atmosphere. Sentimental and slushy, it shows a very different Swift to the dark and defiant version of earlier tracks. She uses a New Year's Day party as a metaphor for her friends and the memories they share. She pleads with them not to become a stranger, nostalgic for a moment, even as that moment is happening. This is a much more relatable track for listeners: it evokes the person who's there for you when the party is over and you return to the mundane details of life.

The album provoked a more interesting smorgasbord of responses than anything she had put out before. It is a 'big, brash, all-guns-blazing blast of weaponised pop' that 'grapples with the vulnerability of the human heart as it is pummelled by 21st-century fame', said the *Daily Telegraph*. It added that 'whatever else she's known for, Swift deserves a reputation as a genuine musical talent'.

Reputation 'shows the darker, deeper side of the pop mastermind', said *Rolling Stone*, while *Entertainment Weekly* said it showed she was 'no longer America's sweetheart'. *NME* felt it was an 'exhilarating, tank-like sixth album', and told readers that 'if you've ever wanted to exact revenge on someone', this was a 'relatable record'. *Re-Edition* magazine said the album was a 'dark and angry record' about 'revenge and betrayal'.

The album was not without its critics. *Consequence* said it was a 'bloated disaster' and added that 'part of the charm of *Reputation* lies in its density of failure', where 'every gesture sounds so poor, each decision so ill-advised, so many of the mistakes sound so avoidable'. *Cinquemani* said it was tarnished by 'tired, repetitive EDM tricks'.

Not for the first time, while everything seemed to have changed for Taylor's music, in one sense it had stayed the same: she had continued to openly express her thoughts and feelings, documenting the reality of her life and how she felt about its ups and downs. The reason it felt so different was because her life had become different.

She promoted the album on a new tour, where a grand total of 2,888,922 fans crammed into stadiums to see the shows, earning her a respectable $345.7 million. The stage set-up included the serpentine imagery of the hour. Alongside the Goth subculture and audacious theatricality, snakes were everywhere on the tour – from a customised snake microphone to massive snake props. The iconography was far from subtle, and it wasn't really meant to be subtle.

Midway through her opening concert, in Glendale, Arizona, she said to the audience: 'You might be wondering why there are so many snakes everywhere, huh?' She then embarked on something of a speech about the serpentine fixation. 'A couple of years ago, someone called me a snake on social media and it caught on,' she told her fans. 'And then a lot of people called me a lot of things on social media. And I went through some really low times for a while because of it.'

She added that the snakes were meant to be a 'message' to the fans that 'if someone uses name-calling to bully you on social media and even if a lot of people jump on board with it, that doesn't have to defeat you' because 'it can strengthen you instead'. She then turned to the theme of the album that the evening was based around – reputation. She said the lesson she had learned from recent trials and tribulations was one she had been telling them from the stage 'for about 10 years, but I never had to learn it so harshly myself'.

'That lesson has to do with how much you value your reputation,' she said. 'And I think the lesson is that you shouldn't care so much if you feel misunderstood by a lot of people who don't know you, as long as you feel understood by the people who do know you, the people who will show up for you, the people who see you as a human being.' Those people, for her, she told them, included her fans. Once again, her words had magically transformed a vast, packed stadium into a small, intimate setting.

Ironically, after a period of doubt, Swift's darkest album actually lightened her up once she took it on the road. 'During the *Reputation* stadium tour, my life felt different,' she said. 'I really do credit the fans for the complete resurgence of exuberance and excitement towards music and making new music.' She realised the fans saw her as a 'flesh-and-blood human being', which brought a feeling of 'humanity' to her life. For the second album running, getting on the road had given her an emotional boost. She said it was liberating to relinquish her 'America's sweetheart' title and the accompanying pressure to be 'always smiling, always happy'.

She welcomed the chance to be more open and honest. Ever since fans pored over the lyrics of *1989*'s track 'Bad Blood', it had been rumoured that Swift and Katy Perry were at loggerheads. Without naming Perry, Swift confirmed that the track was about another woman in the pop scene. 'For years, I was never sure if we were friends or not,' she said in the interview. 'She would come up to me at awards shows and say something and walk away, and I would think, "Are we friends, or did she just give me the harshest insult of my life?"'

But it wasn't until 2017 that either woman spoke on the record about the issue. During an appearance on *The Late Late Show with James Corden*, Perry broke the silence on the issue and confirmed that she did indeed have a suboptimal relationship with Swift. 'Honestly, it's really like she started it and it's time for her to finish it,' Perry said of the disagreement, which began in the form of a row over back-up dancers. She later claimed to have tried to talk to Swift, but said her attempt to reach out was less than successful. 'It was a full shutdown and then she writes a song about me, and I'm like, "Okay, cool, cool, cool, that's how you want to deal with it? Karma!"' It was all a far cry from 2009, when the two singers had swapped compliments on Twitter. Perry had even suggested a collaboration.

But Swift was doing okay on her own: *Reputation* sold two million copies worldwide within one week of release, outselling all of the other 199 albums on the chart combined. It was the bestselling album by a female artist of 2017, selling over 4.5 million copies, and was nominated for Best Pop Vocal Album at the 61st Annual Grammy Awards. So, coming three years and much drama on from her previous album, *Reputation* may have been the most successful comeback in pop history. Personally, it was a triumph too. Taylor had shown herself that she could emerge from difficult times by transforming them into creative work.

Meanwhile, she had embarked on what would become her longest-lasting relationship to date. In one important sense, the actor Joe Alwyn was not a natural fit for a relationship with a star as high profile as Swift, because, though a successful British thespian, his philosophy was to keep his private life as private as he could. 'It's not really [because I] want to be guarded and private, it's more a response to something else,' the shy actor told *Elle* magazine. 'We live in a culture that is so increasingly intrusive … The more you give – and frankly, even if you don't give it – something will be taken.'

Obviously, it would take a miracle to date Taylor without anyone noticing, though. Rumours of a relationship began in October 2016 when they both attended a Kings of Leon concert. A month later, Swift was spotted attending the premiere of Alwyn's movie, Billy Lynn's *Long Halftime Walk*, but it was not until May 2017 that news broke of their relationship, when a source close to them leaked details to the *Sun* newspaper. In the following December, Alwyn was spotted in attendance during her performance at iHeartRadio's Jingle Ball in New York City.

Then, on 8 May 2018, at the opening night of the *Reputation* tour in Glendale, Arizona, several audience members spotted Alwyn, despite him wearing a baseball cap in an attempt to hide his face. As she sang the song

'Gorgeous', which is said to be about Alwyn, some Swifties noticed that she was pointing to her boyfriend in the crowd as he recorded the moment. As far as they were concerned, this made it official. The fanbase quickly took kindly to Alywn, 'shipping' – or approving of – the couple.

Taylor wanted to get to know Joe in private, and she even moved to London to be with him. It felt from the start that Swift was taking this one more seriously. She said that *Reputation* wanted to speak to finding love through the noise, and she hoped she had managed that.

However much public criticism she was facing, Swift had shown during this chapter of her life that she could turn any negativity into art. If *Red* had been an album of evolution and *1989* had seen her dive right into pop, *Reputation* was the album that was a million miles from the happy-go-lucky country girl of her teenage years.

Swift had stepped away from the spotlight in this era. She was less likely to be spotted on red carpets and was snapped less by paparazzi photographers. Her social media posts became rarer and she gave almost no interviews. Even when she was the cover star of British *Vogue* and *Harper's Bazaar*, the features inside consisted of a poem for *Vogue*, and Taylor taking on the role of the interviewer, speaking with 1960s star Pattie Boyd for *Harper's*.

It was almost as if, with this withdrawal from the public glare, on some level Swift sensed that an almighty storm was coming her way. And it was. When Taylor moved record company it should have been an occasion for celebration. Instead, it thrust her into the biggest controversy of her life to date.

Chapter Eleven

Taylor's biggest trial began in November 2018, when she signed a record deal with Republic Records and Universal Records after her Big Machine contract expired. Republic/Universal had offered her a deal that would give her ownership of all her future masters – the original recordings of the songs from which all copies are made – which her first record deal hadn't done. It was a development that thrilled her, but the following summer all hell broke loose when American entrepreneur Scooter Braun bought Big Machine from its founder Scott Borchetta for a tidy $330 million, funded by various private equity firms.

Having signed Swift when she was just 15, Scott Borchetta helped guide her from a raw country newcomer to a global music giant. Swift had spoken of a close relationship between them, even going so far as to say that she thought Borchetta regarded her 'as the daughter he never had'.

So when he sold Big Machine for a reported $330 million to Ithaca Holdings, a mini-conglomerate of media and tech companies owned by Braun, a man Swift already considered a mortal enemy, it was a deeply painful moment for her. She could have been forgiven for feeling betrayed. Swift had already accused Braun of bullying her and she denounced the deal as 'my worst-case scenario'.

She said she learned of the sale the same day as everyone else; a powerful claim that found its way into the heart of the row. Writing on Tumblr, she said: 'This is what happens when you sign a deal at fifteen to someone for whom the term "loyalty" is clearly just a contractual concept. And when that man says "Music has value", he means its value is beholden to men who had no part in creating it.' She added that 'any time Scott Borchetta has heard the words "Scooter Braun" escape my lips, it was when I was either crying or trying not to'.

She said Braun was responsible for 'incessant, manipulative bullying', referencing an incident when West's wife, Kim Kardashian, leaked a recording of a phone call between Swift and West. The Kanye West link was central to the tensions between Swift and Braun, as the pop maestro had managed West off and on since 2015, and relations between Swift and West were still strained after his VMAs behaviour and the controversial release of 'Famous'.

Tensions rose even more when Swift noticed that Justin Bieber, the client who made Braun famous, posted a photo to Instagram showing himself FaceTiming with three men, including Braun and West. He captioned it: 'Taylor Swift what up'. Swift used this image in her Tumblr post, drawing a red circle around the image of Braun, with the message: 'This is Scooter Braun, bullying me on social media when I was at my lowest point. He's about to own all the music I've ever made.'

Bieber responded later by uploading an old picture of himself and the singer on Instagram, apologising for his 'distasteful and unfair' actions in 2016. However, he was less conciliatory when he turned more directly to her disagreement with Braun. He accused Swift of whipping up her fans to bully the executive. 'For you to take it to social media and get people to hate on Scooter isn't fair,' he wrote. He insisted that Braun hadn't been a part of the 'what up' joke three years ago and had even told Bieber not to behave that way. He wrote: 'Scooter has had your back since the days you graciously let me open up for you!' He continued: 'What were you trying to accomplish by posting that blog? Seems to me like it was to get sympathy. You also knew that in posting that your fans would go and bully Scooter.'

A sense of a concerted pushback from the Braun camp to shore up support for their man became stronger when Demi Lovato, another of his clients, also leapt to her manager's defence. 'I have dealt with bad people in this industry and Scooter is not one of them,' she wrote on Instagram Stories. 'Personally, I'm grateful he came into my life when he did. Please stop "dragging" people or bullying them. There's enough hate in this world as it is.'

Braun's wife Yael weighed in, telling Swift: 'You were given the opportunity to own your masters, you passed. Interesting that the man you're so "grossed out" by believed in you more than you believe in yourself.' She was similarly blunt and dismissive as she rejected Swift's claim of bullying, telling Taylor: 'The world has watched you collect and drop friends like wilted flowers. My husband is anything but a bully.'

However, critics of Braun also got involved. YouTuber, singer and actor Todrick Hall posted his thoughts on the matter, writing on Twitter that he had left Braun 'a long time ago'. He said he was 'saddened' but 'not shocked' by Swift's allegations. He said Braun was an 'evil person whose only concern is his wealth and feeding his disgusting ego', adding that 'I know from his own mouth that he is not a Swift fan'.

Braun, said Swift in her Tumblr post, had now 'stripped her' of her life's work, which she 'wasn't given an opportunity to buy'. She added that her 'musical legacy is about to lie in the hands of someone who tried to dismantle it'. She wrote that she was glad to be 'signed to a label that believes I should own anything I create' and called for artist ownership of songs. She said she hoped that the next generation of singers and songwriters would 'read this and learn about how to better protect themselves in a negotiation'.

Swift knew she was centre stage in the saga because her material was at the heart of the original deal. Although Big Machine was also home to other successful artists, including Sheryl Crow, Lady Antebellum and Rascal Flatts, her catalogue accounted for 80 per cent of the label's revenues at the time of sale. A master is the first recording of the music, from which copies are made for sales and distribution. Therefore, the owner of the master owns the copyright to all formats, which meant Swift's masters were a major asset in the transaction.

By now, the story was on the front pages and her former label boss had his say. Borchetta swiftly uploaded a rebuttal, denying that the deal had come as a surprise to her. 'I truly doubt that she "woke up to the news when everyone else did …"' he wrote. 'Taylor had every chance in the world to own not just her master recordings, but every video, photograph, everything associated to her career. She chose to leave.'

He uploaded messages between the pair talking about the deal, and he also added that Braun was a supporter of her, despite her turning down playing at the Manchester One Love concert, or the Parkland March: 'Scooter was never anything but positive about Taylor. He called me directly about Manchester to see if Taylor would participate (she declined).'

His words were very much supportive of Braun and seemingly designed to cast Swift in a negative light. 'Scooter has always been and will continue to be a supporter and honest custodian for Taylor and her music,' he said. Both men deny any wrongdoing.

After Swift said she would re-record her old albums, offering fans a way to buy her music again on her terms after her deal with Big Machine expired, things naturally got even more complicated.

During an interview on *Good Morning America*, correspondent Tracy Smith asked if she was planning to make new versions of all her masters. 'Oh yeah,' Swift replied. 'That's a plan?' Smith asked. 'Yeah, absolutely,' said Swift. 'I'm going to be busy.'

Taylor claimed that Borchetta and Braun had told her at the AMAs that she could not perform the works they currently owned as masters unless she dropped the plan to re-record the albums. Swift was keen to perform her material at the gala, where she was to be named no less than Artist of the Decade. She also claimed the two businessmen had told her she would not be allowed to use her old material in the impending Netflix documentary. 'The message being sent to me is very clear,' she wrote on social media. 'Basically, be a good little girl and shut up. Or you'll be punished.' She complained that she was talking about not just any music, but music she 'wrote on my bedroom floor and videos I dreamed up and paid for from the money I earned playing in bars, then clubs, then arenas, then stadiums'.

There were precedents for this sort of dispute. In 2012, during an epic quarrel with Universal over digital royalty rates, Def Leppard forbade the label from using its own music for anything other than physical product, and began recording 'forgeries' of their old hits – from which they would take 70 per cent of the revenue – for use on download and streaming services. Previously, the UK band Squeeze had released re-recordings of their old songs as the album *Spot the Difference*. Again, they were in dispute with Universal.

Normally, these kinds of disputes are resolved behind closed doors, with boring lawyers boringly combing through boring contracts and statutes, until a solution is found. But this one was played out in front of the watching world. Every time Swift spoke about the issue on her social media, her words instantly reached 85 million followers, many of whom immediately reshared her words, helping them to reach many millions more. The hashtag #IStandWithTaylor trended on social media, and Swift showed that the corporate world does not intimidate her.

It didn't take long for Braun and Borchetta to be bombarded with death threats. They backed down on the AMAs issue, though their statement didn't provide anything specific on the Netflix question. The discord rolled on all the way up until the Friday before the awards, when Braun posted an open letter to Swift, laying out the death threats that he claimed his family had received from Swifties. Taylor was asked to tell her fans to stop sending threats to Scooter and his family, according to the US *Sun*.

At the AMAs Taylor arrived in quite the costume, which she wore while performing a medley of her greatest hits to celebrate being crowned Artist of the Decade. Her simple white shirt prominently featured the titles of her earlier albums – *Taylor Swift*, *Fearless*, *Speak Now*, *Red*, *1989* and *Reputation* – in what was inevitably interpreted as a less-than-subtle dig at Big Machine, particularly because it didn't include the title of her newest album, *Lover*, which was not owned by the label. Some interpreted the style as akin to a prison uniform, comparing the stance to when the artist Prince appeared with the word 'SLAVE' on his face at the 1995 BRIT Awards, in protest at his label, Warner, owning his name and any music released under it.

When she accepted her Artist of the Decade gong, she gave a speech laced with messages. 'The fact is that the last year of my life had the most amazing times and the hardest things I've gone through, a lot of things that haven't been public,' she said. 'I wanted to thank you for being the thing that's been constant in life. This industry is really weird.' In April 2020, Taylor disowned a live album released under her name, describing it as tasteless and 'shameless greed'. The album, *Live from Clear Channel Stripped 2008*, had been recorded when Swift was 18, during the *Fearless* period. It was released by Big Machine.

Writing on Instagram, she made it clear where she stood. 'This release is not approved by me. It looks to me like Scooter Braun and his financial backers, 23 Capital, Alex Soros and the Soros family and the Carlyle Group have seen the latest balance sheets and realised that paying $330 million wasn't exactly a wise choice and they need money.' She added: 'In my opinion ... Just another case of shameless greed in the time of coronavirus. So tasteless, but very transparent.'

In the autumn of 2020, Braun sold the masters to Swift's first six albums to the Disney family's investment firm, Shamrock Holdings. The deal, worth a reported $405 million, was seen as a major victory for Braun, who profited handsomely from his initial investment. Swift was less happy: she said that the master recordings 'were not for sale to me'.

'This was the second time my music had been sold without my knowledge,' she claimed. 'The letter told me that they wanted to reach out before the sale to let me know, but that Scooter Braun had required that they make no contact with me or my team, or the deal would be off.' Her statement claimed that Braun will continue to profit from her catalogue 'for many years'.

Looking back on the controversy, Braun admitted he had regrets over the episode. 'I learned an important lesson from that,' he said. He admitted he had certain assumptions over how it would play out. 'So the regret I have there is that I made the assumption that everyone, once the deal was done, was going to have a conversation with me, see my intent, see my character, and say, "Great, let's be in business together." I made that assumption with people that I didn't know, and I learned … that I can never make that assumption again.' He admitted that he understood that Swift 'probably felt it was unfair', and added that he 'wished everyone involved well'.

As for Swift, she told *Variety* that she had a clear conscience. 'Well, I do sleep well at night knowing that I'm right, and knowing that in 10 years it will have been a good thing that I spoke about artists' rights to their art, and that we bring up conversations like: should record deals maybe be for a shorter term, or how are we really helping artists if we're not giving them the first right of refusal to purchase their work if they want to?'

As she stood up for herself on her music, she found the strength to be more outspoken on bigger issues, too. Once an apolitical celebrity, in May 2020 Swift weighed in on one of the more inflammatory issues of the day. George Floyd was an African-American man who was murdered by a police officer in 2020 in Minneapolis, Minnesota, during an arrest made after a store clerk suspected Floyd to have used a counterfeit 20-dollar bill.

As Minneapolis and other places in the US burned with anger over the death of Floyd, Donald Trump started threatening online that 'when the looting starts, the shooting starts'. Some, including the Swift of yesteryears, would have carefully avoided getting involved in such a divisive debate, but the Swift of 2020 was different. 'After stoking the fires of white supremacy and racism your entire presidency, you have the nerve to feign moral superiority before threatening violence?' she wrote in a tweet addressed to Trump. 'We will vote you out in November,' she vowed.

Her tweet immediately attracted thousands of likes and shares. Within hours, it had been liked more than 800,000 times and retweeted more than 200,000 times. It had been a remarkable outburst because of its direct forcefulness – Swift had not tiptoed gingerly into the political sphere, she had come all guns blazing into one of the fiercest culture battles of the moment, which many celebrities avoided. But Swift got right in there, even referring to 'white supremacy' – a term that many of Trump's fiercest critics were too scared to level at the Republican.

Her message also brought to a crashing end the perception that she was somehow a Trump sympathiser. Like many country singers, Swift was assumed by some to be right-leaning. In 2017, the *Guardian* had said that Swift's songs 'echo Mr Trump's obsession with petty score-settling in their repeated references to her celebrity feuds', adding that she seemed 'not simply a product of the age of Trump, but a musical envoy for the president's values'. These arguments seemed a stretch, to put it mildly, but the fact that they appeared in the leader comment of a respected national newspaper showed that they were not without their believers.

Swift also spoke out on Twitter when footage surfaced of the killing of Ahmaud Arbery by a white former policeman and his son while Arbery was out jogging. 'I'm absolutely devastated and horrified by the senseless, cold-blooded, racially motivated killing of Ahmaud Arbery,' she wrote. Then, in June 2020, she spoke out again. Taking to Twitter, she wrote that 'racial injustice has been ingrained deeply into local and state governments, and changes MUST be made there'. She added that to get the level of change needed, the US would 'need to elect people who will fight against police brutality and racism of any kind'. To back up the latter statement, she shared a link to an essay written by Barack Obama, in which the former US president argued the same point.

Part of this journey was noticeable in the *Miss Americana* documentary, which was released on Netflix in 2020, in which the cameras followed Swift during her tours of 2018 and 2019 and she discussed her life and career. In one scene, Taylor is told that there could be some media trouble after she revealed she was planning to vote for a Democrat candidate in the Tennessee midterms. 'In the past I've been reluctant to publicly voice my political opinions, but due to several events in my life and in the world in the past two years, I feel very differently about that now,' she wrote at the time. She added that she believed 'in the fight for LGBTQ rights', and also denounced discrimination on the basis of gender or race.

In the documentary, Swift is told she could lose fans and spark headlines that she is coming out against Trump. 'I don't care if they write that!' she said, adding that she is sad she didn't speak out at the 2016 election, but that there is nothing she can do about that now. 'I'm saying right now that this is something that I know is right … I need to be on the right side of history,' she said. 'If I get bad press for saying, "Don't put a homophobic racist in office," then I get bad press for that. I really don't care,' she said.

Part of her previous reticence can be laid at the door of the musical community from which she emerged. For many people, anyone involved with country music is quickly linked with Republicans and right-wing views. This is only a partially justified assumption. In 2020, Tim McGraw and Faith Hill donated to Democratic presidential candidate Joe Biden's campaign, according to Federal Election Commission filings. The Chicks, formerly the Dixie Chicks, spoke out against George Bush during the Iraq War that began in 2003 and later performed at a Democrat Party event. Indeed, in its earliest years country music had strong and proud connections to organised labour and struggles for social justice.

Country music has its roots in the music of Black musicians, but its artists are now almost entirely white in its numbers. It is also one of the least protest-based of musical genres. Country songs cover a variety of themes, but speaking truth to power has rarely been one of them. But that has started to change, and Swift was only a part of it. In 2020, CMT, formerly Country Music Television, joined the other channels on social media in supporting the Black Lives Matter movement and condemned police brutality. The network also joined a multi-network blackout of 8 minutes and 46 seconds, to symbolise the amount of time that a police officer knelt on Floyd's neck. Dolly Parton told *Billboard* that 'of course Black lives matter', adding: 'Do we think our little white [behinds] are the only ones that matter? No!'

But the right-wing image of country music didn't come from nowhere. A Gallup survey during the George Bush era found that around 60 per cent of fans of country music identified with Republicans, and the backlash that the Chicks got from the country world for speaking out against Bush was severe.

Meanwhile, the wheels of Swift's career continued to turn. She had appeared in the 2019 film version of the Andrew Lloyd Webber musical *Cats*, which proved to be a mixed experience. In what amounted to little more than a cameo, she appeared as Bombalurina, an impish orange Bengal cat who first appears about 90 minutes into the movie. The character is a flirty, proud and naughty cat with a distinctive red coat. She also wrote the lyrics for a Lloyd Webber song, 'Beautiful Ghosts', for the adaptation. 'We sat around the piano, I played her a melody,' Lloyd Webber recalled. 'It was a joy. She's a real pro. Talk about being a pro.'

Alluding to how difficult the filming experience was, he said of 'Beautiful Ghosts' that it was 'one of the few enjoyable experiences' on the project, and 'probably *the* enjoyable experience'. This was a low bar: the movie lost a reported $113.6 million at the box office and was widely described as one of the worst movies of all time. The *Los Angeles Times* said it was 'as uneasy on the eyes as a Hollywood spectacle can be', the *Detroit News* said it was 'the biggest disaster of the decade, and possibly thus far in the millennium', while *Rolling Stone* gave it zero stars and said it made the audience 'want to cry for mercy'.

Swift's track was sung by other cast members during the production – which *Vox* said 'might be the best part'

– then she sings her version over the closing credits. Speaking to *Billboard*, Taylor described the yearning song poetically, saying it was 'sung from a young voice who is wondering if she will ever have glory days', who is 'longing for the sense of belonging she sees everyone finding' and 'reaching for it, desperately afraid of never having beautiful ghosts of days gone by to cling to in her older years'.

While the film was a widely mocked flop, Swift took positives from it all. 'I'm not gonna retroactively decide that it wasn't the best experience,' she said. 'I never would have met Andrew Lloyd Webber or gotten to see how he works, and now he's my buddy. I got to work with the sickest dancers and performers. No complaints.'

'I really had an amazing time with *Cats*,' she told Andrew Lloyd Webber himself, who interviewed her for *Vogue* magazine. 'I think I loved the weirdness of it. I loved how I felt I'd never get another opportunity to be like this in my life.'

While her brief foray into moviemaking may not have resulted in a resounding success, Swift would quickly make up for it with a new album. Described by the lady herself as a 'love letter to love', her seventh album was the calm after the storm. With the widest range of styles she had attempted for one album so far, *Lover* featured electropop, pop rock and synth-pop, from country and folk to funk and bubblegum pop. She said the invitation was to celebrate love in 'all of its maddening, passionate, exciting, enchanting, horrific, tragic, wonderful glory'.

The album emerged from the renewed glow she felt in the aftermath of the *Reputation* tour. 'This time around I feel more comfortable being brave enough to be vulnerable, because my fans are brave enough to be vulnerable with me,' she said. Her drive to succeed remained, but it was framed in a more healthy way. In short, she had remembered that music was supposed to be fun.

Swift recorded her new album across six different studios: three in Los Angeles, one in New York, one in Auckland and one in London, with much of the collection done in 'whole takes'. This meant that the emotion and narrative of the songs was captured more authentically, she told *Vogue*. 'When you perform live, you're narrating and you're getting into the story and you're making faces that are ugly and you're putting a different meaning on a song every time you perform it,' she said.

Lover was her most ambitious effort to date, and it was also her most opinionated release. She wrote 'Miss Americana & the Heartbreak Prince' after the 2018 midterm elections, using high school as a metaphor for American politics. 'The Man' was inspired by the double standards that women experience in the record industry, while 'You Need to Calm Down' speaks up for LGBTQ rights. It was all a long way from her teenage years, when she was told not to get involved in anything remotely political.

Swift wrote the title track alone at a piano, late one night at one of her properties, in Nashville. When it felt complete, she took the track to her longtime collaborator,

Jack Antonoff, at a studio in New York. They spent six hours one day building the final version. Conceptually, she told the *New York Times*, the track was fairly clear in her imagination. 'In my head I had like, just the last two people on a dance floor at 3am swaying,' she said. 'Whatever that would sound like.'

For Taylor, it was as if the sunshine had come out after a long dark period: conceptually, she wanted *Lover* to be 'a barn wood floor and some ripped curtains flowing in the breeze, and fields of flowers'. The bright pink and pastel style of the cover art was quite the departure from the dark, black-and-white art and aesthetic of *Reputation*.

When it was released on 23 August 2019, the album was like a breath of fresh air for a tired music scene. It sold nearly one million copies on pre-orders alone. In its opening week, it outsold all of the other 199 albums on the chart combined, the first album to do so since her previous release, *Reputation*. Remarkably, all 18 songs from her new album charted on the *Billboard* Hot 100, as she rewrote the record for the most simultaneous Hot 100 entries for a female artist.

It was her sixth consecutive album to debut at number one on the US *Billboard* 200, and it also topped the charts in a range of other regions, including Australia, Canada, Mexico, the UK, New Zealand, Latvia and Greece. It sold more than 3.2 million copies worldwide in 2019 alone, becoming the year's bestselling album by a solo artist.

To sweeten the taste even more, as her love letter to love flew off the shelves, she herself was very much in love – not that her relationship with Joe was something she felt comfortable speaking about publicly. 'I've learned that if I do, people think it's up for discussion, and our relationship isn't up for discussion.' Alywn had sounded a similar note whenever the subject of their relationship came up in interviews. 'I'm aware people want to know about that side of things,' he told British *Vogue*. 'I think we have been successfully very private and that has now sunk in for people … but I really prefer to talk about work.'

During a separate interview with *Total Film*, Alwyn explained a bit more. 'For me, I just don't feel it's something I want to offer up to be picked apart by people who don't know about it, and it's just not theirs to have,' he said. But he did admit he was flattered by the fact that she had written songs about him. Asked by the *Sunday Times* if he minded, Joe said: 'No, not at all. No. It's flattering.'

But she did include a diary entry alluding to the relationship in the deluxe edition of *Lover*. 'I'm essentially based in London, hiding out trying to protect us from the nasty world that just wants to ruin things,' she wrote in an entry from January 2017. 'We have been together and no one has found out for 3 months now.'

The *Telegraph* described *Lover* as 'zippy, feminist electropop about young love' and 'an album well stocked with bright, light, snappy tunes'. It said that, 'broad-brush politics aside', Swift's 'principal subject remains pop's oldest staple: love in all its aspects'. It 'leaves behind the anger that fuelled its predecessor', instead 'opting for open-hearted love songs', said *Rolling Stone*. 'Let's just say that the old Taylor can't come to the phone right now – cause she's busy writing songs that suit her again,' it concluded. The *New York Times* said it saw her 'emerge from the darkness unbroken', while *Vanity Fair* said the production ties together 'a lot of the best impulses in recent pop'.

In the *Guardian*, Alexis Petridis wondered whether Swift was 'treading water' with *Lover*. It 'offers plenty of evidence that Swift is just a better songwriter than any of her competitors in the upper echelons of pop', he wrote, 'but its something-for-everyone approach feels like consolidation, not progress'. *Slate* magazine felt the album was weakened by Swift's efforts to satisfy her audience, and the *Observer* wondered if it was 'at least a partial retrenchment until Swift decides what to do next'.

What Taylor would do next would be full of surprises. In December 2019, she turned 30; she had spent roughly half her life in the public glare. A key lesson she learned around this milestone, she said, was that you 'cannot micromanage life'. Just a few months later, Covid-19 would show everyone that you cannot manage life at all, but you can choose your response to it. As a pandemic that was unprecedented in modern times swept the globe, Swift saw it as a prompt to mix things up in how she recorded her music, what she recorded and how she released it.

Chapter Twelve

Before sickness struck the globe, it struck Taylor's beloved mother. In 2019, Andrea was diagnosed with cancer for a second time, having gone into remission following her first diagnosis in 2015. Announcing the news, Swift confirmed that her father, Scott, had also had the disease. 'Both of my parents have had cancer, and my mom is now fighting her battle with it again.' She said the news had given her a newfound perspective. 'It's taught me that there are real problems, and then there's everything else,' she wrote for *Elle*.

Then, in 2020, Andrea was diagnosed with a brain tumour while battling breast cancer. Swift said the medics discovered the brain tumour when Andrea, 62, was undergoing chemotherapy. 'She was going through chemo, and that's a hard enough thing for a person to go through,' Swift told *Variety*. 'While she was going through treatment, they found a brain tumour.' She added that 'the symptoms of what a person goes through when they have a brain tumour is nothing like what we've ever been through with her cancer before,' so it's 'just been a really hard time for us as a family'. As in song, she was open and vulnerable in print, and hoped her public remarks would help others who were facing the same troubles as her.

Taylor confirmed the speculation that she had shortened her tour to be able to spend more time with her mother. It would have been unconscionable for Swift to take to the road for her usual nine months of concert dates while her mother faced the many challenges of cancer. 'Everyone loves their mom,' she said, because 'everyone's got an important mom'. But for Swift, her mother had been 'really the guiding force' because 'almost every decision I make, I talk to her about it first'. Taylor has paid musical tribute to her mother in several songs, including 'Best Day' and 'Soon You'll Get Better'. Both the tributes are poignant.

Meanwhile, the wheels of her career kept turning. It's so hard to sustain Taylor's level of success while changing as much as she has creatively. The scale of that change was thrown into sharp clarity when she pulled the surprise release of her next album, *Folklore*. Writing during Covid quarantine, the songs came together as 'a collection of songs and stories that flowed like a stream of consciousness', she said. The mellower nature of the songs reflected that the workaholic Swift had been forced to slow down.

The Covid pandemic presented its own challenges for recording and production, but Swift and her two main producers, Aaron Dessner and Jack Antonoff, were able to work together remotely. Dessner and Antonoff were based in recording studios in the Hudson Valley and New York City, respectively, while Swift recorded her vocals in a studio at her Los Angeles home. She named this studio Kitty Committee, and from there she and her two producers were in regular contact, pinging music files back and forth between each other.

'It turned out [Dessner] had been writing instrumental tracks to keep from absolutely going crazy during the pandemic as well, so he sends me this file of probably 30 instrumentals, and the first one I opened ended up being a song called "Cardigan",' she told *Rolling Stone* magazine. 'He'd send me a track; he'd make new tracks, add to the folder; I would write the entire top line for a song, and he wouldn't know what the song would be about, what it was going to be called, where I was going to put the chorus,' she said.

Somehow this game of distant tennis worked, with Dessner in particular. The guitarist in the band The National, he was used to working virtually, as he and his bandmates lived in different parts of the world. Speaking to *Billboard*, Dessner explained that he had written a lot of songs in the early stages of lockdown, which he shared with Swift. 'I thought it would take a while for song ideas to come and I had no expectations as far as what we could accomplish remotely,' he said. 'But a few hours after sharing music, my phone lit up with a voice memo from Taylor of a fully written version of a song – the momentum never really stopped.' He added that Swift is 'one of the most talented, hardworking and deeply caring artists I've ever encountered', with a 'palpable humanity and warmth and raw emotion' in the songs.

It was a curious time for Swift, because the only people who knew she was making the album were the team that she was making it with, her boyfriend Joe, her family and her management team. Alywn got involved in the writing of two tracks on the album – 'Exile' and 'Betty'; he later told *GQ Hype*, 'It was really the most accidental thing to happen in lockdown. It wasn't like, "It's three o'clock, it's time to write a song!"' he explained. 'It was just messing around on a piano and singing badly and being overheard and then thinking, you know, what if we tried to get to the end of it together?' He said it was 'fun' to write together and he was 'proud' of the 'positive reception' the songs got.

The isolation that much of the human race felt during Covid influenced the tracks on Swift's new album, which explored several themes, including escapism and wistfulness. Casting aside her usual focus on autobiographical themes, she instead toyed with fiction. Its relaxed, easier pace chimed well with the lifestyle that people were forced into by lockdown restrictions. The introspective tone, which was a far cry from previous tracks such as 'Bad Blood', 'Shake It Off' and the like, also felt perfect. Having captured her own life so well in previous albums, here she was capturing the story of a planet. It felt like the quintessential quarantine album.

Swift penned a 'primer' on the album, which was published on *Billboard*. Positioned as an 'explainer' for

Folklore, it was a beautiful piece of art in its own right. In it, Taylor wrote that the album process had 'started with imagery', in the form of 'visuals that popped into my mind and piqued my curiosity'. Then she revealed some of those visuals. 'Stars drawn around scars. A cardigan that still bears the scent of loss twenty years later. Battleships sinking into the ocean, down, down, down. The tree swing in the woods of my childhood.'

She also wrote of 'the sun-drenched month of August, sipped away like a bottle of wine', 'hands held through plastic' and 'a single thread that, for better or for worse, ties you to your fate'. She wrote that these images in her head quickly 'grew faces or names and became characters'.

The sudden news of the album's release blindsided almost everyone. On 23 July 2020, Swift uploaded nine photos to her Instagram account. None had captions, but together they formed a black-and-white image of Taylor standing alone in a forest. People were naturally curious. A follow-up post announced that her eighth studio album would be released at midnight. She wrote: 'Most of the things I had planned this summer didn't end up happening, but there is something I hadn't planned on that DID happen. And that thing is my 8th studio album, *Folklore*'.

Stand-out tracks on the album include 'The Last Great American Dynasty', an upbeat folktronica/indie effort, 'Cardigan', which is a minimalist ballad fusing folk, soft rock and indie, and 'Betty', with its harmonica, pedal steel and overall production offering a nod to times past. The album sold 1.2 million copies in 2020 alone, as locked-down fans delighted in the unexpected material.

The album got full-score ratings in the *Sydney Morning Herald*, *i News* and the *Daily Telegraph*. *Rolling Stone* said it was Swift's most intimate effort to date, thanks to her songwriting skills and 'deepest wit, compassion, and empathy', and the BBC said, 'This is a more subdued singer than we've met before,' and 'she's hit on a rich seam of melancholy that chimes perfectly with the times'. *Folklore* is 'an unconventional record – at least for the world's biggest pop star', said the *Independent*. 'It's also brilliant.' Chris Willman of *Variety* said *Folklore* was a 'first-rank album', and its shift in musical style was a 'serious act of sonic palette [sic] cleansing'.

The closest there came to a negative review in any respected publication was the mixed response from the *New York Times*. The 'desolate, stubborn, overcomposed' indie rock is a 'tough thicket to tame', it said. 'Sometimes she triumphs, wrestling it until it's slack,' it added, 'but when it stifles her, it deserves all the eye rolls it gets.'

You wait years for a new Taylor Swift album and then two come along at once. Having surprised the world with *Folklore*, she did it again with *Evermore*. 'To put it plainly, we just couldn't stop writing songs' – that was Swift's basic explanation, shared on Instagram, of why she was releasing a new album less than five months after her last one. 'To try and put it more poetically,' she continued, 'it feels like we were standing on the edge of the folklorian woods and had a choice: to turn and go back or to travel further into the forest of this music.'

They chose to travel further. Taylor and her team recorded it in Los Angeles, the Hudson Valley and London, but the real journey was within the music itself, expertly marshalled by her producers Aaron Dessner, Jack Antonoff and Bryce Dessner. It produced a cosy vibe with simple arrangements and vulnerable lyrics. From the Sheeran-esque 'Willow' to the more energetic 'Gold Rush', with its *1989*-era vibes, and the Christmas glory of ''Tis the Damn Season', it is a fine collection.

For the second album running, the release was announced only a matter of hours in advance. On 10 December 2020, with her thirty-first birthday just days away, Taylor shared nine photos on Instagram. Together, they formed an image depicting the singer's back, with her hair in a braid, facing a forest. 'You've all been so caring, supportive and thoughtful on my birthdays and so this time I thought I would give you something!' she wrote in her follow-up post, which formally announced the impending release.

A metaphor-rich chamber folk song, 'Willow' features picked guitars, glockenspiel, flute, strings and percussion, to create an atmospheric wonder that towers above much of Swift's output. Following a waltz tempo, the rockier 'Coney Island' was also an early fan favourite, and the honky-tonk piano and folk drums of 'Dorothea' were a fine backdrop to some of the richest lyrics of her career to date. The album sold a million copies in its first week on the shelves.

Giving a second successive Swift album a full scoring, the *Sydney Morning Herald* said she was 'stronger than before', and that the album reveals 'Swift's ability to assume a character, write it until it's entirely wrung dry, and move on to her next method role while keeping herself entirely intact'. The *NME* said *Evermore* was a 'freewheeling younger sibling' to *Folklore*, which was the 'introspective, romantic older sister'. The *Guardian* said that 'not everything here works', but, taken together, *Folklore* and *Evermore* 'make a convincing case for Swift's ability to shift shape and for her songs' ability to travel between genres'.

Negativity was thin on the ground. 'She's still a little muted on *Evermore*,' said the *Observer*, with 'pastel music that smears Vaseline on her otherwise keen lens'. The *Washington Post* said the album was overlong, and the *Los Angeles Times* cast the album as *Folklore*'s leftovers. *Evermore* 'may lack the impactful frisson of *Folklore*', felt the *Telegraph*, 'but is nevertheless another treat of classy, emotional songcraft'.

Swift's two 2020 releases showed again that she is a lover of literature. Both albums were rich with literary references. From the 'road less travelled' in 'Illicit Affairs' to 'Peter losing Wendy' in 'Cardigan' on *Folklore*, and the Daphne du Maurier themes in 'Tolerate It' on *Evermore*, these were two literary collections.

In the aftermath of the two releases, Swift felt more comfortable to share something of her relationship with Alwyn and how 'scary' it can be to fall in love with someone who has a 'very grounded, normal way of living'. Speaking to *Rolling Stone*, she explained that 'I oftentimes, in my anxieties, can control how I am as a person and how normal I act and rationalize things, but I cannot control if there are 20 photographers outside in the bushes and what they do and if they follow our car and if they interrupt our lives.' She added: 'I can't control if there's going to be a fake weird headline about us in the news tomorrow.'

Swift also said that Alwyn 'absolutely' understood and sympathised with Swift's life as a public figure. 'But I think that in knowing him and being in the relationship I am in now, I have definitely made decisions that have made my life feel more like a real life and less like just a storyline to be commented on in tabloids,' she said.

At the 63rd Annual Grammy Awards in LA, in March 2021, Alwyn enjoyed a win for his contributions to the album. Although he didn't appear on stage with his girl-friend to accept the award, Swift gave him a shout-out in her speech. 'Joe is the first person that I play every single song that I write, and I had the best time writing songs with you in quarantine,' she said.

While her new records travelled into pastures new, it was also time for Taylor to return to more familiar territory, as she started to release her new versions of her back catalogue. It was remarkable that she managed to be so mellow and mild on *Folklore* and *Evermore*, yet so determined and brimming with energy as she reclaimed her work. She started with her second album, *Fearless*, because she wanted to reconnect with the 'effervescence', she said. The team produced all but the unreleased tracks to replicate the original recordings, which feature indistinguishable arrangements, but with instruments and vocals that are more defined and controlled in parts. The production was sharper and had a warmer feel overall. As for her vocals, her more mature sound occasionally sat less than ideally with the youthful sentiments of *Fearless*, but the 'vault' tracks were welcome inclusions, giving as they did an insight into Taylor's mind at the time of the original album's composition. 'Only she could make bare-knuckled capitalism feel like a moral act,' said the *Los Angeles Times*. It sold 980,000 copies in 2021.

Next up came her version of *Red*. It turned into an epic, 30-track affair. As with all the Taylor's Version releases to date, the new recordings were not meant to recast the music; instead, the tracks were diligently re-recorded note for note, to supplant the originals and reduce their value. The tracks would not be noticeably different to the casual listener, and they weren't meant to be. However, to the more closely tuned ear, aspects of the instrumentation were a bit more dynamic, giving it the feel of a live performance. The drums are brisker in 'I Knew You Were Trouble' and the guitars are more prominent in '22'.

Some differences made the new collection a little more sophisticated than the original. Swift's vocals had inevitably improved since she recorded the original versions, so she lends a layer of class. The 10-minute version of 'All Too Well' was the most remarkable feature of the new version. It fuelled the full running time of the album of two hours and 11 minutes. The cover artwork portrayed her wearing red lipstick, a beige peacoat and a burgundy-coloured 'Matti' fisherman velvet cap. She was sat in a vintage 1932 Chevrolet Cabriolet convertible with a Swiftian autumnal background.

The album 'feels a bit like a cherished garment after it's been through the wash', said the *New Yorker*, while the *Guardian* said Swift's new vocal maturity 'slightly blunts the rabid, deliciously vindictive edge' of the original, the *NME* loved the 'sprawling collection', and the *Independent* said it was a 'better, brighter version of a terrific pop album'.

The *Wall Street Journal* looked more at the album's wider impact, rather than the tracks themselves. *Red (Taylor's Version)* is 'reshaping the music industry', it said, noting how the re-recorded songs were outperforming their original counterparts on streaming services, going viral on TikTok, and landing 'lucrative' licensing deals for usage in motion pictures. For the big release, various business brands hopped onto Swift's bandwagon. From confectionery companies like M&M's and Skittles to sports teams like the Kansas City Chiefs, many were adding Taylor's Version to their social media brands.

Taylor's influence was strong. *Billboard* named her their number-one artist of 2021, saying that she 'rewrote industry rules and had one of the most impactful years of her storied pop career without even releasing an entirely new album'. She was the highest-paid musician of 2021 globally, earning an estimated $65.8 million in take-home pay. Surely, she had reached the ceiling of success and could not climb any higher? In reality, though, 'Taylormania' was only just beginning.

Chapter Thirteen

How does Taylor Swift do it? She gave the world a glimpse into her songwriting formula one evening in September 2022, when she attended the Nashville Songwriter Awards and gave a speech for being named the Songwriter-Artist of the Decade. It was quite the address, right from her opening gambit of: 'Oh hi.'

'I love doing this thing we are fortunate enough to call a job,' she said. Explaining that 'writing songs is my life's work and my hobby and my neverending thrill', she said she was 'moved beyond words that you, my peers, decided to honour me in this way for work I'd still be doing if I had never been recognised for it'.

Admitting that it was 'dorky', she said she had 'secretly, established genre categories for lyrics I write … three of them, to be exact'. She explained that they were 'affectionately titled Quill Lyrics, Fountain Pen Lyrics, and Glitter Gel Pen Lyrics'. She said songs in the 'Quill' style came about if 'the words and phrasings are antiquated', or if she was 'inspired to write it after reading Charlotte Brontë or after watching a movie where everyone is wearing poet shirts and corsets'.

Her most common style, 'Fountain Pen', meant 'a modern storyline or references, with a poetic twist', such as 'taking a common phrase and flipping its meaning'. She said these tracks 'sound like confessions scribbled and sealed in an envelope, [that are] too brutally honest to ever send'. 'Glitter Gel Pen' is her third style and 'it lives up to its name in every way', she said. These songs were 'frivolous, carefree, bouncy, syncopated perfectly to the beat' and their lyrics 'don't care if you don't take them seriously because they don't take themselves seriously'. Naturally, these words were pored over in depth by the Swifties.

In conclusion, she said that 'writing songs is a calling, and getting to call it your career makes you very lucky', so 'you have to be grateful every day for it, and all the people who thought your words might be worth listening to'. Nashville was, she said, 'the school that taught me that'.

During that speech, she also revealed that one of her new tracks on her next album was called 'Mastermind'. Her tenth album, *Midnights*, was a modern affair, released at midnight on 21 October 2022. Throughout the tracklist, she sounded like she was having the most fun, and that's because she was. From the dreamy and scene-setting 'Lavender Haze' and its equally blissed-out 'Snow on the Beach', through the distorted vocals of 'Midnight Rain' and ending with the upbeat, electropop confessional of 'Mastermind', it is Taylor as she had never been heard before. 'Haze' stood out in particular, given that it was inspired by her relationship with Joe. 'My relationship for six years, we've had to dodge weird rumours, tabloid stuff, and we just ignore it,' she said. 'So this song is sort of about the act of ignoring that stuff to protect the real stuff.' She was helped on the track 'Sweet Nothing' by Alywn.

Not that either of them were about to give more away about their relationship status in interviews. Amid persistent rumours that they had got engaged, Joe said: 'If I had a pound for every time I think I've been told I've been engaged, then I'd have a lot of pound coins. He added that 'the truth is, if the answer was yes, I wouldn't say, and if the answer was no, I wouldn't say'.

There were full-score marks for the new album from *Rolling Stone*, the *Guardian* and the *Independent*. The 'variously minimal, eerie, heartfelt and intense songs do have a crepuscular quality that is out of keeping with her usual cheery brightness', said *The Times*, but 'in the main' *Midnights* appeals because, 'for all its modern touches, it is essentially an old-fashioned singer-songwriter album about human weakness'.

The *NME* said it was a 'shimmering return to pure pop', adding that the album 'could possibly see Swift at her most candid, taking us through the sorts of revelations that only come to light – or can be vocalised – in the wee hours'. The *Observer* described *Midnights* as 'an album of fascinating small-hours contemplation', and *Variety* said it was a 'return to electronic, confessional pop that's worth losing sleep over'. Clash said, 'for those already swayed by her craft', *Midnights* 'may reasonably go on to be recognised as her best album to date, a reminder that magic prevails beyond the frustrations, fantasies and damnations she casts across her latest near-perfect body of work'.

However, some outlets, including the *New York Times* and *Washington Post*, felt she played it too safe. *Midnights* 'represents Swift at a turning point', said the *Telegraph*, but it wondered 'if it is the sign of a curtain falling on her imperial phase or a new pop dawn'.

Rather than embarking on a *Midnights*-specific tour, instead Taylor hit the road to support her new album and all the ones that had come before. The *Eras* tour was her sixth major concert tour and, naturally, it was the biggest. Taking in 146 dates across five continents, it began on 17 March 2023, in Glendale, United States, and was inked in to conclude on 8 December 2024 in Vancouver, Canada. Conceived as a journey across her various 'eras', the show lasted over three hours, with a set list of 44 songs divided into 10 distinct acts that render the albums conceptually.

Typically for Taylor, the tour had an impact far beyond the dates and performances themselves. The astronomical ticket demand alone became a saga discussed around the globe. Over 22 million customers across Asia virtually queued for tickets for the shows in Singapore. In the US, some 3.5 million people registered for Ticketmaster's Verified Fan pre-sale programme. When the sale went online on 15 November 2022, the website crashed in an hour, with frustrated users logged out or in a frozen queue. Even with this disaster, some 2.4 million tickets were sold, breaking the record for the highest single-day ticket sales ever by an artist. It leapfrogged Robbie Williams, who had sold 1.6 million tickets for his *Close Encounters* tour in 2005.

Ticketmaster said there was a 'historically unprecedented demand with millions showing up', but there was further upset when scalpers purchased a large number of tickets and put them on resale websites for exorbitant asking prices. The issue went political: several members of US Congress called for the cancellation of the 2010 merger of Ticketmaster and Live Nation, and the US Department of Justice launched a federal probe. US President Joe Biden was quoted as saying that 'capitalism without competition isn't capitalism, it's exploitation'.

In a development that legal scholar William Kovacic called the 'Taylor Swift policy adjustment', Ticketmaster announced that it would begin disclosing 'junk', or add-on, fees up front after angry Swift fans demanded change and the Federal Trade Commission proposed new regulations. Months later, Ticketmaster apologised to Swift and her fans during a US Senate hearing. 'We need to do better and we will,' Joe Berchtold, president of Live Nation, Ticketmaster's parent company, told lawmakers. Swift said it had been 'excruciating' to watch fans struggling to get tickets, and insisted that she had been assured Ticketmaster could handle the demand. A group of fans decided to sue Ticketmaster, alleging that the company is guilty of fraud, price-fixing and anti-trust violations.

There was a surge in commercial activity and economy in cities visited by the tour, which significantly boosted local companies, including hospitality, clothing, public transport and tourism. According to *Fortune*, the tour's net consumer spending was $4.6 billion in the US alone. Politicians, including Canadian prime minister Justin Trudeau and Chilean president Gabriel Boric, petitioned Swift to tour their countries. The mayor of Budapest, Gergely Karácsony, penned a letter to Swift requesting she tour in Hungary.

Those who managed to catch a date were in for a treat. Starting with tracks from *Lover*, the setlist for the shows kicked off with 'Miss Americana & the Heartbreak Prince' and 'Cruel Summer'. Other stand-out tracks included 'Fearless', an epic, 10-minute version of 'All Too Well', a rousing 'We Are Never Ever Getting Back Together' and two surprise songs, which varied from show to show. The shows received full-star ratings across a range of publications, with the *Telegraph* describing it as one of the most ambitious, spectacular, and charming stadium pop shows ever seen' and *The Times* said it showed Swift as 'a pop genius at the top of her game'. *Variety* claimed the tour had grossed $2 billion, as of October 2023.

The tour was immortalised in a film that itself became a cinematic monster. A classic concert documentary, it was put together from Swift's six-night stint at the SoFi Stadium in Inglewood, a suburb of Los Angeles. 'You're stuck with me, because I'm going to sit with you and watch this thing,' she told the crowd at the packed 2023 premiere, which was held at the sprawling Grove shopping complex in Los Angeles. She wore a pale blue Oscar de la Renta gown and complemented it with a matching shade of blue eyeshadow along with her signature cat eye and red lip. She also wore a diamond string necklace and styled her curls into a low updo. She danced in her seat for much of the film. The fans screamed, sang and danced from start to finish, with many hardly taking their seats for even a moment during the near three-hour runtime.

Many of the fans wore sparkly dresses and cowboy boots; even the odd ballgown was spotted. Swift told fans at the premiere they were the 'main characters' in the film and said they made the tour 'magical'. She added that 'the fact that this tour was such a grand adventure has everything to do with the ways in which you cared about this tour and about these shows'.

Before the film was even released, it was already breaking records. US cinema chain AMC Theatres distribution said it had beaten its record for the highest ticket-sales revenue during a single day in its 103-year history. Within 24 hours of its release, AMC Theatres announced worldwide ticket pre-sales had already exceeded $100 million (£81.5 million). First-day sales alone topped $26 million, smashing box-office records.

The film 'more than justifies the hype' and is a 'spectacular, lovingly crafted movie that somehow captures everything great about the live show', said *The Times*. 'The Swift steamroller shows no sign of stopping, like, ever,' agreed the *Telegraph*. 'Whether weepy or accusatory, shattered or sarcastic', Swift 'puts all of her different selves on display in *The Eras Tour*,' said *Screen Daily*. 'You'll sing along with all of them.' The *NME* declared it a 'staggering feat', because 'in the space of one seamless performance, Swift is at turns a playfully eccentric artist, a country star and a genuine pop icon'. It was a 'cacophonous testament to megastardom', reckoned the *Guardian*.

Yet the *Eras* film was a rare example of Swift not *quite* living up to numerical expectations. It was certainly a big hitter, opening to a record $92.8 million domestically and $123.5 million globally over the weekend of 13–15 October. But forecasts had predicted higher takings: $100 million opening in North America and $150 million globally. Questions were asked over whether the encouragement for cinema-goers to dance and sing throughout the two-hour-48-minute showing might have put off some would-be ticket buyers. In the UK, an Odeon spokesperson said fans could 'absolutely celebrate by singing and dancing', while Cineworld said fans were welcome to 'shake it off and dance along'. Independent cinemas had also complained about poor liaison with the movie company regarding the rollout, which may have dented sales.

But there was so little doubt about the ongoing influence that Swift was continuing to wield. As cinemas were echoing to the sounds and steps of the Swifties, a university had launched what was billed as the first Taylor Swift-inspired literature course of its kind in Europe. The elective course at the University of Ghent, in Belgium, focuses on the themes, styles and techniques of famous historical literary writers from the perspective of Swift. It noted that her material 'brims' with classics of English literature and draws on themes that also appear in *Romeo and Juliet*, *Jane Eyre* and *Alice's Adventures in Wonderland*, among others.

Naturally, the course drew criticism from some literary purists. A Flemish journalist wrote witheringly that 'it's an auditorium, not a kindergarten'. But others were more supportive. A professor of Shakespeare, Jonathan Bate, argued that Swift was a 'literary giant', declaring that he would 'compare her (favourably) to the greats of poetry and prose'. The head of the course, Elly McCausland, wrote that she had 'received emails from students and teachers worldwide, whose interest in literature has been rekindled by its connections with Swift'. Speaking to the *Sun*, she added: 'Enough books have already been written about Shakespeare and other dead white men.'

There had been other academic studies of Swift. Taylor Swift and Literature was the name of a summer course at Queen Mary University of London. There was a Taylor Social Psychology module in Arizona and an All Too Well 10 Week Version course at Stanford University. The Clive Davis Institute in New York ran a course exploring 'Swift's evolution as a creative music entrepreneur, the legacy of pop and country songwriters, discourses of youth and girlhood, and the politics of race in contemporary popular music.' Some wondered how long it would be before a full Taylor Swift university was opened.

In April 2023, a source close to Joe told *People* that he and Swift had split, due to their 'differences in their personalities'. Speculation had been mounting about the status of their relationship after Alywn didn't make any appearances during the opening leg of the *Eras* tour, but this was initially explained away by the fact that he didn't like the limelight. When, after four shows, she dropped *Folklore*'s track 'Invisible String' from the setlist and replaced it with the song about past love, 'The 1', in Arlington, Texas, some thought this was her way of dropping a hint that Joe was in her past.

'They've had rough patches before and always worked things out, so friends thought they would take some time apart but eventually come back together,' said the source, but ultimately, they 'weren't the right fit for one another'. When she subsequently released a new song from *Midnights*, 'You're Losing Me', many felt this was a reference to how her relationship with Joe had broken down. The lyrics complain that the man would not marry her and that he was a 'pathological people pleaser'. There had been speculation that the couple had married secretly at one point, but this has been denied.

'They had plenty in common and fell in love in a safe bubble while she was retreating from the world during *Reputation*,' a source told *People*. 'Then, the pandemic hit, and they were locked down together and able to continue growing their relationship in this insulated way. But he didn't really "know" her yet outside of that bubble.' This was a break-up that was less expected than previous ones. Many of Swift's fans and much of the media had believed that her relationship with Alwyn was going to last for the long term.

According to reports, just three months later she had a new partner – the American football star Travis Kelce. Born in 1989 in Westlake, Ohio, Kelce took part in football, basketball and baseball at school. He starred at football, and represented Cleveland Heights and the Cincinnati Bearcats, before being forced to sit out a year after he failed a test for marijuana. After bouncing back, he was drafted by the Kansas City Chiefs.

Kelce had experienced brushes with celebrity before he met Swift, thanks to his part in a reality series, *Catching Kelce*, and after appearing as a fictionalised version of himself in the first episode of the comedy series *Moonbase 8*. He had also hosted *Saturday Night Live* in March 2023 and appeared in adverts for a string of brands, including Pfizer and Bud Light. He had also dated the winner of his reality show, Maya Benberry, and a social media influencer, Kayla Nicole.

But these experiences barely prepared him for the attention he started to receive from the moment the first rumour surfaced linking him to Swift. Following weeks of feverish speculation, Swift was spotted at Arrowhead Stadium to watch Kelce and his Chiefs defeat the Chicago Bears 41–10. When she followed up with an appearance at MetLife Stadium to watch the Chiefs' showdown with the New York Jets, the tongues were wagging out of control.

The famed Swift effect was quickly felt in Kelce's sport. There was a more than 400 per cent increase in Travis's replica jersey sales, and the Jets sold more tickets for their game against the Chiefs in a single day than since the start of the season. NBC cashed in on the hype to promote the Chiefs' game at the New York Jets the following week, producing a promo set to Swift's song 'Welcome to New York'. It worked: the game – which Swift also attended – averaged 27 million viewers, making it the most-watched Sunday-night NFL game since Super Bowl LVII.

The excitement around the relationship coincided with the hype around her most anticipated Taylor's Version release to date – *1989*. 'I was born in 1989, reinvented for the first time in 2014, and a part of me was reclaimed in 2023 with the re-release of this album I love so dearly,' she wrote, announcing the release.

The moment didn't pass without some typical numerical drama. Users of the Apple streaming service experienced issues downloading and streaming the new release. One of the new tracks, 'Slut!', referenced one of the tracks on the original release – a meta moment that the Swifties loved. Whereas in 'Blank Space' she had referred to herself as a 'rose garden filled with thorns'; in 'Slut!' she sang of 'love thorns all over this rose'.

The new version was 'a triumph', said *The Times*, and the tracks, old and new, added up to a 'masterclass in mainstream songwriting'. Her 'best album' will 'never go out of style', said *NME*, while *i News* said the re-release confirmed that 'few pop stars can compete with Swift's effervescence as a songwriter'. The songs are 'some of the best pop of the 21st century', said the *Independent*, and 'a few bits of middling production or some slightly-too-good vocals won't change that'.

As if to underscore how successful she had become, the sales of *1989 (Taylor's Version)* in week one out-performed those of the original album. With 1,287,000 sales in the United States, the original *1989* had been the biggest start for any album in more than a decade, but Swift topped the first-week total of her original with the remake, with the equivalent of 1,653,000 sales in the United States – the biggest opening sales week of her career – and 3.5 million around the world, according to her label, Republic Records.

Taylor's influence and popularity continues to grow and grow at such a phenomenal rate, that sometimes it feels as if all of humanity is a fan. When the Public Enemy rapper Flavor Flav attended the premiere of the *Eras* movie, he said he had seen the 'awesome' Swift on two previous tours. 'I've been a Swiftie for the longest, bro,' he said. Haven't we all? Swift has been active since 2004, a star since 2006, America's sweetheart since 2010, a superstar since 2013 and has since eclipsed even megastar status to become something that the pop world hasn't known for a long time. 'There is Taylor Swift and then everyone else,' said *The Times* in 2023, but even this hardly did justice to her status as she lived out her early thirties. *Bloomberg Businessweek*, not a publication given to any hyperbole, said Swift *is* 'The Music Industry', the leading paper *USA Today* advertised for a Taylor Swift correspondent who would *only* cover Swift. It has been a momentous journey for a kid from Pennsylvania, who was meant to knuckle down into a career in business.

She is more than a pop star, or celebrity, though. More even than a megastar, perhaps. She's a once-in-a-generation cultural phenomenon. How did she become so popular, famous, successful and influential?

We can start with the music itself. She is a consummate performer, of course. She nails it live and even if her vocal range does not quite match the likes of Adele, Mariah Carey and Beyoncé, her concerts are at least as powerful, impressive and impactful as those of that trio of female artists.

Some of her songs take place in an instant, while others, like 'Fifteen', become narrative stories whose verses unfurl over a period of time and a sequence of events. Although Swift's music is sophisticated in pop terms, it never comes over as too highbrow or exclusive. Indeed, her chord progressions are nearly always standard and uncomplicated. As verses and then choruses develop, you continue to hear what you expect to hear. But her verbal hooks are more than memorable – they are almost impossible to shake off. A pop star can have all the vocal talent in the world – and some do – but precious few, if any, on the current pop scene, have Taylor's ability as a songwriter.

Swift has managed to reinvent her musical style over the years, transitioning from country to pop, then incorporating indie and alternative elements in albums like *Folklore* and *Evermore*. This ability to evolve attracts a broader audience and demonstrates her versatility as an artist, only adding to her appeal. Yet as we have seen, while her styles have changed, Swift's core strengths have remained.

Compared to the relatively safe-playing Adele, Swift has pushed her boundaries, and the esteem in which she is held by fans and critics alike reflects that. Having noticed that, fairly or unfairly, female artists are expected to keep reinventing themselves, Taylor has stepped up to that plate. And it has worked: she never goes out of style.

Ultimately, there is an incredibly powerful social and emotional bond between Swift and the public. She connects with their identity in an incredibly effective way. She has retained her relatability, even as she became a multi-millionaire celebrity. Her lyrical content, musical emotion and public statements are all very relatable, particularly for millennials, who grew up alongside Taylor, passing life's milestones at similar times. Then a new generation of fans discovered her thanks to her prolific releases of material and punchy TikTok content during the pandemic, which was quickly dubbed 'SwiftTok'. She came into these youngsters' lives just as they needed something, or someone, new.

Many of the fans that have grown up with Swift over the past two decades have in that time become parents themselves, and some have even started to bring their children along to the concerts, posting videos of them set to the bridge of 'Long Live'. Meanwhile, those fans who are older than Swift can vicariously relive their youths by following her. We've seen her grow up in front of us in real life. She's developed from a young girl to a powerful, strong woman, but one who is not afraid to show her flaws and mistakes. Her songs are painstaking and detailed cuts into life's emotions; she does not just sketch over them, she gets deep. This relates and resonates across generations and cultures. Her songs are more than songs – they feel like novels or films to the listener.

When she is writing, Swift is not just churning out generic pop songs; she's telling stories, painting pictures, and conveying such deep emotions that it feels like she's reading straight from the diaries of her fans' lives. Every song is like a chapter in a novel, and not just hers, but theirs too. In her lyrics, Taylor is sharing a piece of her soul, and as far as her fans are concerned, that's something you don't see with other artists today.

This openness is incredibly potent. In an era when so many people, whether famous or not at all famous, share inaccurately positive takes on their lives through social media, authenticity has become all the rarer and therefore more valuable. Swift regularly conveys vulnerabilities, including a desire for vengeance, in her music. While many artists pretend to be vulnerable, and some occasionally touch on the theme of revenge, Swift spends much of her songwriting time in these fields. This touches on her listeners' own personal experiences. Thanks to her authenticity, they can find their own story in her stories.

Swift has encouraged her younger fans to develop a connection not only with her, but with each other. This unity among 'Swifties' has seen them become a more connected and friendly fanbase than that of other huge pop acts of recent times. Fans of Justin Bieber and One Direction became quite the armies, but there was often an inherent distance among fans who were all craving the romantic attention of their idols. Nearly all of them would have trampled over each other for some facetime with their heroes. But most Swift fans don't want that sort of relationship with her, so they have been able to connect more deeply with each other.

This unity has been utilised well. Her output, whether in song, packaging or on the online page, is rich with Easter eggs. She's become known for hiding messages, references and clues in her lyrics, music videos and even album art. She created her own world and invited the Swifties to unravel its mysteries together. This is much more than a marketing gimmick; it's a way of communicating with her fans, directly and personally, which creates an incredible shared experience that's about so much more than just the music. Ahead of the release of *1989 (Taylor's Version)*, Swift unveiled a series of word puzzles on Google, which would pop up as little blue vault icons when 'Taylor Swift' was typed into the search bar, which she tasked her fans to solve together in order to reveal the names of the upcoming vault tracks. Her fans collectively solved the 33 million of these puzzles in less than 24 hours.

Taylor reaches out to Swifties personally, replying to fans on social media, where she now has 220 million followers, and even inviting some to her home for secret sessions. Despite her huge fame and fortune, she does not seem to be squirrelled away in some celebrity ivory tower; she's right there with her fans, sharing in their triumphs and their struggles. She feels like a friend to them and for them, she does not just belong on stage, but in their very hearts. Swift is their guiding light, a fierce protector of artistic integrity and a true friend. She's touched their hearts with her music, her courage and her unwavering kindness. Expect them to continue to stand by her, fearless, forever and always.

It's not just her music that her fans relate to, but her wider character. The way she has stood up to other celebrities, to streaming giants and to leading industry figures such as Scooter Braun is enormously inspiring to younger fans. She hasn't been bullied and she has found ways to either leap over obstacles, or to knock them down completely.

She is known for her savvy business decisions and her struggle for artists' rights, especially evident in her battle over her masters' ownership. Her public fight for her music rights has garnered respect and placed her in a unique position compared to other artists, highlighting her as a figure standing up for autonomy in the industry.

Swift's ubiquity is also part of the answer. Unlike Adele, who consciously withdraws from the public spotlight between album releases, Swift keeps putting herself out there, aside from her retreat in the run-up to *Reputation*. Yet there is a class underscoring her ubiquity. She is not desperate for attention and therefore she is consistently granted it. Her creative stamina is notable when you measure it against other household names. At the equivalent stage of their career, the Rolling Stones, Bob Dylan and Bruce Springsteen had long since released their most important output. But who doesn't feel that, for Swift, the best is yet to come? Perhaps the only peer who contradicts the claim that Swift is a 'once in a generation' star is Beyoncé, who has sold over 200 million records worldwide and enjoyed influence similar to that of Swift. Tellingly, when Beyoncé attended the *Eras* movie premiere, Swift wrote on Instagram that Beyoncé had been a huge influence on her, teaching her to 'break rules and defy industry norms'.

Then there are her views. Swift's actions extend far beyond music; she's known for her political endorsements and advocacy for the LGBTQ+ community, women's rights, copyright law reform and a host of other hot topics. Her willingness to take a stand on significant issues has solidified her role as more than a musician, but as a cultural influencer. She might not have been a slogan-eer originally, but once she started speaking out, it added to her brand's potency.

All of these many factors have combined to put her on a level that is without equal in the current cultural scene. She has become a colossus, and she wears it so well. Her esteem can also be traced in the respect she draws from some of the industry's biggest and most revered figures. Pop contemporaries often big one another up, frequently to draw on each other's fan bases, but when musical royalty praise an artist, it is usually a more pure and sincere praise.

Speaking of Swift's success, Billy Joel told the *New York Times* that 'the only thing I can compare it to is the phenomenon of Beatlemania'. One of The Beatles, Sir Paul McCartney, said that he had been inspired by Swift's songwriting, while another, Ringo Starr, confirmed that he, too, was a Swift fan. Carole King said Swift was a rarity in that she was a great songwriter, great singer and great performer. Dolly Parton said 'she's just right up there, probably number one', while Shania Twain called Swift 'incredibly brilliant'. Bruce Springsteen, meanwhile, hailed Swift as a 'tremendous writer'. None of these artists need to praise her for their own benefit, so their words carry enormous weight.

The benefits of Swift's stratospheric fame and success can be measured in many ways. Money is only one of them, but it is a good marker. According to reports in October 2023, Taylor has become a billionaire. Bloomberg announced that she had acquired a net worth of $1.1 billion (£907.2 million), becoming one of the few billionaires to reach that milestone through the route of music. 'Swift has evolved from a teen pop-country phenom to a world-famous celebrity', it said.

Swift made more than $500 million of her fortune from music royalties and touring, with an estimated $190 million after taxes from the first leg of the *Eras* tour alone, and another $35 million from the first two weeks of screenings of the companion concert film. Another $500 million of her earnings came from the increasing value of her music catalogue, and she has an estimated $125 million in real estate, including six homes and a $10-million private plane. As the sole songwriter for around a quarter of her biggest hits, and the co-writer on many of the others, she has made more money out of her success than less creatively minded pop stars.

Most pop stars and other entertainers who have reached billionaire status have had to lean into profitable 'side hustles' such as beauty brands, fashion lines and alcohol investments to amass that much wealth. Jay-Z had drinks brands and a stake in Uber, while Rihanna got a big slice of her billion from her cosmetics brand and lingerie line. Bruce Springsteen is one of the few musicians who has, like Swift, hit the billion-dollar mark through music.

As we have seen, when Taylor was a child her parents hoped that she would become a stockbroker, earning a fortune in the world of business. Instead, she has achieved enormous wealth through a much prettier path. But the true wealth she enjoys is not financial. In an era of manufactured artists who crash and burn soon after finding fame, Swift has lasted the course and has done it her way. She's connected with both her strengths and her vulnerabilities, and presented them to the world, harnessing them as she navigates the unforgiving path of fame. Further twists and turns, challenges and dilemmas will come her way as she continues to record and tour through her thirties and beyond, but, for now, no one can compete with Taylor Swift. She is simply imperious.

Bibliography

Blair, Linda, *Birth Order* (Piatkus, 2013)

Cameron, Julia, *The Artist's Way* (Pan, 1994)

Govan, Chloe, *Taylor Swift: The Rise of the Nashville Teen* (Omnibus Press, 2012)

Jepson, Louisa, *Taylor Swift* (Simon & Schuster, 2013)

Newkey-Burden, Chas, *Adele: The Biography* (John Blake, 2011)

Spencer, Liv, *Taylor Swift: The Platinum Edition* (ECW Press, 2013)